Linda Hampshire and Karima El-Hakkaoui

THE
WEDDING
a to Z

EVERYTHING YOU NEED TO KNOW*

*and Stuff You Never Thought to Ask

POTTER STYLE

Published in the United States by Potter Style, an imprint of the Crown Publishing Group, a division of Penguin Random House LLC, New York.

POTTER STYLE is a trademark and POTTER STYLE with colophon is a registered trademark of Random House, Inc.

Grateful acknowledgment is made to the following: Condé Nast: excerpt from "Kiss Me Kate" by Hamish Bowles, originally published in *Vogue* Magazine, September 2011, copyright © 2011. All rights reserved. Reprinted by permission of Condé Nast. Warner Bros. Entertainment Inc.: excerpt from the New Line Cinema film *Wedding Crashers*. All rights reserved. Reprinted by permission of Warner Bros. Entertainment Inc.

Library of Congress Cataloging-in-Publication Data is on file with the Library of Congress

ISBN 978-0-7704-3508-0

Printed in the United States of America

Book and cover design by Karima El-Hakkaoui

10 9 8 7 6 5 4 3 2 1

First Edition

Congratulations!

Planning a wedding is exciting. We can't promise you it'll always be easy, but it should be enjoyable. What's the secret? Stick with what will make your day happy, memorable, and, above all else, enjoyable for you and your guests. You don't have to follow tradition or preconceptions about how a wedding "should" be, unless you want to. Whether you're raring to go or a bit overwhelmed, you've probably got a ton of questions.

Maybe you're wondering when to have your wedding? Or who pays for what these days? Do you have time for Botox/a boob job/lipo? What is the best way to lose weight and get fit without going hungry? How can you have a wedding you'll love, whatever your budget? How do you choose a photographer? What's the secret to a long and happy marriage?

To help you navigate your way through all these questions (and plenty more), we've put together hundreds of answers, insider tips, and inspiration from world-renowned experts on everything from the very traditional to the not-so. You can flip directly to the subjects you're most interested in (Alcohol? Registry? Family? Elope?), but take a look at the contents pages to see topics you might not have thought of. And if you're searching for specific items and don't see them listed, check out the Resources section in the back, where we've grouped all the amazing experts in this book into categories and noted where they're quoted.

So, on your mark, get set, go . . . have fun.

contents

Aa

Accessories

Accessories are such a fun part of getting ready, so enjoy picking them out.

"There are no absolute rules for accessories," says fashion stylist Desirée Lederer, who's worked with A-listers like Scarlett Johansson.

There are a few pointers that can help . . .

DON'T stick to bridal accessories. "They're often more expensive and really predictable," she advises. Shop around.

DON'T overdo it if you're wearing a dress with lots of embellishment. "You might only need one extra thing—some sparkle in a pair of earrings, or maybe your hair and makeup will give the finishing touch. Less is more."

DO look to the red carpet for inspiration. A-listers often wear just one piece of statement jewelry with gowns.

DO try on everything, even things you're sure you wouldn't be seen dead in, from traditional veils and tiaras to sashes, gloves, and jewelry that's outside your comfort zone.

DO look at vintage accessories and costume jewelry.

WHAT COUNTS AS AN ACCESSORY?
Earrings, necklaces, bracelets, tiaras, headdresses, headbands, clips, combs, crowns (only if you're the Queen), hats, fascinators, veils, gloves, shoes, scarves . . .

WANT TO BUY VINTAGE ACCESSORIES? Clare Borthwick, Christie's vintage couture and accessories specialist, who catalogued Elizabeth Taylor's vast accessories wardrobe, has this advice for brides:

BUYING VINTAGE ACCESSORIES

1. Always buy what you love. Then you'll be happy with it for years, regardless of its value.

2. Buy the best of what you can afford.

3. Buy well-known brands. Designers like Chanel and Yves Saint Laurent will always be popular and they have both classic and contemporary designs.

4. Care for things, and they will last.

5. Always buy from a reputed source. Not only will one be able to answer all your questions and advise you, but you'll be able to buy with confidence.

TOP
5
TIPS FOR BUYING VINTAGE ACCESSORIES

GUESTS NEED TO KNOW . . .
- Websites and contact information of hotels.
- An idea of price range so they can go straight to the ones that suit their budget.
- Where to find the info—post on your wedding website or slip a printed sheet in with the invitations.

Accommodation
If you're having a destination wedding or there'll be overnight guests, put together a list of local hotels, motels, inns, and B+Bs. Don't forget . . . check guest reviews on sites like www.tripadvisor.com beforehand.

GROUP DISCOUNTS: Hotels often give discounts if you reserve a block of rooms for your guests and are prepared to give a credit card as advance guarantee. But, warns Jody Value, event manager at Kauai Marriott Resort, it's not always the best thing to do. "In the early stages you don't always know exactly how many guests will need rooms, so it can become stressful. It's better to e-mail your guests two or three website links to hotels that are near the ceremony and reception site, so they can choose where they want to stay and which hotel fits their budget." If you do arrange preferential room rates, let your guests know the cutoff date for confirming rooms.

Acne

Ah, crap. Acne can make you self-conscious and generally not on bright, shiny form. If you want to improve it before your wedding day, start early, says dermatologist Dr. Debra Jaliman. "Acne can clear in three to six months depending on how bad it is." See your dermatologist, but try these approaches, too.

HOW TO FIX IT: From the inside out

"The first thing to do is remove the things that make acne worse," says naturopath and author Roderick Lane: stress and bad diet.

- **Hormones, stress, and inner cleansing:** "Balancing your hormones and reducing stress is vital for treating acne," says Margo Marrone of the Organic Pharmacy. "Take calcium and magnesium before you go to bed to help your body cope. For balancing hormones, agnus castus is brilliant, and herbs like dandelion and burdock help cleanse the blood and liver."
- **Detoxing your diet:** "Very poor dietary choices make acne worse," advises Lane. "Increase your intake of raw foods and fruit and vegetables, cut back on processed food, and eat plenty of fresh fish like salmon, sardines, and mackerel. Finally, get juicing for a liquid nutrition hit that's far healthier than any amount of vitamin pills."

911!

Gahhhh! Holy crap, you've woken up with a huge zit. "The best treatment is an injection of hydrocortisone by a dermatologist," says Dr. Jaliman. "If that's not possible, use a drying salicylic acid or benzoyl peroxide gel; toothpaste works in a pinch."

"One of the best ways to prevent acne is via regular exfoliation."
Erin Flaherty, Health and Beauty Director, *Marie Claire*

"BEAUTY does come FROM WITHIN. The skin reflects on the outside of your body what's going on inside."

RODERICK LANE

SCARRING: How to treat it

"If you have acne scars, use the Medlite laser with microdermabrasion; it'll help smooth the skin without any downtime," says Dr. Jaliman.

CAN FACIAL ACUPUNCTURE GO HEAD TO HEAD WITH BOTOX?

● Yes. "It's a realistic alternative. It improves muscle tone, lifts drooping eyelids, and improves the color and tone of the skin," says acupuncturist Annee de Mamiel.

● Start two months before your wedding and have eight weekly treatments. Leave a week between your last one and the wedding. Better than injecting nerve toxins into your face . . . no?

Acupressure

A vital part of the bride-to-be's armory, acupressure uses the same meridian of pressure points as acupuncture but with finger pressure instead of needles. Once you know the points you can do it yourself pretty much anytime. It might also make you look better: the Chinese have used the Heavenly Appearance acupressure points as beauty treatments for thousands of years. Check online for websites detailing each acupressure point or invest in a good acupressure reference book.

Acupuncture

Need stress relief? Help sleeping? "Acupuncture's highly effective against stress. It's been proven to lower levels of the stress hormone cortisol and increase the release of serotonin and also epinephrine," explains acupuncturist Shellie Goldstein. "A single treatment can leave you feeling calm, relaxed, more focused, and clear headed." It's also a well-documented treatment for chronic pain and even cellulite and acne, and the World Health Organization has officially recognized that it works.

● To find a fully qualified practitioner in your area, contact the National Certification Commission for Acupuncture and Oriental Medicine.

Acupuncture can help ALLEVIATE physical stress-related symptoms like trouble sleeping, ANXIETY, DEPRESSION, and headaches.

Address book If you're anything like the rest of us, a good few of the contact details for your guests are probably hopelessly out of date. Update your address book while you're still getting your guest list together and before your save-the-dates or invitations are ready to be sent out—it'll also minimize the time searching for the random bits of paper and bills you've jotted everyone's new details on when you go to send out your thank-you cards after the wedding.

Adventure Isn't the future an adventure? Full of ups, downs, and excitement. Try to see your wedding day this way, too, without putting pressure on it to be perfect.

For the ULTRA-ADVENTUROUS COUPLE, get married here:

While scuba diving (yes, the marriage certificate will be signed underwater)

On a yacht, hot air balloon, horseback, or Harley

At one of the world's most famous archaeological sites

Under a waterfall

While sky-diving, skiing, or swimming with dolphins

Advice is great.

But, when it comes to weddings, everyone has an opinion and we're bombarded with well-meaning suggestions. So, we rounded up the experts to ask what their single most important piece of wedding guidance would be.

THE HEALTH AND BEAUTY EDITOR

"Don't make any drastic hair or cosmetic changes close to your wedding and avoid facials the week before because they can make you break out," says Erin Flaherty of *Marie Claire.*

THE CAKE DESIGNER

"I love making cakes for special occasions, but let's not forget that a cake is a cake; it's the marriage or relationship that is the most important!" says Ron Ben-Israel.

THE PHOTOGRAPHER

"I can't overstate the importance of good posture," says Ian Martin, whose award-winning work has appeared in *Rolling Stone* and the *New Yorker.* "The most flattering thing anyone can do for herself is stand, or sit up, straight."

THE WEDDING PLANNER

"Do fewer things and do them fabulously," says Lindsay Landman. "Just focus on what's important to you. So often I see couples trying to do too much . . . cram every color palette, type of music, and style of food and flowers into one six-hour event. There isn't enough time or space for them or their guests to enjoy any of it!"

THE MAKEUP ARTIST

"Beware of concealers that have light-reflecting properties," says Amanda Wright. "They look beautiful in daylight, but you'll look like a panda in all your photos that use flash!"

THE FLORIST

"Choosing flowers in season is hands down always the best way to go. Aside from being green or budget friendly or any of the buzz words, seasonal flowers simply look the best," says Liza Lubell.

Afterparty

This is where the drunk get drunker, tears start flowing (that's just the bride), the desperate are on the hunt, and the really bad drunks either pass out or get ejected. Yes, the good old afterparty.

SHOULD YOU PLAN ONE IN ADVANCE? If your venue is asking for an early finish and you know everyone will be in full swing just as the lights come up, yes. If your guests aren't big partiers or all have young kids, let it happen spontaneously, rather than plan another bash when everyone will be ready for bed.

Alcohol

We were going to pepper this entry with tales of overindulging brides, babies being conceived, and other normal alcohol-related wedding behavior, but we all know how to get drunk and make a fool of ourselves, so it doesn't need saying. Aside from that, alcohol has an important and traditional part to play. Drinks should start being served when you arrive at your reception and finish when the lights go on for everyone to go home. It's not a side issue—it fills up the boring bits for your guests, is used for those very important toasts, and gets the evening party going.

WE TAKE IT BACK
OK, we lied, we're going to throw in a few stories . . . see page 18.

ASK YOURSELF three questions:

1. Are you providing the alcohol, or is the venue or caterer?
2. What alcohol will you serve?
3. When?

WHO'S PROVIDING THE ALCOHOL?

You: One of the biggest ways of making your budget go further is to bring in your own alcohol. Look for a venue right from the start that allows it—taking corkage into account (see the Corkage fee entry on page 94 for more on that). Use warehouse clubs like Costco or BJs that have discounts of around 10 to 30 percent for bulk purchase. When you're buying in bulk always ask if it's returnable; that way, you can get a refund on unopened bottles.

The venue: Set your budget and then negotiate the best deal you can; prices are not always set in stone and many venues will be flexible. Make sure they stipulate on your contract exactly what they'll be serving, down to the names of specific wines and brands of spirits if necessary.

WHAT TO SERVE? The most important thing is to offer drinks that will please the majority and work well with your menu. For much more detail on how to choose wine, cocktails, beer, and Champagne, go to the separate entries on pages 314, 87, 39, and 81.

WHEN TO SERVE IT? You could begin with a cocktail hour but also fill gaps between the ceremony, reception, meal, speeches, and evening party with drinks—these are the times guests really start to grumble if they're left milling around.

DID YOU KNOW . . .

The rule of thumb for ordering alcohol is to cater for two drinks per hour, per person, from cocktail hour through your reception, plus Champagne for toasts.

PREMADE=NO LINES

Have some drinks set out for guests to help themselves. If you're outside, fill troughs with iced beer; lay out trays of soft drinks and signature cocktails; fill ice buckets with white wine and Champagne, or have on-tap ready-mixed drinks.

"ALWAYS serve food!
It's crucial not to serve your guests alcohol
on EMPTY STOMACHS."

MIXOLOGIST TONY ABOU-GANIM

Alcohol, drunks, and the rules of engagement . . .

Alcohol before the ceremony needs to be rationed.* "One groom showed up to the wedding drunk and spent the first three hours of the reception in the emergency room on oxygen and intravenous fluids."
ANGELA GREGORY, WEDDING COORDINATOR AT RIVERSIDE CHURCH, NYC

*Nerves and booze aren't always a good mix.

If someone gets so drunk they start thinking it's a good idea to strip, it's only polite to cheer them on. "My brother took all his clothes off halfway through the night—he did a full monty. Welcome to the clan. . . ."
Real groom

Drunks always think they're the greatest dancers on the planet . . . avoid the temptation to put on what seems an inspired performance after a few drinks. "The groom grabbed the bride's mother and was aggressively spinning her around. Next thing, he was lying on top of her. On the dance floor."
Lindsay Landman

Allergies

Weddings need a bit of negotiating for anyone with an allergy to flowers, pollen, grass, and all that stuff. If you can't afford to be without an antihistamine, start taking it at least four weeks before you usually get symptoms, says Boots UK pharmacist Angela Chalmers. "Prevention's always better than cure. If your antihistimines make you sleepy, take your dose early in the evening before your wedding and the next day's dose before you go to bed. This will avoid the hangover effect early on your wedding day."

KICKING HAYFEVER: THE NATURAL WAY If you want to take a more natural approach, allergies need to be addressed long before the wedding, says naturopath Roderick Lane. "If you're a long-term sufferer, avoid two of the most common foods that irritate hayfever—dairy and gluten. This type of sensitivity can be triggered when you're stressed, overloaded, or lacking in vitamins or minerals. It takes time, though; avoiding dairy or gluten for a week before your wedding won't have any effect."

BUSTING ALLERGIES

1. If you know there's a flower that sets off you or anyone else in the bridal party, tell your florist.

2. Ask the florist to recommend flowers that aren't strongly scented or won't leave trails of allergy-causing pollen.

3. If the flowers in the church or venue are not under your control, tell whomever's responsible for them in advance.

4. Do what you can to minimize the risk. Choose a time of year for your wedding when pollen counts are low, and take into account tree pollen is abundant in the early spring, and flower and grass pollen and mold in the fall.

5. Instead of real flowers, have a bouquet made of paper blooms, shells if you're having a beach wedding, or brooches and jewelry. Check out Pinterest for inspiration and search online for tutorials on how to put one together.

PLANNING AHEAD
Download the National Allergy Bureau's pollen and mold app for up-to-date pollen counts and see how medicated you need to be.

TIPS
FOR
ALLERGY
BUSTING

Altar The altar is the focal point of a ceremony. Tradition has it that the bride normally stands on the groom's left. It's a practice going back to Anglo-Saxon times, when brides were often forced to marry or had been stolen by the groom. He was then free to pull his sword with his right hand if he had to defend himself against angry family trying to get her back.

Reinterpret the tradition any way you want, however. You might like to face your guests as you say your vows, and there are no laws about who stands on what side. Note: Ministers often see the altar as sacred and take issue with photographers snapping away over their shoulders. Always talk to your officiant to check if they have a particular way of doing things.

Animals

GOATS, horses, cats, dogs, elephants, chickens, REINDEER, guinea pigs, LIONS—you name it, they've all been to WEDDINGS.

It's cute, but it's another thing that can go wrong, so unless your middle name is Chill and your threshold for dealing with stray poop and unscheduled interruptions is high, know that it might send your stress levels through the roof. "I've done lots of weddings with dogs," says event planner Lindsay Landman. "If what the couple wants on their wedding day includes their pet, as long as there's a plan B, it's fantastic."

"Have a person whose job it is to pick up the leash and KEEP YOUR PET SAFE no matter what's going on."

KRISTEN THEISEN, THE HUMANE SOCIETY

ANIMAL HOW-TO'S

1. "Consider if your pet's personality is suited for the frenzy and limelight of a ceremony," says Kristen Theisen, director of pet care issues at the Humane Society. "If they're nervous in crowds or around loud noises, giving them a safe place away from the chaos might be best. Include shy pets or small animals by arranging photographs before or after the ceremony."

2. Your pet will need food, water, regular exercise, and toileting. Allocate someone who's not part of the wedding party, not allergic, won't be drunk by 6:00 p.m., and is familiar with looking after animals.

3. "If you want to include your pet in the ceremony, practice, practice, practice. If you want them to be a ring-bearer, let them get used to wearing a doggie-tux or having a pillow tied to their harness," says Theisen.

4. If you don't have someone who can care for your animal all day, consider a pet sitter.

5. Ask your guests not to feed your pet or give it alcohol. You'll be amazed at how many get offered a sip of Champagne. "Receptions can be risky. Common foods like onions, raisins, and chocolate are toxic for dogs."

ANIMAL HOW-TO'S

PLANNING AHEAD
Check with your minister and venue that they're happy to have animals present (some want to avoid a possible mess).

anniversaries

BEING CLEVER and saving a few things from your wedding means you can plan very cute gifts for the future. (Go easy, though, or you could end up as a crazy hoarder. . . .)

- **Photos:** Turn your favorite snaps into anything from iPhone and iPad covers to mugs, pictures, and T-shirts.
- **Words:** Record your "I dos" and print them as giant sound wave posters with your names underneath.
- **Music:** Find the vinyl of your first dance song and frame it.
- **Cake:** Dig out the layer of your wedding cake that's buried somewhere in your freezer and serve it up with the personalized cake knife from your wedding day.

PLANNING AHEAD What do you think your partner might like for your first anniversary? We'll start you off . . . What about wheeling out your bridal lingerie?

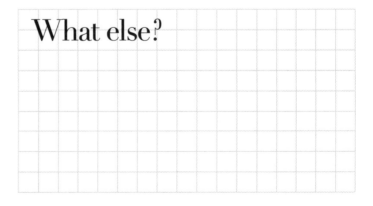

What else?

WANT TO PLAN AHEAD FOR YOUR ANNIVERSARIES? These are the traditional anniversary gifts and some more modern alternatives, including wine selected and compiled by Master of Wine Jennifer Simonetti-Bryan.

ANNIVERSARY	MODERN GIFTS	TRADITIONAL GIFTS	WINES
1st	Paper	Clocks	NV Champagne
2nd	Cotton	China	Red Bordeaux
3rd	Leather	Crystal/glass	Chianti Classico
4th	Fruit/flowers	Appliances	Malbec/Viognier
5th	Wood	Silverware	Napa Valley Cabernet Sauvignon
6th	Candy/iron	Wood	California red Zinfandel
7th	Wool/copper	Desk sets	Super Tuscan
8th	Bronze/pottery	Linens/lace	Rhone Valley red
9th	Pottery/willow	Leather	Brunello di Montalcino
10th	Tin/aluminum	Diamond jewelry	Vintage Champagne
11th	Steel	Fashion jewelry	Chablis
12th	Silk/linen	Pearls	Red Burgundy
13th	Lace	Textiles and furs	California Pinot noir
14th	Ivory	Gold jewelry	White Burgundy/white Bordeaux
15th	Crystal	Watches	Provence rosé
20th	China	Platinum	Aged red Bordeaux
25th	Silver	Silver	Aged red Burgundy
30th	Pearl	Diamond	German Auslese Riesling
35th	Coral	Jade	Tokaji 5 Puttonyos
40th	Ruby	Ruby	Eiswein
45th	Sapphire	Sapphire	Vintage port
50th	Gold	Gold	Sauternes
55th	Emerald	Emerald	Tawny port/Madeira
60th	Diamond	Diamond	Champagne demi-sec

Announce For an engagement, it's more a matter of good sense than set rules about who you tell in what order. According to tradition, the bride's parents are told first, but that's because historically they had to gird their loins to pay for the thing. Then come the groom's parents, both sets of grandparents, siblings, other close relatives, and then your friends.

But tell your news in whatever order suits you. Families can be scattered and disjointed, and you should share your news first with those you love and care about the most. The only rule is to make sure that children from previous marriages, especially if they're still young, don't hear your news from other people. Tell them yourselves, face to face if you can.

any cool ideas pop to mind?

How to ANNOUNCE your ENGAGEMENT

TEXT IT

It's not very personal and likely to be pounced on as Not Good Form, but texting makes life easier if you don't want to speak to anyone but want them to hear the news. For example, let's say you are marrying a Colombian drug lord and your parents don't approve, or the groom-to-be's divorce hasn't quite come through yet, or just because you hate fuss.

GO DIGITAL

Facebook, Twitter, websites, and e-mail announcements are cool if all your family and friends are on them. You can send out an e-announcement or e-card, or create your own wedding website page and e-mail links to everyone.
CONS: Not everyone gets the news as soon as they should. Do you really want your parents to find out at the same time as (or after) your Facebook friends?

Surprise!

Throw a party where you announce your engagement. A fun option and good practice for the wedding.

DO IT THE OLD-FASHIONED WAY

Announce your engagement in the paper or send out cards. If you want to follow the etiquette for formal announcements, the name of the groom comes first, followed by his parents' names and where they live, then the bride's name and her parents'. You could also include a line about where and when you got engaged. If you are including a picture, follow these guidelines. . . . At the minimum, you should BOTH look good and hands shouldn't be wandering anywhere you don't want your parents to see.

Q Can any Catholic request an annulment from the church?

A Yes, but there's no guarantee you'll get it. The first step is to talk to your priest because you'll need his support to be successful. Being in America gives you a greater chance— the U.S. has just six percent of the world's Catholics but accounts for two thirds of the annulments handed out by the Vatican every year.

DID YOU KNOW...

"It's a good idea to switch up your deodorant brand every six months to prevent resistance."
Dr. Han Lee

Annulment
This has a bad reputation as a get-out-of-jail-free card for the powerful, rich, and famous who don't like the inconvenience of a divorce, but there is more to it. Why would you need to know about annulment? If you want a marriage legally dissolved by the courts, or if you have one that you want to be annulled in the eyes of the church—and they're two very different things.

COURT ANNULMENTS: If you annul a marriage in court, it never legally existed. Grounds for legal annulment are
- it hasn't been consummated
- either party was still married to someone else or underage
- it's between very close relatives prohibited by law
- it was made under duress
- either partner was under the influence of alcohol or drugs
- either partner was suffering from mental illness.

CHURCH ANNULMENTS: These have no legal bearing on divorce proceedings and the status of children born within the marriage; they just leave you free to marry again in church. In the Catholic Church, a couple must be legally divorced before the Church will begin the process of annulling a marriage.

Antiperspirant
It sounds simple enough, but nerves make you perspire far more than normal, so choose wisely. It's not just about the potential for BO; choose one that guarantees no yellow stains on your wedding dress and won't leave big chunks of white snow in your armpit from a spray-on gone wrong. For die-hard, excessively sweaty people, Botox injections in the armpit, blocking the nerves that stimulate sweat glands, will do the trick. They start working after about a week and last for around three to six months.

Apps All those planning tasks that used to take weeks and use a rain forest of paper can now be done in real time.

Apps can handle ANYTHING from your SEATING PLAN to your to-do list. They can pinpoint your WEDDING COLORS OR STREAM your wedding live.

APP APPLICATIONS

- **RSVPs.** Your guests can respond instantly, and you can keep track of numbers in real time.
- **Seating plans.** All the changes used to take forever but can be done with a few clicks.
- **Hotel reservations.** If making block reservations, allow your guests to link directly to the booking.
- **Registry.** Some registry websites are so advanced you can scan items in any store with your phone and they'll go straight onto your digital list.
- **Sharing photos and streaming.** See your guests' photos, share your own, and let absent friends watch the ceremony.
- **To-do lists.** You can share lists with anyone from your partner to family and friends, your wedding planner or vendors.
- **Music.** Yes, even the reception music can be run from an app that controls timings and what songs play when, or you can use Spotify to create playlists.

TOP TIP
Use an app to gather your RSVPs and think of the money (and time) you'll save on printing and stamps.

Can you feel the tension rising around you? Emotions are running high. Money has been spent left right and center.

Arguments, squabbles, and fights

"As happy as weddings are, nerves get frayed, patience limited, and misunderstandings happen more frequently," says psychologist Yvonne Thomas. Want to know how to avoid everything from silent sulks to huge blowouts? Here's how, she says.

TOP 5 WAYS TO AVOID A FIGHT

WAYS TO AVOID A FIGHT

1. Be precise. Communicate clearly and directly. Don't be vague, be detailed, because it helps avoid arguments down the line. For example, say to your florist, "I want pink and purple roses, some green leaves, and a candle in the middle for my centerpieces," rather than, "I like pink and purple." Ask them to repeat back to you what they understood—it identifies misunderstandings really quickly.

2. Write it down. When it comes to vendors, write down everything you think you've agreed to—including prices, timings, and time lines. Have them confirm, clarify, or correct anything they don't agree with, and you should rewrite the update. Have vendors verify that they're in agreement, then you can draw up a contract if you're having one.

3. Be open-minded. Listen to anyone involved in your wedding—vendors, close family, or friends—with an open mind, and don't be defensive. Try not to shut down and take things too personally—by really listening you might see things from a whole new angle or recognize a good point. Sometimes two heads are better than one for seeing the full picture.

4. Turn a negative into a positive. When you're having a discussion with someone about your wedding plans and you don't agree with him or her, use what I call the sandwich approach.

- Start by telling them something genuinely complimentary.
- Get to the "meat" of the sandwich—talk about why you don't agree with what they said.
- End on an authentic positive note.

5. Stay true. Be appreciative of others' feedback and emotions, but stay true to what most represents you and your partner. Don't lose control over what you envision for your wedding, and don't feel guilty.

Assumptions

Think everyone's on the same page as you? That sort of thinking will trip you up, so clarify everything (see Arguments entry, above). Don't assume that people (from guests and vendors to your partner and members of the wedding party) always know what you mean or what time to turn up, or are picturing the same things as you. Always double-check and explain; show examples—draw pictures if it helps. Confirm everything in writing, and then again just before your wedding day.

(see Arguments entry, above)

DID YOU KNOW . . .
Getting angry raises adrenaline, blood pressure, and heart rate—and, if you are chronically cranky, eventually damages the immune system. Reason enough to stay chilled out.

KNOW HOW TO MINIMIZE ANGER
Learn to be assertive rather than aggressive. Be clear about what you want while respecting others' needs. Speak up, but do it calmly.

ASSUME NOTHING
- Double-check
- Explain
- Show pictures
- Draw pictures
- Confirm in writing
- Confirm again

How about your friends and family? In the whirl of planning your wedding, don't take for granted how much time or money they have to spare for you. Be sensitive. Not everyone speaks up when they can't afford things, and they often give their time when they have other commitments.

Astrology

We called Buckingham Palace to see if, when planning the wedding of William and Kate, they had consulted an astrologer to make sure the date was an auspicious one. They declined to comment. But, according to Sydney-based astrologer Mystic Medusa, a "bad" date astrologically doesn't necessarily equal a marriage that goes down the tubes faster than you can send out your thank-you cards. "Astrology is all about timing, so it's not that anything bad will happen if people get married on the wrong date; some people are just meant to be together. But it's more that, given the choice, why not choose an awesomely auspicious date?"

ASPECTS AN ASTROLOGY-LOVING BRIDE SHOULD MARRY UNDER: "You want harmonious Mars and Venus aspects for sexual chemistry and zing, Jupiter for luck and prosperity." If you really want to pinpoint the perfect date, aside from consulting an astrologer, Mystic's advice is "at the very least, schedule it in the two weeks following a new moon."

WHAT NOT TO DO: To maximize your all-around good wedding timing, try to avoid:
- Periods when Mercury is retrograde, and especially when Mars or Venus are retrograde.
- Having your wedding during the Dark Moon. "These are the days right before the New Moon. It's a time for endings, not beginnings, and very low energy for a party," explains Mystic.

DID YOU KNOW . . .
"Don't buy an engagement ring with Mercury in retrograde," says astrologer Susan Miller.

Attraction Do you need it for a long and successful marriage? Apparently not. According to biological anthropologist Helen Fisher, human attraction and romantic love are all part of a biological setup designed to get us from attraction, to sex, to mating, and then to long-term partnership. In this latter stage we form a strong attachment that lasts for long enough to bring up children together. And, adds relationship and sex expert Dr. Jane Greer, attraction goes up and down like crazy throughout the life of a relationship. "It's not just normal, it's the norm. As Dan Hill sings, 'At times I think we're drifters, still searching for a friend, a brother or a sister, but then the passion flares again.'"

Avoid There are no hard-and-fast rules for weddings, but we think every couple should steer clear of these things if they want to stay sane:

- Spending more than you can afford. Be clever and work within your budget.
- Asking your parents to donate more than they can without having to downsize to a garden shed or continue working until they are 90. Adjust your expectations if you know it's hard for them. And, if your parents will also want to contribute toward the weddings of siblings, don't get overenthusiastic and spend all their cash on yourself.
- Getting so strung out and hung up on the details of just one day that everyone is secretly avoiding you.
- Partying so hard the night before your wedding that you end up walking down the aisle shaking and wishing you were lying down in a dark room. Getting married is so much nicer with a spring in your step.

What do you think you need to avoid?

Bb

Bachelor party The thought of the bachelor party can make even the most laid-back bride break out in a cold sweat.

Will he END UP NAKED and tied to a lamppost in Vegas?

Cavorting with lap dancers? DO YOU CARE?

If you think the groom might head off for *The Hangover*–style antics, or anything close, and it's a step too far for you, speak up now. Naked lap grinding isn't the only way to celebrate. At the other extreme, one groom's bachelor party included an afternoon helping out at the Los Angeles food bank. "This was a great way to have fun and serve the community at the same time," he says.

WHERE DO YOU DRAW THE LINE? Be open with your partner about what is and isn't acceptable for you; personal boundaries are different for everyone. Have a quiet word with the best man if you think you need to (and he'll listen). Other than that you'll have to relax, and leave it in the lap of the Gods, so to speak.

PLANNING AHEAD
Would you and your partner like to have a joint bachelor-bachelorette party?

Bachelorette party

Bachelor party rules apply to you, too. Don't do anything to upset anyone, don't have it too close to your wedding, and play fair (if strippers are OK for you, they are for your partner). Most important, do something that you want to, not what you think you should be doing. You don't have to eat a penis cake, wear a sash or tiara, and have a gyrating dancer's oiled butt in your face to make it a bachelorette party.

WHO'S INVITED? Girlfriends, male friends, family, mom, mother-in-law . . . anyone you want to celebrate with. Just tell whoever's doing the invites who you definitely *don't* want there.

WHO PLANS IT? Normally your bridesmaids and maid of honor, but if you're not having any bridesmaids, throw it yourself.

MOST IMPORTANT THING? Make sure everyone can afford it. Don't make huge plans if your best friends are broke.

Try this:

"When you're planning a bachelorette party you can and should preface all reservations with: 'This is a bachelorette party with X amount of girls.' Every club and restaurant benefits from having a group of girls at their venue." **Kendra Cole, manager, Skybar at Mondrian, Los Angeles**

Bad behavior

Weddings are a bit of a magnet for bad behavior, with all those heightened emotions and family dynamics. Throw alcohol into the mix and you can guarantee that someone, somewhere will need to be put in the naughty corner.

PROBLEM Got wild guests or family tensions?
SOLUTION Have a plan and a peacekeeper. Make mugshots of the overemotional potential drunks and troublemakers for your wedding planner or a discreet and unflappable friend or relative. Ask them to intervene if they see trouble brewing. "I often spend time negotiating peace treaties, I've suggested that the groom apologize, removed obnoxious drunks, and separated warring relatives. It's important to have a third party with authority who can step in and take control before it becomes unfixable," says wedding planner Sandy Malone, star of TLC's *Wedding Island.*

Bad breath
No one wants to be stinky on her wedding day, but the worst offenders for bad breath can't be quickly brushed away with half a tube of extraminty toothpaste. Want to know the five secrets of fresh breath?

WAYS TO STOP THE STINK
1. Stop drinking coffee. A dry mouth equals a smelly mouth. Coffee dries up your saliva, creating a happy home for bacteria.
2. Ditch the diet. If you're on a very low-carb/high-protein diet or aren't eating nearly enough, you'll have bad breath. If you don't want to change your diet, try eating lots of parsley, mint, and cloves or taking parsley oil capsules and drinking more water.
3. Stay cool. When you're nervous, your mouth dries up as the body's fight-or-flight response reroutes resources to more important things than eating and digestion. Learn how to turn off your body's stress response—go to the Meditation entry on page 210 (and no, you don't have to sit and chant your way out of bad breath . . .).

TOP 5

WAYS TO STOP THE STINK

DID YOU KNOW . . .
Mouthwashes containing alcohol can give you bad breath. They dry out the mouth, resulting in a buildup of bacteria.

Q How can I tell if my breath is bad without making some poor person smell it?

A You'll get a good idea by licking a clean patch of skin. Wait a few seconds and sniff—if it smells bad, you know.

4. Cut some of the fun stuff. That's drinking, smoking, and smelly food. Celebrity cosmetic dentist Dr. Thomas Connelly explains:

- Smoking will make your lungs smell—you can brush your teeth all you want, but your lungs aren't getting cleaned by your toothbrush.
- Alcohol gets released when you exhale (think about it—that's how a Breathalyzer works), which is why brushing your teeth won't hide the fact that you've been drinking.
- Some strong foods like onions and garlic carry into your blood too and get released when you exhale. The only real cure is not to eat them or to wait them out.

5. Schedule a checkup. If you can't put stinky breath down to any of the above, you might just need to step up your oral hygiene or check for gum, tonsil, or lung problems, advises Dr. Connelly.

Bartenders

Good BARTENDERS are worth their weight IN GOLD.

They're the ones who'll serve everyone with a smile all evening, keep the event flowing, and bear the brunt of overindulgence at the end of the night without raising an eyebrow.

A DRINK TOO FAR: If you want an advance plan in place, ask the bar manager to tip someone off if anyone has had one too many. Make sure everyone is treated like adults, though; bar staff shouldn't be eking out drinks like your guests are teenagers.

WHO DOES THE TIPPING? If there's no service charge included in your contract (and even if it is, you need to check that the staff actually get it), tip at the end of the night or allow your guests to tip as they go. Don't want a tip jar on the bar? Say so in advance.

HOW MUCH SHOULD YOU TIP? Unless the bartenders really sucked, start at 10 percent and work up. You can calculate the tip as a percentage of what you've paid for a package, or of the total sales. If you brought in your own drink, do the same—tip a percentage of how much you paid for it.

BEWARE OF BARTENDING SCAMS: The desire to skim cash or booze you've paid for can be a temptation for the less than honest. "A barman at our wedding hid half the alcohol we'd provided and made our guests pay," said one bride. "We only found out the day after. The catering firm refunded our money after a fight but it wasn't the experience I'd wanted for our guests." How can you help prevent scams?

● Always get barstaff through a reputable company and check references.

● Ask who'll be supervising the bartenders.

● If you're having an open bar that's not on a prepaid per-person package, ask someone who's likely to be sober to check the final bill at the end of the evening and see if it seems to tally with the number of guests that are old enough to drink. One bride realized after her wedding that each man, woman, child, and baby would have had to drink two bottles of Champagne to get through what she was billed for.

PLANNING AHEAD

The rough rule of thumb is one bartender to every 50 guests, but ask yourself:

● Are your guests big drinkers who'll be spending a lot of time getting refills?
YES / NO

● Will your guests all be descending on the bar at the same time?
YES / NO

● Will you be serving cocktails? No one wants to be in line behind the order for a string of complicated drinks.
YES / NO

How many **YES** did you score?
1 YES: You need more barstaff.
2 or more YES: You need lots of extra barstaff to avoid lines.

Bathrooms

Don't underestimate how much time people spend in bathrooms at parties. Women do makeup, people sneak in to make out, brides try to pee in their wedding dresses . . . it's all going on in there. If you're responsible for providing the bathrooms, don't skimp. You could even hire a whole trailer/restroom setup.

RULES FOR PORT-A-POTTIES? Light the way for your guests; they don't need to be stumbling into ditches in the dark. And, even though we know you want the facilities out of sight of your event, don't put them miles away. Think: women, alcohol, high heels. Put some extra toiletries in the bathrooms—hand creams, tissues, Q-tips, bobby pins, hair bands, hairspray, mouthwash, deodorant, eye drops, face wipes, perfume, nail files, and clear nail varnish.

GO THE EXTRA MILE

If you want to go a bit further, add some emergency kit items from page 127.
- stain wipes
- static guard
- tampons
- sewing kit

Beauty

"Beauty is being able to laugh easily and feeling confident."

MARIE CLAIRE HEALTH AND BEAUTY DIRECTOR ERIN FLAHERTY

MAKEUP IS YOUR FRIEND

Even the world's biggest natural beauties look better in a bit of makeup. Go to the makeup entry on page 203.

Real beauty may come from within, but you can help it along.
- Get proper sleep, eat well, relax, exercise, and get some facial treatments.
- If you're not great at putting on your makeup, take some lessons. If you never wear any at all, consider practicing wearing a little for the day.
- Ditch bad habits—smoking, drugs, drinking—and see what beauty emerges.

Beauty sleep

" It's no myth. If you don't get enough sleep, your skin will look worse. Try to sleep 7 to 8 hours a night. "

DERMATOLOGIST DR. DEBRA JALIMAN

Beer Don't forget your beer drinkers—most of them feel as strongly as wine drinkers do about wine. If you're not a beer buff, here's what you need to know from Matt Simpson, owner of the Beer Sommelier.

1 NO, ALL BEER IS NOT THE SAME. "Some beers are clean, light, and easy to drink, but others are rich, chewy, and complex. . . . Serve a selection of different types, but don't overwhelm them with choice."

NEVER SERVE BEER IN CHILLED OR FROSTED GLASSES. "It condensates into the beer, and nobody wants their beer watered down." **2**

3 GOING LOCAL IS BEST. "You'll get the freshest beer, it's greener, and your hard-earned money stays in your own community," says Simpson. "Do an internet search for local breweries."

STOCK THESE
"Three beers is enough to give a good variety while still catering to varying tastes, and no matter what food's being served, you've got your beer-pairing covered," says Simpson. Offer:
● One relatively light, unassuming style: cream ale, Pils, saison
● One hoppy ale: pale ale, IPA/India pale ale, or American red ale
● One big, complex, full-bodied beer: Belgian strong ale, barleywine, Imperial stout

Belts and sashes

A sash can be anything from a simple length of satin to one decorated with ornate vintage crystal, or a dramatic bow with floor-length ties.

SASHES MADE EASY

1. Don't go overboard. "Think about how you'll look once you add your other accessories, like jewelry and a veil, and about how you're wearing your hair. The sash should balance everything, not compete or detract," says Stephanie McQueen of SparkleSM Bridal Sashes.

2. Stitch, sew, and alter. Have a seamstress tack your sash to your dress. If you have buttons or fastenings that you don't want covered, have it sewn on, stopping before the fastenings with a clean end.

3. Time to party. "Wear a plain belt for the ceremony and change into a beaded, blingy statement sash for the reception," says McQueen. "It costs far less than changing into a whole new outfit."

Bespoke

Whether it's the design, finish, fabric, size, or even smell, in the case of a fragrance, a bespoke piece will be yours and yours alone. For your wedding, bespoke options can include stationery; dress and shoes for the bride; suit, shirt, and shoes for the groom and ushers; accessories such as hats and gloves; a fragrance; and jewelry for both bride and groom. There's a whole industry out there ready to make things exactly as you want—if you've got the cash.

PLANNING AHEAD
Bespoke takes time. Shoes can take six months, suits three months, perfume from one to six months, and jewelry a couple of months or more.

These items are the FINAL LUXURY.

BESPOKE VS CUSTOMIZED: Don't confuse bespoke with off-the-shelf items that are tweaked and personalized for you. Underhand sellers call these customized items bespoke. For example, a wedding dress that you selected from a preexisting design and tweaked is customized. If you're not involved in the design process from the floor up, it's not bespoke. It's important to know the difference because bespoke commands a higher price.

Best man

A best man ISN'T just for the grooms ANYMORE.

Either of you or both of you can have a best man. Grooms—you can have a man or a woman. Brides—the same applies . . . but the female version of this is your maid of honor.

WHAT ARE THE BEST MAN DUTIES? The traditional duties are listed on the next page; if it doesn't feel right to ask the person you've chosen to be your best man to undertake any of these, just ask another member of the wedding party if he or she would mind helping out, or split the tasks between a few people.

TRADITIONAL BEST MAN DUTIES
- Arranging the bachelor party
- Helping arrange suits (purchase or rental) for groom and groomsmen
- Getting the groom to the ceremony on time
- Directing the ushers, ensuring they all know what to do
- Standing at the altar with the groom until the bride arrives
- Taking care of the wedding rings
- Settling fees after the ceremony such as choir, organist
- Making sure all guests have transport to the reception after the church
- Giving a speech at the reception
- Returning the groom's suit, if it's a rental

A NERVOUS BEST MAN? The best man has to be super-organized, together, charming, and flirty, and then deliver a speech that will have everyone on the floor laughing and crying simultaneously. It's no easy job. Don't be fooled by bravado; if no one buys the best man a how-to book and you think he's secretly sweating about the day, choose one yourself that suits his personality.

Bigamy
If you marry another person while you're still married to someone else, you're a touch crazy, but also committing bigamy (or even polygamy if you want more than two). It's still illegal in the U.S. although there are campaigns afoot to decriminalize it in some states. It's worth noting that out of more than one thousand societies worldwide that practice polygamous marriages, there are only four where women choose to take more than one husband. No one out there wanting two husbands then? Apparently not.

WORST BEST MAN?
What if you think your partner's selection of best man sucks? Well, how would you feel if he bad-mouthed your choice of maid of honor? Unless the best man is so bad your wedding could implode, you have to respect his choice.

POLYGAMY IN PRIME TIME
Catch some clips of reality show *Sister Wives,* which followed the lives of slick Kody Brown, his four wives, and their many, many, many children.

Big day Sure, it's momentous, but wouldn't you rather enjoy it than be uptight because you want everything to be perfect? "The hardest weddings to shoot are those where someone is so concerned about something that they're no longer enjoying themselves. It's really a shame to watch someone remove some of the joy on their own wedding day," says photographer Brian Dorsey.

"Go with the flow."

MARIE CLAIRE HEALTH AND BEAUTY DIRECTOR ERIN FLAHERTY

Bikini, bridal Yes, you can wear a bikini to your wedding if you want to. Your number one inspiration will obviously be Pammy at her 2006 Saint-Tropez wedding to Kid Rock. Make sure any guests know the dress code, too—can everyone join in or is the bikini just for you? There are bridal bikini ranges (lots of lace and crystal) and upmarket designers who carry white and embellished swimwear, even if they don't label it bridal. On Etsy, you can even find mini–ribboned tulle tutus designed to tuck into your bikini bottoms.

BEAT THE BUSH
Read more about how to groom that bikini line on page 173.

This is not a trick question . . .

What's the best way to be a **bitch**?

Locked away with your friends, a glass of wine, and a sense of humor. Get everything off your chest in private, bitch to your heart's content, and go home with a lighter heart.

Blessings

Dr. Seuss, the Bible,
and song lyrics . . . they're all some of the popular
sources of wedding blessings.

For more inspiration, go to the Readings entry on page 246.

WHAT DOES IT MEAN IF YOUR CEREMONY'S CALLED A BLESSING? Normally, that it won't make you legally married and you'll also need a civil ceremony for the sake of paperwork. If you're getting married abroad and can't satisfy the local residency requirements for a legal marriage, they'll often do a blessing (which for all intents and purposes looks exactly like a normal ceremony), and you can whiz off to the courthouse once you're home.

Bling If you're the kind of girl who likes sparkle, a wedding really can bring out your inner Christmas tree fairy. Don't just limit it to your dress and jewelry; also think about veils (Kate Moss's Galliano-designed floor-length veil was studded with glittering sequins), shoes, table decorations, floral centerpieces, and your bouquet. You can spell out your names in lights on the floor when you walk into the reception, hang crystals from the ceiling, or drape your bridesmaids in sparkly things. And even less subtle: there are dresses that will light up like the Eiffel Tower at night courtesy of fiber optics.

911!

Stock up on Dr. Scholl's antifriction sticks and cushioned strips for strappy sandals. Take an emergency pair of shoes to change into that are completely worn in.

Blisters No one wants to spend her wedding day limping or sticking Band-Aids all over her feet, so if you've bought new wedding shoes, wear them around the house first in tights or superthin socks for a few hours. It's also a good way of getting in some practice if your heels are outside your normal comfort zone. (To learn how to manage high heels like a catwalk model, go to the Footwear entry on page 152.) If you get even a hint of blister, gently rub the part of the shoe causing it—obviously not with grubby hands—until it's completely softened up.

ON THE DAY . . . Spray your feet with an antiperspirant. Blisters love warm, damp flesh, and with 250,000 sweat glands in each foot you can see why a quick spritz might be worth it.

Blues Want to know how to head off postwedding blues? The best way, say neuroscientists, is not a holiday or shopping spree, but to take stock of the good things in your life every single day. Studies show that when we make a habit of being grateful, our happiness increases. Consciously put your attention on being thankful and you'll light up the reward center in your brain: you'll boost the pleasure neurotransmitter dopamine and bonding hormone oxytocin, which is also released during orgasm.

Try this:

Write a list every morning of what you're thankful for, even if it's just your favorite coffee and a bagel. Helping other people out triggers the same reward center in the brain (yep, dopamine) as when you're on the receiving end.

Boobs There are only two things you need to know . . .

Try to avoid racking up your boobs (as fantastic and as perky as they may be) on display with excess cleavage at a religious ceremony. Breast spillage in a house of worship is generally a no-no. You can show them off later at the party. And wear the right bra for the shape of dress. For more advice, turn to page 293 for underwear and bras.

If you want a boob job in time for your wedding, you won't be able to shop for a dress or have fittings until you've had the procedure and the swelling and bruising have worn off. "Your new breasts will alter significantly in the weeks and months after a boob job, so expect changes and plan ahead for your wedding," says Dr. Miles Berry MS, FRCS (Plast).

WANT TO KNOW HOW TO GET THE PERFECT BOOB JOB?

Dr. Miles Berry, author of *The Good Boob Bible,* gives the essential need-to-knows. See also the Cosmetic treatments entry on page 96 for his tips on finding the right doctor.

TOP CONSIDERATIONS

● Because a breast implant won't last forever and will definitely require maintenance surgery in the future, expect this and prepare for the cost it entails.

● Ignore what friends and celebrities have. They are highly unlikely to share your size, shape, or individual tissue characteristics, so why should the same implant fit you? A good surgeon will not only listen, but try and guide you to the best possible outcome for you personally.

● Listen to and follow your own surgeon's advice during and after the operation, because there are different techniques in addition to individual tissue characteristics,

JINGLE BOOBS

"Remember a boob job is 'not just for Christmas, but for life.' Even if the implant is removed, the effects, including scarring, will remain with you always," says Dr. Berry.

boobs cont

JUST THIS ONCE . . .
SMALL IS BETTER

"Try to select the smallest implant that does the job, rather than the largest possible, as the vast majority of the negative effects are directly related to implant size and weight."

Dr. Miles Berry

therefore unique individual needs. The same is true for healing time, return to work and the gym, or other physical exercise.

● A boob job is real surgery and comes with a risk of side effects and complications. While all surgeons have patients who suffer them (unless these doctors are not actually operating or they're being economical with the truth), the best tend to have fewer and should look after you in the uncommon event that a problem arises.

● Your breasts are not static organs, but dynamic as they alter throughout life, particularly with pregnancy, breast-feeding, and weight changes. So, even if the implants last 15 to 20 years, the breast envelope changes and this generally manifests itself as droop.

Botox™

Love it or hate it, you can't deny
THAT BOTOX HAS
got gazillions of devoted followers.

If you've never tried it but are tempted, here's what you need to know. It's a registered trademark of Allergan for injectable botulinum toxin A—if you see the brand names Vistabel and Dysport, they're the same toxin used for the same purpose. Botox temporarily freezes facial muscles, meaning they can't contract.

WHAT DOES IT DO? It sort of smoothes you out. Done properly, it should be subtle—as the experts say, you can only spot Botox when it's been done badly. Effects last three to six months.

SIDE EFFECTS? You may get bruising and slight swelling at the site of the injection for 24 hours. "To minimize this, stop taking omega-3 fatty acids, NSAIDs like ibuprofen (Motrin, Advil) or naproxen (Aleve), aspirin, vitamin E, licorice, garlic, ginger, ginkgo, and other herbal supplements at least ten days before," says dermatologist Dr. Mitchell Schwartz.

RECOVERY TIME: Don't take a flight within two hours of treatment, go shoe shopping on the same day (too much time with your head down), do aerobic exercise or Bikram yoga, or take a sauna or hammam, says expert Dr. Daniel Sister. Other than that you're good to go.

WHEN TO DO IT: Never have Botox close to your wedding. The week before is a complete no-no, two weeks before is the minimum, and for best results, go around a month before.

WHERE TO FIND THE BEST BOTOXER: Start by asking friends and family—then you can tell instantly if you like the work. Find the best you can afford; it's an art, and you get what you pay for.

CAUTION! It can be really badly overdone; your face can become frozen in unexpected spots, stuck in weird expressions, or you can get a droopy eye. One of the biggest Botox mistakes, says Dr. Sister, is when people demand more than they need.

TOP TIP
Your practioner should be looking at your whole face and aiming to make it as symmetrical as possible. If they give you a cursory once-over and jab you between the brows, you're probably not at the right place.

❝Don't go for budget Botox.
It can be diluted, or worse, counterfeit.❞

DR. DEBRA JALIMAN

bouquet

Throw out any advice that says you have to design your bouquet around the size of your venue (big venue equals big bouquet, etc.), size or shape of your body, or what you're wearing. "That's all bullshit. Anybody can have anything," says event designer Lewis Miller. "It's our job to make it look fantastic."

Is a bouquet a must?

NO . . . ALTHOUGH IT CAN BE HARD TO RESIST THE PRESSURE FROM OTHER PEOPLE TO HAVE ONE. YOU COULD WEAR A CORSAGE OR HAIR WREATH INSTEAD.

TOSSING THE BOUQUET

It's a tradition that signifies passing on the bride's luck to the unmarried females—whoever catches it will be the next to get married. Got friends who'll think this is fun? Throw away . . .

Making it more personal

Get your florist to fix mementoes or charms into your bouquet; include your mom's favorite flowers or the flowers she used in her own bouquet.

Delivery date?

BOUQUETS ARE NORMALLY DELIVERED ON THE DAY OF THE WEDDING. IF IT COMES THE DAY BEFORE, YOU'LL PROBABLY NEED TO PUT IT IN THE FRIDGE.

Flower alternatives

Your bouquet doesn't have to be fresh flowers. Use paper flowers, vintage brooches, or something relating to where you're having your wedding—for example, shells for an event at the beach.

The language of flowers

A really sweet way to put a bouquet together is to use the language of flowers—all blooms have a meaning. For more on this, go to the Flowers entry on page 149.

Boutonnieres A single flower is normally worn on the left lapel by the groom, best man, groomsmen, both fathers, and sometimes the mothers of the bride and groom, too, but you can extend it to include anyone you want.

Even though tradition calls for it, we don't know many men who willingly attach too many flowers to their body as decoration.

Most couples keep it simple and classic, but there's no rule that says you can't do something different. "I LOVE big boutonnieres on guys. . . . Only guys with big balls wear big flowers," says event designer Lewis Miller. For expert tips, go to the Flowers entry on page 149.

FLORISTS' CHOICE
"We love small field-picked flowers loosely tied with custom velvet or silk," says florist Holly Flora.

Brand Just for fun, ask yourself, If my wedding was a brand, what would it be?

Is it UPMARKET CHIC and SOPHISTICATED, YOUNG and FUN, DOWN TO EARTH and a bit hippie?

Once you decide which words describe your brand, let it guide all your design decisions, from the location to the colors, stationery, dress, rings, cake, and music.

Bridal shower

How much better can it get? A party thrown in your honor, where, although you know it's theoretically about friends and family showering you with good wishes, they're likely to shower you with gifts as well.

WHAT DO YOU DO THERE? Get together with the people you love and, if we're being honest, unwrap presents. The good news is that the bridesmaids usually organize it.

IF YOU DON'T HAVE ANY BRIDESMAIDS? Etiquette fanatics say bridal showers shouldn't be hosted by the mother of the bride, sisters, or even future mothers-in-law, in case it looks like they're asking for stuff—but that's nonsense. Anyone can throw you a shower.

WHEN DO YOU HAVE IT? Because it's normally thrown by someone else, you might not even know when it is. If anyone asks you, space it out from the bachelorette party and wedding to give everyone a break from spending money on you.

AND FINALLY: Whatever form your shower takes, smile. Not like a crazy Stepford wife. Just keep a genuine upbeat attitude, even if you're secretly disappointed they haven't done something more glamorous or up your alley.

A LITTLE BIT OF CONTROVERSY

Can you put registry details in with the shower invitation? We're not fans of all the intrigue regarding registries that some people go to for appearance's sake. If you think your friends and family won't get offended by a direct approach (some do), then go ahead. Read more in Registry, page 250.

Try this:

Ask the most organized bridesmaid to make a gift log at your bridal shower, so your thank-you's aren't guesswork. Try to make the shower fun for everyone else, too. Watching someone else unwrap gifts for an hour is boring, no matter how much you love her.

It's always better if your bridesmaids are a team and can get along. It makes sense to avoid bringing together people you know will squabble and bitch. Include at least one sane person who is always good in a tight spot.

brides

Is there a "right" number?

No,

how many bridesmaids you have is up to you
and how much room you have.

any ideas whom you'll ask?

maids

Bridesmaids: What do they actually do?

"Brides, please remember that your bridal party is there to offer you emotional and moral support. They're not at your beck and call. They'll occasionally need to be out of your sight for small reasons, such as using the bathroom. Treat them with kindness."

ANGIE NEVAREZ,
WEDDING PLANNER

1 Be honest about your clothing, hair, and makeup choices. If they're hideous, someone should be letting you know.

2 Help you organize the wedding without letting their phone go to voicemail when you call because they're sick of talking about weddings.

3 Organize a bridal shower and bachelorette party you'll love.

4 Get their outfits and accessories together and turn up on time for all fittings no matter how otherwise occupied they are.

5 Help ensure everything goes smoothly on the day, leaving you free to enjoy it.

6 Mop up tantrums—yours or anyone else's.

7 Reapply your makeup (nicely).

8 Keep small flower girls and page boys under control with bribery if necessary.

9 Run interference with guests/relatives/parents who are getting on your nerves.

10 Generally be a pillar of happiness, light, and calm in the storm and make the day wonderful.

WHAT TO WEAR

You want to look good, but so do your bridesmaids. Don't insist on dressing them all in the same style or color just to suit a theme if they look like satin sausages and feel crappy. It's not rocket science; different body types don't all suit the same shapes.

Consider this . . .

Let your bridesmaids choose a style that suits them and, when it comes to color, think about having different tones that work with their hair and skin colors. Let's say, for example, that you want them in purple—what looks good on a blond won't necessarily on a redhead, but tones of purple range from palest lilac to deep lavender and aubergine.

A little bit of controversy

Do you expect your bridesmaids to pay their own way? "The participation of a bridesmaid is an honor bestowed on a friendship," says bridal expert Renée Strauss. "But some brides expect that to come with the investment of the bridesmaid 'buying in.' I think a bride should show appreciation of her friends by paying for the attire she wants them to wear." You should be footing all or some of the bill, especially if you're being very particular about what they wear. "If budget's a factor for you," says Strauss, "choose a less-expensive dress."

SAYING THANK-YOU

It is traditional to thank your bridesmaids with a gift. Something personal to each girl has much more meaning than a few identical pendants snapped up online. See the Thank-you's entry on page 285 for some inspiration.

Brunch If you're not flying straight off on honeymoon, a next-day brunch is a fantastic way to recap the wedding and catch up on all the gossip you missed. Let your friends and relatives know in advance you'll be hosting it, even if it's informal.

Budget Being clear about your budget is the biggest wedding planning time-saver—it stops you from wasting time on things and people you can't afford. And, to be honest, it stops the heartbreak of lusting over things you just can't have.

Set your budget as early as possible.
It will define everything you do from how many guests you have to the vendors you short-list.

DO THE MATH

If you want to save, how much can you put aside every month?

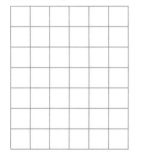

TIPS FOR SETTING YOUR BUDGET
- Write it down in black and white. Learn to love it.
- If you've got savings, consider whether you want to use them.
- If the number you come up with is not what you hoped for, set up a savings account for your wedding and add to it every month. If you know your savings plan is likely to be wishful thinking by month two, don't increase your spending.
- If parents offer to pay for something specific, check their budget for it. Don't overspend and assume they'll be able to make up the difference.
- When you're penciling in prices, always verify that they include tax. Tradesmen often quote without it.
- Be businesslike; if you overspend in one area, cut down in another.

- Make accurate notes on your checklist about when deposits and final payments are due and check them off when they're done.
- Be honest about what you've spent on everything wedding-related, from clips for the bridesmaids' hair to underwear. All the little things add up.

BUDGET BREAKDOWN Putting together a wedding on the tightest of budgets? Planner Amy Nichols pins down what to spend where:

- **$1,000:** Keep the guest list VERY small—immediate family, maybe a best friend each. Keep it to Champagne and cake, or do a morning breakfast or brunch. Ask family members to help make a cake or arrange flowers.
- **$3,000:** Go with the above, and add some stellar photos from a professional. Snag a deal by getting married on a weekday, and asking for a four-hour package. If you love food and wine, go to an amazing restaurant for dinner.
- **$5,000:** Include the above but add a few more splurges that are important to you. I'd add flowers. Find someone local to design inexpensive boutonnieres, bouquets, and arrangements, or visit your local flower market and design yourself. With the leftover $$, invite a few more people— taking it from a small family party to perhaps another 20 friends and family members.

Butterfly release

This practice is still legal, but it's condemned by conservation groups. "The potential for harm is tremendous," says Jeffrey Glassberg, president of the North American Butterfly Association (NABA). "The butterflies released are often outside their natural habitat and die very quickly or impact local wild populations. And why would you treat animals like party favors?"

PLANNING AHEAD

- Leave an allowance for unexpected extras.
- Don't forget to factor in tips—they can add up to a sizeable chunk of cash.

FURTHER READING

For ideas on what you can use instead, see the Confetti entry on page 92.

Cake and cupcakes

"There is no RIGHT or WRONG when considering **wedding cakes."**

CAKE DESIGNER RON BEN-ISRAEL

But you need a starting point . . . so think about whether you want just a simple, delicious cake or something that'll be more of a focal point, too—part of the décor.

ARE YOUR HANDS TIED? Does your venue or caterer have a list of bakers you're required to use? If they don't, you're free to buy from local cake makers and bakeries, specialist celebration cake bakeries, big-name cake designers, delis, in-store bakeries; have a friend or relative make it for you; or do it yourself.

HOW MUCH CAKE DO I NEED? If you're using it as dessert, you'll need a serving for every guest. If you're dishing it up on top of dessert, allow for around 70 to 80 percent of your guests. If you're making it yourself, use online guides to determine how many servings you'll get from different-sized cakes. As a very rough guide, a three-tier cake—with eight-inch, ten-inch, and twelve-inch round tiers—will feed 100 to 120 guests.

DO YOU WANT . . .
- Traditional tiers?
- Different shapes: hearts, squares, rounds, hexagons?
- A flat sheet cake?
- Cupcakes?
- Towers of profiteroles?
- Cheeses?

WHEN SHOULD I ORDER? If you want a complex or designer cake, or have your heart set on a particular baker, book six months to a year out. Otherwise, try to give yourself around three months.

GROOM'S CAKES AND THEMED CAKES Can you have a themed cake that tastes as good as it looks? "Definitely," says cake designer Greggy Soriano, "but choose a baker with structure and design skill. There's no point having a crazy-weird shape made of rice cereal treats, piled with tons of gum paste, because A: It's ugly, B: Structurally, it's probably not the most safe, C: People want to eat a yummy, lush cake, darn it. Think about flavor profiles, texture, and flavor."

CAKE AND CHAMPAGNE "Don't choose a dry Champagne or sparkling wine to have with the cake," says Master of Wine Jennifer Simonetti-Bryan. "It's as good as drinking orange juice right after you've brushed your teeth with mint toothpaste. The sweet cake makes the wine taste sour and bitter. Instead, choose a slightly sweet sparkler (demi-sec Champagne, Moscato d'Asti, Brachetto, etc.) to pair with it."

TIPS FOR SAVING SOME OF YOUR CAKE Want to save the top tier for your first anniversary, or a christening? Here's what you need to do:

- Remove all the decorations except smaller icing and sugar flowers, which should be fine.
- Check what the tier's resting on: if it's cardboard, transfer onto plastic or a foil-covered cake base.
- Put it unwrapped in the freezer for about an hour.
- Take it out, and wrap it really, really, really well in plastic wrap (foil will stick to the icing).
- Now you can add a layer of foil.
- Place the cake in an airtight container and freeze.

WANT TO DIY YOUR CAKE? Now is not the time to bake a cake for the first time, or attempt something fancy if your repertoire is normally a frosted layer cake.

- **Practice:** If you're set on doing your own, factor in practice time. If it's complicated, do a dry run from beginning to end.
- **Timing:** How long does it take to make a cake? "As a general rule, set aside four separate days for a stress-free cake," says Mary Maher, cofounder of www.thecake girls.com.

> **Day 1:** Bake all your cake layers, let cool, wrap them in plastic wrap, and place them in the freezer.
> **Day 2:** Prepare any decorations that you can in advance, for example, the display board, sugar paste flowers, fondant bow, etc.
> **Day 3:** Three days before your wedding, make the icing, defrost your cake layers, and ice your tiers before placing them in the fridge overnight.
> **Day 4:** Two days before your wedding, stack your cake and decorate. Refrigerate if you have fresh fillings or buttercream.

- **Insider secrets:** Here's how to take the stress out of preparing your own wedding cake, says Faith Durand, executive editor of The Kitchn.

> **1.** Stick with recipes you know.
> **2.** Think many cakes, not one huge one.
> **3.** Have help at the wedding.
> **4.** Think of creative ways to decorate. Garnish with swirls of whipped cream, chopped chocolate flakes, seasonal cut fruit, or fresh organic flowers.

DO I HAVE TO HAVE A CAKE? Of course not. Apart from cake alternatives like profiterole towers and cupcakes (see right) you can go ultracreative. "We had a piñata, which people went crazy over," says Erin Flaherty, *Marie Claire* health and beauty director.

CUPCAKES

Candace Nelson, founder of Sprinkles cupcake bakery, highlights the need-to-knows.

- **Why cupcakes?** No need to settle on one flavor; easy to serve and many ways you can present them.
- **How many?** One per person is usually enough.
- **How to cut costs:** Find out if quantity discounts are available; think about which orders are easiest for that bakery. For example, you might convince a cupcake bakery that ordering 200 cupcakes in one flavor is easier than the same order in eight different flavors.
- **How do you cut the cake if you're serving cupcakes?** Order a small six-inch cake for the photo.

CAKES TOP 10:
tips for getting exactly what you want

1

SET YOUR BUDGET & GET MORE FOR IT
Know how much you have to spend, and work out what you can get for your money. "Ask what your options are within your budget," says Renato Poliafito, cofounder of Baked NYC.

2

GET THE RIGHT BAKER FOR THE JOB
Choose a baker who routinely makes the sort of cake you want, because that's where their expertise is. "Don't push for things they don't normally do," says Erin McKenna, founder of Babycakes NYC. Reputable bakers will turn you down if something's outside their comfort zone, but some won't, and down that road lies disaster.

3

DO YOUR HOMEWORK
"Research before you decide on a bakery or a cake designer. The reliable ones will have plenty of referrals and experience," says Ben-Israel.

4

MAKE SURE THEY'RE INSURED
Bakers have had to handle everything from hurricanes to thieves to good old human error. "Life is unpredictable. Insist on hiring only licensed and insured vendors," says Ben-Israel.

5

GO LOCAL "Choose a local vendor. Shipping is expensive and nerve racking," says Poliafito. The exception is if you're happy to pay for the baker and team to travel with the cake and ensure its safety!

ON THE ROAD
Farthest a top baker traveled to deliver a wedding cake? "To Sri Lanka. I had to ride an elephant for part of it," says Ben-Israel.

6

LISTEN TO THE PROFESSIONALS

If they tell you something's not a good idea, listen. "It's not that he's trying to make your dreams go to hell by not giving you what you want," says Soriano. "He just wants to make sure you have a beautiful cake on the day."

7

SHARE YOUR IDEAS

Take inspiration to the appointment—color swatches, pictures, details from your wedding, including the location and what you're wearing. "Don't be afraid to tell the designer what you love," says Soriano.

8

DON'T JUDGE ON LOOKS ALONE

Always, always try before you buy. "All wedding cakes should look appealing, but it's all about taste at the end of the experience. Make sure it's delicious," says Poliafito.

9

FRESH IS BEST

"Ask when your cake will be made," advises McKenna. "At a tasting, you're eating a fresh cake, but many caterers bake and freeze a week before to save time. Make sure you are getting a fresh one on the day of the event, too."

10

GET IT ALL IN WRITING

Include timings, delivery, add-on fees, rush charges, as well as the specifications for the cake itself. "Include any sketches or photos to illustrate the promised product," says Ben-Israel.

SPECIAL DIETS

Being on a restricted diet doesn't mean you can't have a delicious wedding cake. Specialist bakeries can cater everything from gluten-free to sugar-free, dairy-free, or completely vegan.

Cake-cutting etiquette

"Cut the cake whenever you want."

WEDDING PLANNER CASSANDRA SANTOR

Q **How do I cut the cake?**

A Traditionally the groom puts his hand over the bride's, they cut the cake together— usually the bottom layer—the groom feeds a bite to the bride, and vice versa. If you're a same-sex couple, just clasp your hands together.

PLANNING AHEAD

Buy a server set engraved with your initials or the date you're married and reuse it on special occasions.

"I've seen couples do it before dinner because it's what they were most excited about," says Santor. Around 45 minutes before the end of the evening also works well because it signals the end of the party. For tea or cocktail receptions cut it after speeches and, if it's also dessert, before any food is served.

PROBLEM: The cutting fee trick

If you bring in a cake from an outside baker, the venue or caterers will claw back what they've lost on it by charging you an extra fee. It can be anything from $1 per slice to $10 or more. Their justification is that they need to be paid for their time, dishes, and flatware.

SOLUTION: Try some negotiating

Ask for the fee to be removed from your contract or at least reduced, or negotiate a flat fee for their time before you sign. It should take expert catering servers only "about twenty minutes to cut a cake for 200 people," says caterer Urban Palate. If you'd rather do it yourself, ask if that's an option, or negotiate that into your contract, too.

WANT TO CUT THE CAKE YOURSELVES . . . ?

- Download a chart showing exactly how to cut the shape and size of wedding cake you have.
- Have two people to help: one can slice while one plates.
- Clean the knife after every few cuts or the cake will look like it's been in a car crash.
- Know how to remove any dummy layers, pillars, and cardboard between the tiers.
- Hide away your anniversary tier before it gets eaten.

Cake toppers
There are some strange things out there but also some cute, handcrafted toppers that you can customize with your names, dates, or initials—everything from crystal monograms to wooden figurines, mini-you caricatures, and sugarcraft. Etsy is the best place for these; for antique and vintage, head to eBay.

THINK ANY OLD TOPPER WILL DO? Consider the size of your cake—will your little figures be lost? How heavy are they—will your cake sag under the weight of the statues? And do they actually look good, or clash with the other decorations?

DID YOU KNOW . . .
Sugarcraft and clay figurines break. Easily. Arms snap off, heads will roll. Use caution when handling or transporting for minimal limb loss.

Calligraphy
This is an art. If you're thinking it's all a bit old-fashioned, calligraphers have lots of styles, including clean, modern writing. What can they do apart from your envelopes?

Try this:
Use calligraphy to chalk up menu boards, number your tables, handwrite your vows, or create a personal monogram. "The sky's the limit," says professional calligrapher Anne Robbin. "I've done balloons for flower girls to carry down the aisle saying 'Here comes the bride.'"

BOOKING A CALLIGRAPHER
If looking at the website's not enough, ask for a sample and check past client reviews online. Run through this checklist before you confirm, says Robbin:
1. How much extra stationery do they need to allow for mistakes?
2. When do you pay and do they charge tax?
3. Tell the calligrapher what type of envelopes and paper

TIPS FOR BOOKING A CALLIGRAPHER

calligraphy cont

Q **Can you DIY calligraphy?**

A Not normally. "I can't tell you how many last-minute calls I've had from brides who thought it seemed like a good idea," says Anne Robbin.

you're providing. "They need to know if it's dark or lined because that can mean extra charges."

4. Are they charging per piece (i.e., per envelope) or per word?

5. How much time do they need?

DON'T hand over a handwritten list or one full of typos. Get someone else to double-check spellings.

DO allow the calligrapher more time if you ask for extra work.

DON'T stuff and stamp your envelopes beforehand because the calligrapher will have to take everything apart again.

Calling it off/cold feet

How do you feel about getting married? Excited? Nervous? Or depressed and like you've got a stone sitting in the pit of your stomach?

"A BIT OF WAVERING before a wedding IS NATURAL. Knowing that can help you keep it in PERSPECTIVE."

RELATIONSHIP EXPERT DR. JANE GREER

Although doubts are common, don't ignore them, says Thomas Bradbury of the Relationship Institute at UCLA. A 2012 study showed that newlywed women who'd had doubts were two-and-a-half times more likely to divorce four years later. "Do you think the doubts will go away when you have a mortgage and two kids?" Calling off a wedding isn't easy, but if you know that you don't want to go through with it, here's what you have to do:

HOW TO UNRAVEL A WEDDING

1. Guests. Ask sympathetic friends or family to help let guests know immediately, and keep explanations simple.

2. Vendors. "Notify them quickly, but don't feel obligated to go into detail; just let them know the wedding won't be taking place. Do it by phone, then follow up with confirmation in writing via e-mail," says wedding planner Amy Nichols.

3. Gifts. Start sending them back once you've notified the guests.

RECOUPING COSTS
Brokerage companies act as middlemen between couples who've canceled and couples or wedding planners looking for deals at short notice.

Cameras

Do you want the sea of iPads, cameras, and phones your guests are waving to get the pics of your wedding, or would you rather leave it to your photographer?

CAMERAS ALLOWED

PROS: Your guests will capture all the candid moments your photographer can't. And picture sharing is easy. Wedding apps let guests log on and download their shots; you can even set up a laptop for it at the reception. Or use Instagram; ask your guests to hash-tag their pics with a name you choose, and you'll have access to those, too.

SOME CAMERAS ALLOWED

PROS: Have cameras but put some restrictions on when. Maybe you want a camera-free ceremony and then guests can shoot away. Win, win.

NO CAMERAS ALLOWED

PROS: You won't have this: "It's guests gone wild," says photographer Corey Ann Balazowich. "They are jumping in front of the photographer—in the aisle, onto the altar, and in front of the first kiss."

TOP TIP
If you'd like an unplugged wedding, have the officiant read out a request before the ceremony starts, says Balazowich. If you put up a sign, people will pretend they haven't seen it.

TOP 3 REASONS FOR A CAMERA-FREE WEDDING . . .

Faces: "You'll see your guests' faces as you walk up the aisle instead of the backs of their cameras and iPhones, and they'll see yours, instead of looking at you through a screen."

Eyes: "When your photographer tries to take the shots you've paid them to take, your eyes will be on them. When guests are taking pictures, no matter how many times I ask people to look at me, they're not, because it's instinct to look at the person you're most familiar with."

Flashes: There's only one set going off. "Fewer pictures will be ruined by someone else's flash or focus beam and there's less blinking!" says Balazowich.

SOCIAL MEDIA ETIQUETTE

Do you want pictures of you getting ready on social media before you've even made it to the ceremony? If not, lay down some advance rules. Do you mind if guests share pictures, comments, Tweets, or live video feeds? If so, have your officiant ask guests not to post on social media.

Candles/candlelight
What's the simplest and cheapest trick in the book for transforming ANY venue? Candlelight. Apart from the fact that everyone is suddenly better looking and ten years younger because it's basically the Botox of lighting, candlelight is the best way to create romance, mood, and atmosphere. It's magical.

TRICKS OF THE LIGHT

1. There aren't many times you can say this—more is definitely more.

2. Use candles to replace flowers if you're on a budget.

3. Spend a few dollars more on slow-burning candles.

4. Check your venue's policy. "The restrictions we face are mostly to do with candles—whether we can use live flame, or if they need to be enclosed in glass," says event designer Lewis Miller.

5. Avoid putting tapers in the line of breezes (use hurricane lamps or votives) and placing votives on buffet tables (people drop food and drink in them).

TRICKS OF THE LIGHT

Try this:

Group together different sizes, styles, and colors of candles.

Think about tiny colored votives, tall candelabras, rustic iron holders, storm lanterns, or pretty mercury glass holders.

UNITY CANDLE Lighting a unity candle during the ceremony is a recent tradition, so if you're having a religious ceremony, check whether your minister will allow it. How does it work? You are each passed a taper candle from a friend or family member, and together you light a single candle.

Carriage "There aren't any cars on the island of Sark [British Channel Islands]," said one real bride, "so we left our wedding in a horse-drawn carriage at midnight. The sound of the horses' hooves and flickering lantern light (no streetlights!) made it completely timeless."

A horse and carriage can be a really romantic means of transport if you don't have far to go and aren't in a hurry.

Don't do it if the weather could be wet (unless it's got a cover), or if you are allergic or afraid of animals bigger than a cat, or aren't very nimble (it's not easy clambering into a carriage in a gown). Use a company that treats its animals well—check reviews.

cash

Would you really love cash instead of traditional wedding gifts? You're not alone.

There are TWO SCHOOLS of thought here.

YES!

Go ahead and ask for cash.

"I swear the only people that care are the 'etiquette' people who tell you not to do it," says one bride who asked for cash gifts. "Even older relatives we thought might be upset, like our grandparents, couldn't have cared less."

NO!

Don't ever ask for cash . . . it's never okay.

"Dear God, please don't write that you want cash even if you'd really, really, prefer it. It'll always be tacky to ask for it in any way, shape, or form. Nothing takes the warm feeling out of a wedding than talking about cold, hard cash," says event planner Annie Lee.

AMERICA VS THE REST OF THE WORLD It's time for common sense. *Cash* isn't a dirty word. We sometimes tie ourselves in knots because we can't be straightforward about money, while the rest of the world showers newlyweds with cash as a blessing. There's no logical reason that cash is "ruder" than other gifts. You can politely and creatively ask for what you need, rather than looking to "rules" to get you what you don't.

HOW TO ASK FOR MONEY The key to not offending people is to give them a choice.

> **DON'T** scrawl demands like "Contributions of $100 each will be gratefully received" on your stationery . . . No surprises, it'll get a bad response.
>
> **DO** say something more along the lines of: "We have everything we need but if you'd like to contribute, we're saving for x, y, z." Some guests definitely prefer it if their contribution has a purpose, a honeymoon for example, or to put toward a house or college funds for your kids.
>
> **DON'T** make it something too outrageous, although one British bride asked for contributions to a DD boob job and guests dutifully donated.

SURVEY SAYS As a note, all the brides we spoke to who asked for cash offended . . . exactly no one. Guests were all relieved they didn't have to go searching for gifts, and grateful for the honesty.

WHERE AND WHEN TO TELL PEOPLE YOU WANT CASH The same as you would for a traditional registry, approach this in a way that suits your family and friends and style of wedding best; there's no single right answer here. Put the info on your wedding website at the same time you send your invitations out or leave the details with someone who's happy to take a gazillion calls. The easiest way? Put a note in with your invitations. But be warned . . . being this straightforward upsets some people.

AROUND THE GLOBE
Brides and grooms are showered with cash . . .

- **Netherlands:** an envelope sign on invitations means cash gifts.
- **Belgium:** guests put cash in mini–mail boxes posted at the reception.
- **Greece:** money is pinned on the bride.
- **Italy:** the bride carries a bag for guests to put money in.
- **Spain:** guests deposit straight into the couple's bank account.
- **Jewish weddings:** money is given in multiples of the number 18.
- **Asia:** cash is put in red envelopes for good luck.
- **Middle East:** guests bring blessings to the couple by gifting money or gold.
- **Mexico:** has the money dance.
- **Brazil:** the bride's shoe is passed around to tuck money in.

Cash bar
A bit like Cash (previous pages), this is a subject where people like to lay down the law. Thou shalt not have a cash bar at a wedding. Thou shalt have a dry wedding rather than a cash bar. But if you genuinely can't afford to fund a bar, ask yourself if you know a single person who'd rather go to a dry wedding than dip into their own pocket to buy a drink. Treat your guests like adults and give them the opportunity to buy drinks for some (or all) of the party if you can't.

TOP TIP
Have the sort of meal you want, not what you think you should have. Julia Roberts served hot dogs, hamburgers, and corn at her 4th of July wedding to Danny Moder.

DO YOUR HOMEWORK
Go to meetings prepared. "Bring photos and examples of food and drink ideas you love. Create a Pinterest board and invite the caterer to follow you."
**Paula LeDuc
Fine Catering**

Catering
What's the secret to getting wedding food right? All you have to do is pay attention to the most common gripes about it: there's not enough, it's cold, or served late.

THE SECRET OF SUCCESSFUL CATERING
- **Have plenty.** No one wants to come away hungry or feel like they're being rationed one potato at a time.
- **Keep it timely.** Hungry people get tired and bored. Feed everyone at the same time, and in between meals always have something for people to nibble on.
- **Have enough staff.** Make sure there is enough kitchen staff and servers to handle the number of guests. You might need extra staff.

GETTING THE MOST FROM YOUR CATERER
DO be honest about your budget. And be realistic about what you can get for it.

DO say what you don't want. "Tell them your least favorite foods and drinks, as well as your favorites," says Paula LeDuc Fine Catering.

DON'T be afraid to ask. "Ask your caterer to develop ideas even if you don't see them on their standard menus."

DON'T take it too seriously. "Food and drink decisions should be fun."

DON'T book a caterer who's never done an event similar in size and location to yours.

DON'T book without trying the food. If it's a food truck or restaurant, go and try it yourself.

DON'T book based on basic prices on a website. There will be add-ons like cutlery and tableware, staff, etc.

FOODIE QUESTIONS TO ASK YOURSELF

1. What's your favorite food? What does your family like?

2. What sort of food is right for the time of day? Are you having breakfast, brunch, lunch, afternoon tea, dinner?

3. What time of year is the wedding? Think in season: what do people naturally prefer to eat then? Most people don't want a light green salad when it's zero degrees outside or heavy, rich food when it's too hot to move.

4. How many guests am I catering for? Some meals can't be catered on big scales.

5. What style do I want? Buffets and stations make it easy to offer multiple choices of meal; a seated dinner is normally more formal and comes with a set menu or a couple of choices. Canapés are good for socializing.

TOP
5

**FOODIE
QUESTIONS
TO ASK
YOURSELF**

FURTHER READING

For more information on service options, turn to page 266.

What kind of catering style will work for you?

CATERERS' TOP 10:
questions you need to ask

1 How many jobs will you be catering on the same day/weekend as mine?

2 What's not included in my price quote? (Ask them to spell out everything that incurs additional cost, from extra bar staff and overtime charges to cake cutting.)

3 How do you charge . . . per guest or per serving of food?

4 Will gratuity and service charges be added to my bill automatically? If yes, will any of that go to the staff?

5 How many staff will you have in the kitchen/as servers/waitresses/bartenders? How much will extra staff cost?

WANT TO CUT COSTS?

● **Have a simple, pared-down buffet.** "You need fewer servers or people in the kitchen," says caterer Urban Palate.

● **Have your meal earlier in the day.** Lunch, brunch, or afternoon tea often costs far less than an evening meal.

● **Book your wedding on a weekday.** You're much more likely to get a deal.

6 Do you have a preset menu or will I be able to customize?

7 Have you worked at the venue before? What information do you need about equipment and deliveries?

8 What happens if the chef is sick or abducted by aliens?

9 How will staff be dressed? How experienced are they? (Don't take it for granted that they'll be clean, sweet smelling, and with intact brains . . .)

10 For a buffet, when will the food be made? Two weeks before, day of, an hour before?

SPECIAL DIETS

● **How do you find out who can't eat what?** Don't assume people will let you know. Write, "Please advise of any dietary requirements or allergies" on your RSVPs—whether that's on a card, by e-mail, or on your wedding website.

● **Want to make the veggies happy?** Don't resort to the lazy caterer's favorites: risotto and pasta. Work with the caterer to make the meal as delicious as the one for meat-eating guests. Need inspiration? Look at menus from vegetarian restaurants, vegetarian recipes online, and veggie blogs. There is no end of delicious options.

Cell phones

Think people won't have messages and e-mails pinging away during your wedding? You can guarantee they will; if it'll drive you nuts, operate a cell-phone coat check. Always give advance warning that there'll be one (people get crazy over their phones), and allow guests to check in with their cell-phone babies once an hour for good behavior. If a phone check seems extreme, ask the officiant to make an announcement asking people to turn them off.

> **DON'T** have crazy people who will forcibly pry cell phones from guests or refuse them entry. If people are visibly reluctant or on call to save the world, just let it go or ask them to turn the phone to silent.

Cellulite

Dimply skin, or good old cellulite, can affect anyone, even the superslim. These are the things you really need to know about it. . . .

1. There is no magic cream that will fix it. "I've yet to come across a product that really works," says *Marie Claire* health and beauty director Erin Flaherty. But anticellulite creams can make your skin look better. The combination of increased blood flow through simply massaging it in and ingredients like retinol and caffeine can make skin look smoother and more evenly toned.

2. Diet and how often you poop make a difference. If you have a couple of months before your wedding, you'll see an improvement if you eat a clean, alkaline, unprocessed diet and drink pure water with lemon first thing in the morning, says nutritional therapist Amanda Griggs. "I'd do a vegetable juice fast." See the Detox entry on page 112 for more information on doing this properly.

3. A tan can hide a multitude of sins. If you don't have time to tackle your cellulite, get a spray tan.

DID YOU KNOW . . .

Dry brushing works. "Instead of spending hundreds of dollars on treatments, women should just dry brush their legs," a therapist at a prestigious spa told us. Starting at the ankles, brush upward with a natural-bristle brush, using light pressure all the lengths of the legs and buttocks in the direction of the heart. Do it every day. This stimulates the lymphatic system to clear toxins.

Centerpieces

The rules for centerpieces are actually very simple, says event designer Lewis Miller. "They go in the center of the table, they're low or high enough to allow for conversation easily, and should be simple enough to create a dynamic vision, but detailed enough to allow for discovery upon closer inspection."

INSIDER ADVICE We asked LA-based Holly Flora what the biggest do's and don't are for centerpieces:

1. Focus on the practical as well as how it looks. "Think about weather conditions and what's appropriate décor for the space."

2. If you're indoors, bring the outdoors in.

3. Don't be afraid of drama; not everything has to be ethereal and organic.

4. Rose balls are done and done.

OTHER THINGS TO THINK ABOUT? Avoid anything smelly that'll trigger allergies or overwhelm food. Play around: See how different ideas, colors, and heights work, but avoid clustering too many things together—it'll drown the table.

STICKY FINGERS Don't forget to put a sticker or card underneath any rented centerpieces saying clearly that they're rented; these have a habit of disappearing with guests at the end of the evening.

SOME FOOD FOR THOUGHT ...
Centerpieces don't have to be flowers, plants, candles, or purely decorative. Try beautiful arrangements of . . .

● cheese and crackers, fruit trays, olives and nuts, baked Brie and bread

● candy dishes, cupcake towers, colored *macarons*, chocolate-covered strawberries.

FURTHER READING
For more information on floral centerpieces, go to the Flowers entry on page 149.

Try this:

"Have a single medium-scale stunning floral centerpiece on a round table. For example, blackberries on the vine with wild groupings of red scabiosa, Sally Holmes roses, other wild vines, and currants in a brass container." **Holly Flora**

"The ceremony plan is the **single** most

P R O C R A S T I N A T E D

item of wedding planning. **"**

WEDDING PLANNER SANDY MALONE

Why does everyone have such a mental block about it? Because it feels "big," there'll probably be an audience, and it might require a bit of homework. You might need to choose a reading or music and write your vows. But the basic ingredients are always the same. If you feel stuck, you can't go wrong with the traditional ceremony and vows. You don't have to dream up something wild, wacky, or original. Whether the ceremony is the most meaningful part of your day or a formality before you get to the party, see below and the Order of service entry on page 223.

MAKING IT PERSONAL

- Have someone you know officiate.
- Share messages from absent loved ones.
- Use readings, songs, poems, or something you wrote yourself.
- If you have children, get them involved, too. See the Children entry on page 84.

RECIPE FOR A CEREMONY

- 1 couple
- 1 officiant
- Witnesses
- 1 exchange of vows
- 1 signing of the marriage license

OPTIONAL

- Exchange of rings
- Readings/blessings
- Singing
- Music

Champagne

Engagements and weddings are all about celebration, and what better way to celebrate? But without Champagne expertise, buying it can be an expensive minefield. We asked Master of Wine Jennifer Simonetti-Bryan, author of *The One Minute Wine Master,* to guide us through the wonderful world of Champagne.

WHAT'S BEST ON A BUDGET? "No question, go for cheaper Champagne, rather than Cava or Prosecco. But you generally don't see Champagne under $25 per bottle," explains Simonetti-Bryan. "A sweet spot for Champagne is around $40 per bottle. If you want a great sparkler for under $25, look for sparkling wines from California or Italy. For under $15, the best values are Prosecco and Cava."

> **Champagne** = citrus, minerals, toast, and biscuit aromas
> **Prosecco** = pear, floral notes, and minerals
> **Cava** = apple, citrus, minerals and earthiness

MISTAKE-PROOF YOUR PURCHASE

Simonetti-Bryan offers the following advice:
DON'T confuse sparkling wine with Champagne. Champagne only describes the traditional method sparkling wine that comes from the French region of Champagne.
DON'T buy the wrong style. See the sidebar (right) for the sweetness classification levels. People often mistakenly assume extradry is drier than Brut.
DON'T assume if it's more expensive, it must be better. Champagne's a luxury product; there's supply and demand and marketing built into the pricing.

PARTY TRICK "It always takes six twists to take off the wire cage when you're opening Champagne. Try it!"

Q Can Champagne ever be too cold?

A "Yes. The proper temperature is about 45°F or 7°C. Most refrigerators are set between 35 and 38°F (2 to 4°C)—too cold for serving. It'll be less flavorful until it warms up."

DID YOU KNOW . . .
Think you know which the driest Champagne is?

DRIEST
Ultra Brut (also known as Brut Zero, Brut Nature, Brut Sauvage)
Extra Brut
Brut
Extradry or Extrasec
Sec
Demi-sec
Doux
SWEETEST

Cheap and chic

Tiny budgets don't mean you can't have a chic wedding. Chic equals simplicity. Lose the fuss, the extras, and the overblown and overpriced details. "We used mason jars as candleholders, brown paper bags filled with sand and a votive candle secured inside, and Tiki torches for extra lighting and a romantic feel," says male grooming expert Diana Schmidtke.

1 LOSE THE NOTION THAT WEDDINGS MUST HAVE . . .

We all have ideas about what we think makes a "wedding." White dresses, bridesmaids, a bouquet—but a wedding doesn't need any of it. All you need are two people and an officiant. That's liberating: From there, add on only the things that have meaning and lose the rest.

2 KEEP IT SIMPLE AND SMALL

You don't have to spend a lot of money. "Simple can be beautiful," says Paula LeDuc Fine Catering. "Intimate ceremonies are often the most memorable and special for the bride, the groom, and the guests."

3 HAVE CONFIDENCE

If you're incorporating some cheap and chic ideas, own them. Runway models walk the catwalk with all sorts of crap draped over them—but they carry it off because they do it with confidence. Take some of that kick-ass positivity and apply it to your wedding. Spending more money never makes a wedding more meaningful, and it definitely doesn't always make it more beautiful.

4 USE WHAT YOU HAVE AROUND YOU

Recycle, use nature, borrow from friends and family. "We collected driftwood on the beach and made our wedding signs with a couple of tubes of paint," said Schmidtke.

Checklist

This is the only way to keep track of what you've accomplished and what's left to do. But, reminds wedding planner Sandy Malone, "You are responsible for keeping your to-do list and actually doing the things on it: create your music playlist, write your ceremony, complete your place card chart, choose your reception menu, etc."

Cheese (cake)

A cool change from the usual stacked-up layer cake affairs is a stacked-up cheese affair instead. "The number one rule is to offer cheeses with different colors, textures, and flavors," says cheese expert Juliana Uruburu. "Your 'cake' should get progressively lighter, softer, and smaller toward the top. For example, you could have a sharp cheddar, a bold blue cheese, a sweet washed-rind mellow cow's-milk cheese, a grassy table cheese (a multipurpose cheese that can be eaten as dessert or used in cooking), and a creamy Brie. Factor in the look of the wheel as well as the taste. Use all white bloomy rind cheeses for a more traditional look, wrapped in leaves or herbs."

SEASONAL IDEAS "In the spring and summer, decorate with fresh berries, and dress fall and winter cakes with dried figs, wine grapes, and fruit and nut crostini," says Uruburu.

BUBBLES AND CHEESE Want something to nibble on while you're doing the toasts? Champagne and wedding cake are disgusting together, explains wine expert Jennifer Simonetti-Bryan. It's far better to have delicious cheese istead. Uruburu recommends some Champagne-friendly varieties:

"Bubbles love buttery and creamy cheese. Offer your guests a triple-cream blue, burrata, or a *crescenza*—a soft, buttery Italian cow's-milk cheese that's also called *stracchino*. The cream from the cheese leaves a richness on the palate that the sparkling wine cuts right through. They are remarkable together."

DID YOU KNOW . . .
- You should serve one to two ounces of each cheese per guest.
- Cheese can be left out for up to two hours before it's served as long as the wheels haven't been cut into.
- Want to DIY? "Put sturdy cheese like cheddar on the bottom, then denser wheels like Manchego, then a top layer of Brie or goat's-milk cheese," says Uruburu.

Children The reasons people most often have for not inviting children are that they want an adults-only party, are trying to stick to a budget, or have a limit on numbers.

Or it could be that KIDS ARE ANNOYING SOMETIMES.*

*we can say this; we have them.

TOP 5

TIPS FOR NAVIGATING CHILDREN AND WEDDINGS

PLANNING AHEAD

Bored children are a magnet for trouble. Offer movies, games, coloring, or outside play areas. You can borrow toys, crayons, and board games, and download free activity packs from the internet or head to the 99¢ store.

NAVIGATING CHILDREN AND WEDDINGS:

1. The golden rule: Let your guests know early on what your policy is, with no room for misunderstandings. If you're saying no children, make it clear what "children" means—under fives, babies, only breast-feeding babies, no one under 18. Put a polite notice on your invitations or wedding website. Try something like this: "Unfortunately, we're unable to accommodate children [under the age of X]. Thanks for understanding."

2. All or nothing: Allowing some children but not others will cause untold trouble. It's better to have them all, or none. The only exception is your own children.

3. Stick to your guns: If you've decided no children, stay strong because parents will seek out the weakest link. If you aren't good at saying no, make your partner the enforcer.

4. Grumpy f*ers:** Having a no-children policy can get nasty. It can be worth making calls to any highly strung friends or relatives (or just ones who think the sun shines out of their kids' behinds) to save friendships.

5. The truth is out there: However, it's no one's business but yours. You don't ever have to tell people why you aren't inviting children, though if you need to soothe ruffled egos, tell them it's about numbers or budgets.

THE KIDS ARE ALRIGHT

● **If children are welcome, put their names on the invitation.** Or send their own mini-invites.

● **Serve healthy, child-friendly meals (okay, some concessions, it's a party).**

● **Provide childcare if you can.** If your budget won't stretch, ask friends and family to make a childcare rotation, an hour at a time.

● **Have a quiet area where young ones can nap.** Borrow playpens and cots if you need to.

CHILD FRIENDLY

Hire someone to entertain them. Be age appropriate, don't scare them with clowns, and let them have fun.

Children are often messy, loud, and unpredictable. If you aren't OK with this, you may prefer an adults-only wedding.

INCLUDING YOUR OWN CHILDREN

1. Get them involved. Ask them to design an invitation for the children; let them help you choose food, movies, and games.

2. Make them part of the ceremony. One bride had all three of her children walk her down the aisle. Include them in your vows; they can say "we do," too, to their new family.

3. Make them ring bearers. See the entry on page 259.

4. Let them join in with the adults. If your children are confident, ask them to do a reading, hand out programs, or show guests to seats.

5. Ring in the new family. Engrave their names on your wedding rings.

TOP 5

TIPS FOR INCLUDING YOUR OWN CHILDREN

Choir

❝There's nothing like a choir to elevate a scene to an ethereal level. Whether it's gospel, children, or amateurs, it just touches the soul. ❞

ANN KLINE, MUSIC SUPERVISOR FOR FILM AND TV

As well as adding atmosphere, if you're getting married in a church, a choir will make hymns sound great, says Joanna Stephens, founder of Canti d'Amore wedding choir. "People feel free to sing if there is a good strong choir leading the way."

DO make sure the choir can fill the space and they're comfortable with the music. You need at least eight people in a huge church, says Stephens.
DO check sound systems. In a small space, overmiked singers are painful.

DO YOU WANT . . .

● A canopy that shelters just you and the rabbi, or your family, too?
● A handheld chuppah or the presence of a freestanding one?

Chuppah

The chuppah is a canopy under which a Jewish wedding is performed. "It represents the home you'll build together. In its simplest and most traditional form, it's a tallith, a prayer shawl, attached at corners to four branches," says Andrea Cohen, owner of Chuppah Studio.

ARE THERE ANY RULES? "It must have four vertical poles, be open on all four sides, and covered on the top," says Cohen. Beyond that, the design is open to a modern interpretation.

86

Cocktails

Cocktails are the perfect wedding drink, says Tony Abou-Gamin, author of *The Modern Mixologist.*

"Cocktails make experiences, bond friendships, establish traditions, and celebrate memories. "

PROBLEM You think your guests will be blitzed before they even get to the meal. They're not good at moderation.

SOLUTION "Serve lower-proof spirits. Don't only serve spirit-only drinks like martinis and Manhattans. Punch can be softened so the alcohol is present but fresh citrus juices, tea, water, and carbonated soda make up the majority of the drink."

KEEPING EVERYONE HAPPY "Look for drinks that can be made in batches and finished to order; that are easy, not overly alcoholic, memorable, and lots of fun."

> **French 75:** Gin, fresh lemon juice, simple syrup, and Champagne. It's refreshing, and easy to make in bulk.
> **Punch:** There's nothing more festive than a punch bowl. I'm not talking about an Everclear, Kool-Aid, and lime sherbet punch, but a well thought-out and balanced classic punch.
> **Sangria:** Use white or rosé in the spring and summer, red or sparkling in the fall and winter. Also, celebrate the fresh fruits and juices of the season.

And remember, don't leave out the nondrinkers; give as much thought to a nonalcoholic cocktail or two as you do to the heavy-hitters. And kids always love them.

Q Can you do cocktails on a budget?

A "Absolutely. Focus on doing less and doing it the best you can. You can find good value, especially vodka, rum, and American whiskey. Find three or four cocktails that can be easily fashioned from each spirit."
Tony Abou-Ganim

FURTHER READING

See the Bartenders entry on page 36 for tips on hiring and managing barstaff.

cocktails cont

FANCY A SIGNATURE COCKTAIL? How do you put one together? Just bear these keys things in mind, says Abou-Ganim. It should:

- Represent both of you and include flavors you love
- Be relatively simple to craft
- Be able to be made in batches
- Be well balanced and not overly alcoholic
- Appeal to both men and women

Try this:

Use local ingredients; pick a color and give your favorite cocktail a twist; rename a classic or think about the first drink you both shared.

SUNSPLASH (with or without alcohol)

Batch mix (makes 25)

"To serve nonalcoholic," says Abou-Ganim, "simply exclude the Stolichnaya Ohranj and Cointreau and top each glass with some chilled seltzer water to give the drink a tickle."

- 1 liter Stolichnaya Ohranj vodka
- 12 ounces Cointreau
- 40 ounces freshly squeezed orange juice
- 40 ounces cranberry juice
- 10 ounces fresh filtered lemon juice
- 5 ounces simple syrup

"Pour into an ice-filled glass or plastic container (you'll need at least a one-and-a-half-gallon volume and preferably with a spigot so you can dispense individual drinks), shake until well blended, strain into an ice-filled 14-ounce goblet. Garnish with an orange slice and a spiral of lemon peel."

Cocktail hour

This is the start of your party, and it sets the mood for the night, so spend some time thinking about the essentials:

EATING, DRINKING, AND BEING MERRY

1. Visualize: Picture in your head how you want it to look and feel—low-key and easygoing, smart, glam, casual, wild, anything goes? Think about the best bars you've been to that had a similar feel: what were the lighting, music, and seating like?

2. In or out? Cocktail hour doesn't have to be inside. On summer evenings take it outside: set up on the beach, under the trees, on the lawn, around the fire, from the back of a car (create your own tailgate); or have a catering truck do the drinks. On cooler nights remember to keep everyone warm— provide patio heaters, fire pits, or piles of blankets.

3. Sound effects: Can you imagine being in a bar with nothing on in the background? Conversation buzzes along much better accompanied by some upbeat music, and your cocktail-hour soundtrack will get your guests in the party mood. See the Music entry on page 214 for more tips on choosing tunes.

4. Room to maneuver: Think about the space you'll be in. You want to make it as easy as possible to get drinks into your guests' hands. Make sure it's big enough for people to circulate but not so big that they'll all disappear in clusters. Will you want waiters moving around with trays of drinks or serving at a bar?

5. Good timing: Cocktail "hour" is a tried and tested formula: anything from 45 to 90 minutes works. Any longer and people start drinking too much or are starving; any shorter and they haven't had a good chance to start winding down properly.

TOP 5

TIPS FOR
EATING,
DRINKING,
AND BEING
MERRY

CROWD CONTROL

● Ask your bartenders to stop serving drinks around 10 to 15 minutes before you want everyone to be somewhere else.

● Allow about two drinks per person per hour.

● Make sure you've got plenty of comfortable seating, including cozy spots, big tables for socializing, and seats the oldies can get up from easily.

Colleagues They'll offer you lots of congratulations and Champagne on your engagement, but work colleagues can get bored quickly if you don't shut up about the wedding . . . sometimes.

HOW NOT TO . . .
Annoy your colleagues: Give them some time to talk about other things and try not to fill every waking moment sneaking wedding tasks into your working day.

HOW TO . . .
Know whom to invite: Ask yourself if they're really close friends, or if it's a strictly professional relationship. This goes for your boss, too. "Don't think you're obligated to invite them just because you get your paychecks from the same place," said one real bride.

Colors

"A life without color is a life WITHOUT LOVE."

INTERIOR DESIGNER KELLY WEARSTLER

TOP 3 SECRETS OF CHOOSING COLOR
1. Head for your closet, says Wearstler. "What color stories are you drawn to? What do you buy consistently?"
2. Colors can make you feel happy, energized, alert, calm, or soothed. They affect your body and your emotions. "Discover which ones evoke the right mood for you and go from there," she adds.
3. The effect of color can be subtle, so try different tones and shades. Choose what you like, not just because they're "wedding" colors or fashionable, and don't be swayed by other people.

COMPLEMENTING COLORS If you find yourself obsessing over one single color, or even one shade, take advice from planner Lindsay Landman: "If a bride tells me she wants green as the main color, I show her how one color's not enough . . . I need to use shades of green paired with other colors to add focus."

PASSION FOR PANTONE
If the thought of non-matching anything makes you want to weep (although you might need to let go, a little), invest in a Pantone color book so you can police your color choices like a pro.

Compromise Willingness to compromise and make sacrifices for the sake of your relationship, states UCLA's Relationship Institute, is what people with fewer problems in their marriage and lower divorce rates have in common.

So if the going ever gets tough, and it will, find ways to compromise.

"Or at least have the conversation that allows you to see things eye-to-eye. Often, we don't have the big conversations that we need. The very act of communicating in difficult times can be as important as the outcome of the conversation. When people are in it for the long term, they are often willing to make sacrifices and view themselves as a team," says psychology professor Thomas Bradbury.

COMPROMISE IN THE REAL WORLD "In the most positive light, you should want to compromise because it's important to the person whom you care most about. As a fallback, you do it to avoid the aggravation that comes from not doing it," says real groom Josh Kline.

OUR FAVORITE CONFETTI
- Biodegradable paper flowers with embedded wildflower seeds
- Bubbles
- Petals: hydrangeas, peonies, lilac, roses, delphinium, and bougainvillea

FURTHER READING
Butterfly release as confetti is never okay (see the entry on page 59) and if you're worried about rice and birds, see the Rice entry on page 258.

Confetti
The traditional confetti of rice, paper, and birdseed—symbolizing abundance and fertility—could equally now be bubbles, sparklers, or tinsel sticks. If you want old-fashioned confetti, check with your venue first. If there's a no-confetti policy, some venues might be open to compromise—biodegradable flower petals, okay; drifts of neon paper dots, not so much.

FRESH VS FROZEN Flower petals are a confetti favorite but fresh ones cost an arm and a leg. Is there a good alternative? "Freeze-dried petals hold their size, shape, and color even if they're stored for many months at room temperature, and don't stain or get slippery like fresh petals, which have a short shelf life," explains Jami Brown of confetti company Flyboy Naturals.

REAL BRIDES SAY . . . "The sweetest part of my wedding day was seeing my dad deadheading flowers for confetti. He picked them from hedgerows that morning." **Jessica**

Contact lenses
Even if you are a die-hard glasses wearer, this is one day you might want to ditch them for contacts.

TOP 3 TIPS FOR THE DAY
1. Have spares. You don't want this to be the time you drop a contact on the bathroom floor and are crawling around sweeping aside dust, scraps of toilet paper, and God knows what else.
2. Put them in before you do your makeup.
3. Carry rewetting drops that'll help dry eyes.

Contracts
These are very, very important to do right with your vendors, so don't skip through and just sign because they bore you.

A contract should cover just about everything.

YOUR CONTRACT CHECKLIST
● **Specifics:** The exact make, model, designer or style, color, and size. If you're buying a service, it should also include locations, dates, and timings.
● **How many:** The precise quantity should be listed.
● **The price:** As you've been quoted, with costs for additional items. The contract should state if tax is included in the price or if it will be added later and at what rate.

- **Date/timings:** When is delivery due?
- **Deposits:** How much is due and when?
- **Cancellation and refund policy:** What is it? Will the vendor refund a deposit if you have to cancel? Some run on a sliding scale.
- **Replacement policy:** What happens in the event of damage or failure to deliver on time?
- **Special-order requests:** These should be laid out in full in the contract.
- **Any other additional costs:** Will there be add-on costs (for example, transport, travel and accommodation, and cleanup)?
- **Gratuities:** Are they included in the price or will you be expected to stump up an additional 10 to 20 percent?
- **No-shows and sickness:** What does the contract stipulate if your vendor is a no-show? Will there be a replacement or just a refund of your money?
- **Postponement or rescheduling:** What happens in the event of having to postpone or reschedule? Is there a provision for acts of God or illness of a family member?

Corkage fee When venues allow you to bring in your own alcohol but then charge you by the bottle for opening it, it's called corkage.

Try this:

Buy extremely large bottles of wine, such as Jeroboams (three liters/ the equivalent of four bottles in a bottle) and Methuselahs (six liters/ eight bottles). You can buy good-quality wines in these sizes, and they mean fewer corks.

CAN YOU HAGGLE IT DOWN? Always try. We've seen couples negotiate corkage from $25 a bottle to zero, but you have to challenge the venue. See the Haggle entry on page 167.

TOP 3 INSIDER NEGOTIATING TIPS
1. If you're paying for a catering package that includes wine you don't want, ask them to improve the food and give you free corkage instead.
2. If you're booking accommodation for guests, too, point out how much that's worth to the venue.
3. If no corkage fees are a deal breaker, tell them. The chance of losing the full price of a wedding could swing it.

Corsages
These are a great alternative to bouquets and boutonnieres for the bride or anyone in the wedding party. "Why doesn't everybody wear huge over-the-shoulder orchid corsages like the goddesses of the silver screen used to sport? I also love wrist corsages—provided they are a single bloom tied to a long silk ribbon," says event designer Lewis Miller.

PLANNING AHEAD
If, as the bride, you like the idea of wearing a corsage, avoid a bouquet too, or you risk looking like a walking flowerbed.

❝Experiment with hip corsages that that affix to belts or sashes. They're a GOOD ALTERNATIVE to bridal bouquets. ❞

FLORAL DESIGNER LIZA LUBELL

Do you fancy being bigger, smaller, smoother, or PLUMPER in time for your wedding day?

TOP TIP

Allow anything from a day to six months or more for recovery, depending on what you have done. Always allow the maximum time your doctor advises between a procedure and your wedding.

SMART GIRL'S GUIDE TO COSMETIC SURGERY: Do your research. "Without the benefit of knowledge, how can you give yourself the best possible chance of an optimal outcome?" asks plastic surgeon Dr. Miles Berry.

- Get reviews of individual doctors and clinics online. "A good reputation invariably beats a cheap price."
- Know the pros, cons, and potential risks before you sign up for a treatment. If no one volunteers the info, ask for it and rethink your choice of practitioner.
- Be realistic about what the treatment can achieve. Go online for real-life reviews, before-and-after photos, and tips on how to deal with side effects.
- Make sure the person doing your treatment has the right qualifications and experience, whether it's a laser or surgery. "Check your surgeon's qualifications and registration with the national regulatory bodies," says Dr. Berry. "Try and get it right the first time because, when it comes to surgery, secondary surgery is generally more expensive and less predictable, and has more complications."
- Ask to speak to some previous clients. "Personal recommendation is usually the most reliable way."

MYTH: My wedding's in four weeks; I don't have time.

BUSTED: You do. "There are plenty of cosmetic enhancements that can be done quickly, with little to no downtime, including Botox, fillers, and many laser treatments. But don't overindulge when your wedding's just around the corner, especially if you've never had the treatments before, and do not use an inexperienced doctor or one you don't know." —Dr. Robert Gotkin

Want to know more about the most commonly performed treatments for brides?

- **Boob Jobs:** See the Boobs entry on page 47.
- **Liposuction:** See page 198.
- **Botox:** See page 48.

DID YOU KNOW . . .

"Don't make radical changes to your appearance when Mercury or Venus is in retrograde. For example, Botox, veneers, or other cosmetic procedures are very popular, but you may not like the results if you get them when these planets are retrograde," says astrologer Susan Miller.

Costume jewelry

Not only can costume jewelry be hard or even impossible to tell from the real thing, but it's been plenty good enough for famous women who have access to some of the best jewels in the world. If you want people to think your costume jewelry is the real deal, keep it simple, avoid cheapo settings that might give it away, and wear something people think you would be able to afford. If you suddenly sport 20-carat drop diamond earrings, you won't be fooling anyone.

"Costume jewelry is not made to give women an aura of wealth, but to make them beautiful."
Coco Chanel

EVEN RICH PEOPLE LIKE FAKE STUFF

- **Jackie O.** always wore fake pearls; she bought her favorite triple strand, her go-to for official functions and photographs, at Bergdorf Goodman for $35.
- **Kate Middleton** is famous for (allegedly) wearing a $75 pair of fake pearl drop earrings for the Queen's Diamond Jubilee celebrations.
- **Liz Taylor** left a mountain of costume jewelry. Coco Chanel, who practically invented it, was the same—fake pearls all the way.

Cotton candy machine

If you let otherwise **responsible** adults loose with a cotton-candy machine, you'll have a big mess.

You'll have guests strung with stray strands of pink goo and airborne melting sugar crystals because it's not as easy as it looks. Children putting hair, heads, or various other body parts in the machine because, well, why not? "If you want fresh cotton candy at your reception, be prepared to wear it," says gourmet cotton candy company Fluffpop. "Cotton candy machines fling cotton candy all over the place." Hire someone to do it for you.

Counseling

Do you know how many kids your partner wants? Where he or she wants to be living in five years? Is his favorite food really deep-fried KFC? Religious weddings often include obligatory prewedding counseling sessions. They might feel like a pain, but in the hands of a good minister they're eye-opening. "So many couples find it easy to get on in the relatively simple world of the immediate present, but don't know enough about their partner's long-term aims and abilities," says rabbi Dr. Jonathan Romain. "Marriage is really about second-guessing how suitable someone will be for you in the future. The more you know them, the better chance you have of making the right long-term judgment about them."

Counseling:
How well do you know your partner?

Take Rabbi Romain's quiz and find out.

"The real message of these questions is that couples need to start talking about deeper issues in each other's lives before making any commitments. Those who haven't should put their plans on hold until they really know the person they think they know. Just as important as the right and wrong answers is the number of 'don't knows.' It isn't necessarily a sign a couple is incompatible, but it does mean they don't know each other well enough, especially each other's deeper influences and characteristics."

1. What is his/her favorite food?

2. Does he/she want a pet?

3. Does he/she have any allergies?

4. What was one of the happiest moments of his/her life before meeting you?

5. What's been the saddest moment of his/her life so far?

6. Does he/she want children? How many, and when?

7. How often does he/she like to visit his/her family?

8. What special family traditions does he/she have that he/she wishes to continue?

9. What type of holidays does he/she like best?

10. Does he/she believe in building up savings or spending what he/she earns?

11. Do you find it easy to know what birthday present to get him/her?

12. Where would he/she like to be living in a few years' time?

13. What person has the most influence on him/her apart from you?

14. What's his/her greatest regret?

15. Does he/she want joint or separate bank accounts or both?

16. What type of education does he/she want for any children?

17. What is his/her ideal view of the future?

18. Are there any habits/characteristics of yours that he/she doesn't like?

19. What would you most like to change about him/her?

20. What are the main values he/she has?

Couture

Any clothes that are custom designed, made, and fitted for you by a dressmaker or designer—whether they cost $100 or $100,000—are technically couture. It's a process that gives you freedom; you can have input into the design down to the tiniest detail.

GOT A FLAIR FOR THE FANTASTIC? Go to town like designer John Galliano, who created a vision around the wedding dress he designed for model Kate Moss. "In Galliano's narrative it is as though the scullery maid had picked up milady's fallen sequins to spangle her own dress. The skirts are symbolically licked with the beaded plumes of a mythical phoenix, 'delicate and defiant, like Kate,'" writes Hamish Bowles in *Vogue*.

TIME FRAME: It depends on your dressmaker. An amazing dressmaker on a rush budget can conjure up an outfit in days, but designer names can take anything from six months to a year.

Craziness

Going nuts can manifest itself in lots of different ways. It isn't all about running wild; it's also about losing your ability to make normal, commonsense decisions.

TOP 3 SECRETS FOR WARDING OFF THE CRAZIES
1. Appoint a crazy-proof guardian. Ask a friend who won't hold out to tell you when you're crossing the line into deranged. You need someone sane: don't appoint another crazy to watch over your own crazy-o-meter.
2. Deal with stress. See the Stress entry on page 278 for lots of tips on eliminating and coping with stress. Once you relax, it's easier not to feel so rabid about everything. . . .
3. Learn to delegate. If people offer help, grab it like your life depends on it.

HAUTE COUTURE
This is a label that can only be handed out to a design house by the Paris Chambre de Commerce et d'Industrie, which issues a list with a handful of names on it every year. Designers who famously show haute couture bridal include Chanel, Jean Paul Gaultier, Valentino, Elie Saab, and Dior.

RETREAT
Stop what you're doing. Have wedding-free hours every day—or wedding-free days—every week. It's the same principle as when CEOs of huge multinationals switch off their electronic devices one day a week.

cutting costs

This isn't complicated, but cutting costs can feel hard if you're emotionally attached to ideas about how you want your wedding to be. Work out your priorities (music, food, wine, how many guests you can have, the venue, how it looks, what you wear). Spend your money there and then let go of the things you can't have.

We asked wedding planners for their top tips on cutting costs.

"Cut costs by using lots of candlelight and fewer flowers."

WEDDING PLANNER CASSANDRA SANTOR

1 Narrow down your guest list to close friends and family.

2 Think about different locations or destinations at times of the year when business is slow for them; they'll be much more negotiable!

3 No favors.

4 Always have a better DJ rather than a mediocre band.

5 You don't have to have a formal seated meal. There are so many fun options: tables that look abundant with help-yourself stations or a cocktail party. And the time of day can save considerably; for example, having a daytime reception when guests are likely to consume less alcohol or when they don't expect a three-course meal.

EVENT DESIGNER JUNG LEE

"Focus on taking care of your guests with the basics: great food and drink and music. You don't need all the fuss."

EVENT PLANNERS
SARAI FLORES AND
MARTHA HUERTA

Dd

Dd

Debt Accumulating debt for the sake of a few hours doesn't make sense, but it doesn't automatically mean disaster.

TOP 3 TIPS FOR DEBT MANAGEMENT

DO note all your current expenses, especially things that are technically luxuries but that you don't like to do without. Then ask yourself if you really can afford it. Is it still worth it?

DO shop around for the best interest rates on credit cards and loans. Don't sign up for crazy, overpriced store credit just because they're waving a form in front of you.

DON'T skip payments. That will land you with a trashed credit rating, possibly debt collectors turning up at your house, and inevitably bad memories of your wedding.

Décor/decorations

There's so much wedding porn out there, you'd be forgiven for thinking that you have to design your day to within an inch of its Pantone color–coded life. But you don't need a complicated theme—or even any theme.

THREE STEPS TO CHOOSING YOUR DÉCOR

Step 1: Get an idea of your big picture first: "Start with big broad strokes and then whittle down to the little details," says event designer Lewis Miller.

RENT AND RETURN

Instead of buying, consider renting . . . anything from chair covers to linens, full-size film-set–style props to seating, lighting, umbrellas, canopies, and even fake florals.

Step 2: Does it feel like "you"?: "It should fit your vibe, be it laid back or formal," says interior designer Kelly Wearstler.

Step 3: Step outside the wedding industry: For inspiration look at magazines with features on entertaining and parties; travel magazines and websites, food blogs, and fashion magazines. Go international—look at European, South American, Asian, and Australian style sites.

"Stick to what makes you feel great and you can't go wrong."

INTERIOR DESIGNER KELLY WEARSTLER

TOP
5
DESIGNERS' TIPS FOR CREATING ATMOSPHERE

CREATING ATMOSPHERE

1. Lights, camera, action . . . and music: "Lighting and music create the mood—they're critical," says planner Annie Lee. For more tips, see the entries on pages 194 and 214.

2. Look at the whole room: "Think about décor beyond your tabletops," says planner Lindsay Landman. "Take into account the whole environment, not just the centerpieces."

3. Create some drama: "Have one or two visual anchors," says event designer David Beahm. "It could be an arrangement that's larger than life; a ceiling hung with brightly colored lanterns; or simply using lighting to color a room a different shade from what it usually is."

4. Excite the senses: "Stimulate all five senses," says event planner Lesley Price. "What are your guests listening to, what do they smell?"

5. Share the love: "Only invite people you love and who care about you. Those who support you unconditionally will contribute to the emotion, and no amount of candles or flowers can fake that," says Jung Lee.

Deposits A deposit is a promise between you and the vendor. You hand over money and, in return, they commit to providing a service/item. It seals the deal. Once the deposit is paid, you're unlikely to get it back just because you changed your mind, saw something better, or broke out in hives at the realization of the final bill. Before you hand over any cash be 100 percent sure you really want what you're signing up for.

PLANNING AHEAD

Think you might have a change of heart? Check the cancellation and refund policies in the contract before you sign.

Dessert Dessert can be any permutation of sugar known to man (plus the healthier options like fruit and cheese if you must). Here are a few suggestions (besides your wedding cake) to get you going:

- desserts or candies that remind you of your childhood
- simple ice cream
- your most-loved comfort food
- something from your favorite restaurant
- a local specialty
- or just accept that excess is always better and pile ten of your favorite treats on a dessert table.

HOW TO SERVE DESSERT

Dessert tables: We know, they rule. "I'd have a small tiered cake in the center, two 10-inch cakes flanking, a few dozen cupcakes or whoopie pies, a couple of bite-size brownies or bars, some biscotti, a bundt or fruit pie, and some candies," advises Renato Poliafito, cofounder of Baked NYC.

Bars: Sundae bars, ice cream bars, pie bars, candy bars . . .

Carts or trucks: Bring in an ice cream cart or go all the way and hire a dessert catering truck.

Minidesserts: Rather than having one big dessert, opt for small portions of lots of yummy treats, like a bite-size tasting menu.

TOP TIP
Want to DIY a candy table? "Order hurricane jars and candy online and have friends help you set it up. It's so easy."
Kendra Cole

Sunshine, mountains, glamour, the city, the ocean . . .

It's no wonder so many of us want to leave our own backyards and head off somewhere else for a wedding.

KEY CONSIDERATIONS If a destination wedding seems like a good idea, you need to figure out if it's right for you and your guests. Start by running through this checklist:

Why here? You may only have a general location in mind, but ask yourself if this destination really makes sense to you, says event designer David Beahm. "Does it tell your story?" It doesn't have to, but many couples head off to a place that has significance.

Is it good for your guests? Would the journey and location really be okay for everyone you want there? "Consider how old your guests are, and how mobile," says Beahm. Will they all be able to take that flight, or climb up to your clifftop sunset wedding? Will it be too hot, cold, loud, or unfamiliar for them to be comfortable? Will it be a nightmare for people with young children?

Do your guests have the money? "Can your guests afford it, and if not, can you afford to pay for them?" says Beahm. This is the crux of destination weddings—unless

SO MUCH CHOICE . . . WHERE DO YOU START?

Work out what your priorities are when you're choosing your destination. Are they...

- Budget
- Weather
- Location
- How long the journey is
- How many guests you can have
- Family- and child-friendliness
- Having a religious or civil ceremony

you can foot the whole bill, there will almost certainly be people who can't afford it, or for whom it'll be a huge financial pressure (even if they don't let on).

But, says wedding planner Michelle Rago, people have gotten hip to the fact that destination weddings are a blast. "Don't bank on the old rule of thumb that twenty to thirty percent won't show. I find that's no longer true."

Can it give you what you want? A destination wedding often means not being able to micromanage everything like you would at home. Can you be relaxed about that or would it spoil your wedding? You also need to determine if what you want is possible. "Are your expectations on a level with what the destination can provide?" asks Beahm. For example, if your venue is a donkey ride from civilization, is a formal dinner-dance realistic?

OVERSEAS If you're dealing with unfamiliar bureaucracies, double-check all legal requirements well in advance.

1. The golden rule: If you're traveling outside the U.S., check with your state Attorney General's Office that your wedding will be recognized as legal.

2. Don't forget the documents: There are a good handful of things you'll need to prepare in advance or sort out when you arrive. If you don't have a wedding planner walking you through it, check the State Department website, travel.state.gov, for information on the country in which you're getting married.

WHAT WAS IN HER BAG? Want to know what beauty essentials a beauty editor packed for her Mexican destination wedding? "Sunscreen, leave-in conditioner (comes in handy for swimming, etc.), concealer, tinted lip balm; Manoi oil (it smells delicious from head to toe), vitamin C serum, and eye cream."

WRINKLE-PROOF TRAVEL

Traveling with a wedding dress? Check the airline's policy—can you book a place in the first-class cabin wardrobe in advance? If not, don't leave it to chance. Buy a hard-sided carry-on cabin suitcase at the maximum size and ask the store to pack your dress in it professionally.

THE WAITING GAME . . .

It can take a long time—and we're talking months, sometimes—to receive your marriage certificate back in the U.S. if you have an overseas wedding. You won't be able to do a name change or receive spousal benefits until you have it.

DESTINATION WEDDINGS TOP 10:
questions to ask potential LOCATIONS

FINDING VENDORS AT A DISTANCE . . .
Use the community Facebook page of the town, village, or resort where your wedding is to locate vendors and entertainers, says celebrity groomer Diana Schmidtke.

1 If a wedding coordinator is part of the service, will he/she be available to you in the run-up to your wedding and on the day? If there's only one coordinator, how will he/she cope with multiple weddings on one day?

2 What's not allowed? For instance, children, your own photographer, minister, flowers or cake, alcohol, etc.

3 Is the size of the wedding party limited?

PLANNING AHEAD
Vaccinations, malaria, insect bites, diarrhea, jet lag . . . factor them all in for overseas weddings and honeymoons. Go to the CDC Travelers' Health website (www .nc.cdc.gov/travel) for advice on vaccination requirements and malaria worldwide.

4 For the ceremony, is there a choice between a religious or civil service? What language will it be in if you're traveling overseas? Will there be a translator, if necessary, and can witnesses be provided?

5 What else is close to the spot where your wedding will take place? Strip clubs, building work, campsites, crack dens, all-night bars?

6 How many weddings take place a day? Is there a limit? How long between each wedding?

7 What's included in the price? What do you have to pay extra for?

8 If hair and makeup is included, will they do a practice session? "Always do a practice run of your hair and makeup and bring plenty of visuals to share with the people doing it," advises celebrity male grooming expert Diana Schmidtke.

9 Do you have to use their photographer?

10 Will the public have access to your wedding area? They often do in hotel and resort weddings, as the venue can't afford to close off grounds, bars, and restaurants for small wedding parties.

INSIDER TIPS
- Use tools like Skype and FaceTime to talk to vendors face to face and get a feel for everything. "If you can't get there beforehand, do a virtual wedding venue site tour."
- "Pictures are KEY to communicating what you want. E-mail bouquets, décor, cakes . . . anything! It helps your coordinator create exactly what you're picturing."
- "Don't send over bulky favors; your guests will probably leave them behind. Look for a local option."

Event planner Jody Value

Detox Why do a detox? And what does it mean anyway . . . three weeks of liquid kale? It's not just about juice. A proper detox will clean you out from top to toe, and from the inside out . . . including your bad habits and bad attitudes (okay, within reason; it's not magic).

"Detox helps with skin, energy, your digestive system, and attitude."

HEALTH AND BEAUTY GURU EDEN SASSOON

TOP 5 KEYS TO A WHOLE-BODY DETOX

KEEP IT FRESH

Stay away from prepackaged juices. "If it's fresh and made in front of you, though, go for it!"

Eden Sassoon

KEYS TO A WHOLE-BODY DETOX

"You have to clear your mind, body, and spirit, because they're interconnected," says nutritionist Amanda Griggs.

1. Poop every day. "If you're not, take psyllium husks or cracked flaxseeds in lots of water, or colon-cleansing herbs without senna, as it's too harsh," says Griggs.

2. Exercise. You need to get off the couch and get moving regularly, preferably enough to make you hot and sweaty. Walking to the car doesn't count.

3. Get some therapy. "Acupuncture, reflexology, manual lymphatic drainage, and colon hydrotherapy are all natural add-ons to a cleansing program."

4. Less drinking, drugs, and staying out all night. Sleep when the sun goes down and get up when it comes up (within limits).

5. Eat decent food, and don't starve yourself. "I advocate a very gentle detox that encompasses good eating habits while deeply cleansing the body. Then it helps skin, hair, nails, energy, weight loss, and bloating," says Margo Marrone, founder of the Organic Pharmacy.

COME TO GRIPS WITH JUICE Vegetable and fruit juices are a detox staple. Why? Because they can help clear all the toxic stuff out of your system, while giving your body high-quality concentrated hits of nutrients. But we've done juice fasts and ended up cranky and too tired to work or play. "The problem is that people don't prepare their bodies. Follow the rules and it's quite easy," explains Griggs.

SUCCESSFUL JUICE DETOX

Griggs says:

1. Stop eating crap: For a few days cut out sugar, alcohol, soda, caffeine, refined carbs, saturated fats in heavy meats and cheeses, and fried foods. Eat lots of vegetables, a little fruit, salads with a squeeze of lime, fish, and lean chicken.

2. Be ready to deal with hunger pangs: Make a potassium broth (see next page) and have it in addition to your juices. Add barley, greens, or spirulina powders to calm the appetite. If you're really hungry, add avocado or almond milk to your juice. Or, start with a balanced meal, have a juice in the middle, and end the day with some solids—fruit, veg, and a little protein. This is sustainable and healthy and means you can carry on with daily life.

3. Don't do it when you're under pressure: You can get all sorts of symptoms: tired and irritable or a headache that can last from one to three days.

4. Time it right: If you have a week, prepare for two days, fast for three, and come off properly for two days. If you want to do a juice cleanse for more than five days, do it under controlled conditions like a spa.

5. Detox/retox: Don't go straight back to whatever you needed to detox from in the first place.

WARNING If you have severe blood sugar imbalance or diabetes, or are pregnant, a juice cleanse is contraindicated.

TOP 5

TIPS FOR A SUCCESSFUL JUICE DETOX

Q What if my green juice tastes like dirt?

A "They're not like cocktails, designed with taste in mind," says juicing expert and best-selling author Jason Vale. "They're liquid medicine. The best thing to do is get over it and drink!"

Detox
RECIPES

Here are two juice recipes that actually taste good and keep hunger pangs at bay. No more excuses, people.

WHAT TO BUY

Vale says keep these juice staples on hand:
- apples (Golden Delicious, if possible)
- beets
- broccoli
- celery
- cucumbers
- ginger
- lemons
- limes
- spinach

WHAT'S GOOD ABOUT THESE INGREDIENTS?

"Apple and cucumber are amazing for flushing out the system. Celery helps flush excess carbon dioxide and reduce acidity. Ginger is a natural antibiotic and decongestant. Lemon is particularly powerful at removing harmful bacteria and toxins from the intestinal tract and clearing the liver and kidneys," explains Jason Vale.

POTASSIUM BROTH (AMANDA GRIGGS)

Use organic vegetables.
- 1 medium potato
- 4 medium carrots
- 4 beets, roughly chopped
- 5 large onions, roughly chopped
- 2 whole cloves garlic
- 3 stalks celery, roughly chopped
- 1 bunch spinach
- Ground chili pepper to taste

Peel the potato and carrots thickly (about a quarter of an inch) and add the peelings to a large pot. Add the beets, onions, garlic, celery, and spinach until the pot is around a quarter full. Add a dash of hot pepper to taste, enough water to cover and simmer on a very low heat for about an hour. Strain, and drink only the broth. Refrigerate and reheat as you wish.

DIY DREAMY DETOX JUICE (JASON VALE)

- 2 apples (Golden Delicious or Royal Gala)
- 1 slice of lemon with rind on (unwaxed where possible)
- 1-inch chunk of cucumber
- 1 stick of celery
- 1-inch piece of fresh ginger
- Ice

Juice the apples, lemon, cucumber, celery, and ginger. Place the ice and juice in a blender. Blend until smooth. You can skip the blender if you wish and just add the ice to your juice, but it's better and smoother blended.

Diamonds

Diamonds For most of us, buying diamonds is a big deal. And when it's for your wedding it's a big emotional deal, too. Use these tips when you're buying, says gemologist Antoinette Matlins, author of *Jewelry & Gems—The Buying Guide*.

1. Use the 4Cs as a reference. No matter how small the diamond, it's graded and priced based on the 4Cs.

- **Carat:** The weight of the stone measured in hundredths of a carat, e.g., ¾ carat or 0.75 ct. If you want to be able to compare sizes in your head, huge stones are 10 to 15 carats and above.
- **Color:** White diamonds are graded from D (colorless) to Z. Fancy colors like pink, blue, and brown use a different color grading system.
- **Cut:** The cut determines how brilliant and fiery a stone will be, and is graded on a numerical scale or using terms such as *excellent, very good, good, fair,* or *poor.*
- **Clarity:** This means how many inclusions or blemishes a diamond has. It runs from the rarest, flawless (FL), through VVS-1 and 2 (very, very small inclusions), VS-1 and 2, SI1 and 2 down to I1, 2 and 3.

2. Be careful who you buy from. Beware of clever dealers with unbelievable scams up their sleeves. NEVER buy from diamond wholesale districts or the internet without the advice of a gemologist. Small, family-run stores with an on-staff gemologist usually offer the best value for the quality you get because they normally have lower overheads than the big chains, explains Matlins.

3. Get everything in writing. On the sales receipt, ask for everything you've been told about the color, clarity, quality of the cutting, and weight of a diamond, whether it's treated, plus the quality of the cutting, to be put in writing, she adds. "Get an independent gemologist-appraiser to verify that what you have is what the seller said it is."

WANT MORE DIAMOND FOR YOUR MONEY?

"For most brilliant-cut diamonds, flaws aren't visible to the naked eye until you reach the SI2 category. Ask for an SI clarity, which has 'twinning wisps' . . . they're invisible to the eye." **Antoinette Matlins**

TOP TIP
To find a reputable gemologist or gemologist-appraiser, contact the Accredited Gemologists Association or American Society of Appraisers.

Disney Dream of a Disney wedding in a Magic Kingdom? Your wish is their command—you can get married at the Happiest Place on Earth, say "I do" next to Cinderella's castle, and be escorted in Cinderella's coach. The only downside? Mickey and Minnie can't be your best man and maid of honor, but, says Disney, they can come to your reception to mingle.

FURTHER READING

DIY ideas in:
- COCKTAILS:
see page 87.
- CAKES:
see page 61.
- PHOTO BOOTH:
 see page 236.

DIY The key to DIY is to keep pesky projects within the limits of what you know your talent and concentration threshold can bear . . . so, don't commit to anything tricky if your attention span is just long enough to paint your nails.

DJ

A good DJ gets your party going and holds it together.

TOP
5
TIPS FOR BAGGING THE RIGHT DJ

BAGGING THE RIGHT DJ

The DJ is a Very Important Person. He can make or break a party. Here's how to ensure success, says DJ specialists Scratch Weddings.

1. Know what you're looking for. What type of music will your family and friends enjoy? This will help you find the best DJ who's on the same vibe.

2. Know your venue logistics. It's the only way you can accurately assess costs and equipment. For example, do you expect the DJ to provide music in an outdoor location?

3. Not all DJs are created equal. A real expert creates a musical "story arc" with high points to build energy and low points for sentimental moments like parent dances. Ask questions about background, experience, and training.

4. Look for value, not price. Lots of companies throw in bells and whistles like fog machines, but is the actual DJ impressive? Don't be thrown off by low-value add-ons in place of an exceptional DJ.

5. Find someone who'll work with you. Music will play a huge part in the memory of your wedding. The music should reflect your tastes, not the DJ's or a generic playlist.

> "You and your DJ have the same goal, to have the dance floor packed all night, so trust their opinions on what, musically, will and won't work." **Scratch Weddings**

Documents

To get a marriage license, you'll always need to provide official documents. Exactly what varies from state to state, so always check your state website. The universal requirement is valid photo ID, like a driver's license or passport.

Double booking

This is when a vendor or venue books two events for the same time slot. If you haven't signed a contract, they can just let you down and walk away. If you have a contract and someone double books you, they should be:

- Bending over backward to accommodate and help you.
- Offering a full refund of your deposit plus compensation.

If they offer nothing but your deposit, check your contract for compensation clauses. If there isn't one, take your money and move on quickly to an alternative. Whatever agreement you come to, get it in writing.

dresses*

"There are no rules for what you should wear on your wedding day, so keep an open mind. You can wear long or short, a dress or trouser suit, white or color. It's entirely up to you, it's your day."

FASHION STYLIST SOPHIE ROWELL

*or anything else you want to wear

NAVIGATING THE WORLD OF WEDDING DRESSES There's a HUGE selection out there, but don't rush straight to the stores. Do a little digging around first.

Get inspired: See which brands and designers, shapes, styles, and details catch your eye. Use fashion magazines and websites, too. A dress in *Vogue* or *Harper's* might not be "bridal," but that doesn't mean you can't wear it or something like it.

BY APPOINTMENT ONLY Most bridal stores have rules. They'll normally ask you to make an appointment if you want to try on dresses, and many have a policy of no browsing. An assistant will bring out what she thinks you're looking for in your budget. If you're willing to go over budget for something special, let her know, so she can wheel out a few extras. Want to know how to get the most out of precious appointment time? Here's how, says bridal designer Rani Totman, founder of St. Pucchi bridalwear.

MAKING THE MOST OF YOUR APPOINTMENT TIME

DO your homework. Know your budget and style and focus on stores that suit both. Select your venues carefully.

DO keep an open mind and a positive attitude. Be curious—try on things you wouldn't normally consider.

DO wear appropriate underwear. It'll affect how dresses fit you. For example, if you think you'll want to try on strapless dresses, wear a strapless bra.

DO take shoes with the same heel height you want to wear on the day.

DON'T take everyone you know. Only bring the person whose opinion you value the most and someone who won't be afraid to tell you if something doesn't look good.

DON'T overbook yourself. Cramming in too many appointments on a single day is a mistake. It's exhausting and overwhelming. Space them out and eat a light breakfast so you'll have energy without being bloated.

AWESOME DRESSES DON'T JUST COME FROM BRIDAL STORES:
- Department store in-house bridal sections
- Online fashion retailers
- Vintage stores and websites
- eBay or Etsy
- Fashion boutiques
- Anyone from a friend or relative to a dressmaker or upmarket designer
- Rent
- Borrow

PIN DOWN YOUR DRESS STYLE
"Think about the location of your venue. It's often the best indicator of your style, and a great place to start." **Shea Jensen, Nordstrom bridal director**

TOP 5

SECRETS OF HAPPY DRESSING

CELEBRITY BRIDES WHO WORE COLOR

- Pale pink: Grace Kelly
- Lilac: Sofia Coppola
- Green: Elizabeth Taylor
- Purple: Dita Von Teese
- Red: Shakira Caine

See the White entry on page 313 to find out why people got used to wearing it. Wear your favorite color instead.

dresses cont

SECRETS OF HAPPY DRESSING

1. What not to do: Don't order a dress several sizes too small in the hope that you'll lose weight if you and exercise/dieting have an on-off relationship. Just buy the size that fits you.

2. No, you haven't gained 20 pounds overnight: Wedding dress sizes can come up supersmall, by two or three sizes. Ignore the numbers and trust the assistant as to what you need. If you're buying online, double-check whether it's standard or wedding dress sizing.

3. Have your own made: "If you can't find anything on the rack that's close enough, have someone make it for you," says celebrity stylist Tara Swennen. There are plenty of talented dressmakers who don't charge designer prices. The best way to find one is through recommendation. See the Couture entry on page 101.

4. On trend vs timeless: "I don't think it matters if what you wear is very trend-led, as long as you'll look back on it with fondness," says stylist Sophie Rowell.

5. Make sure you are comfortable: You'll be standing, sitting, eating, and partying. Can you actually do all these in your dress? Do you feel like you're carrying the weight of a small child on your back and perhaps need some special forces endurance training to get you through it?

You don't have to wear white.
It doesn't make you a "proper" bride or a virgin and it doesn't have any religious meaning.

DRESSES: Tips and tricks

INSIDER TIT TIP

Use double-sided fashion tape to keep everything in place and avoid flashing your nipples/boobs or underwear. "My favorite is Topstick, it's the strongest and stickiest on the market," says stylist Clare Mukherjee.

ALTERATIONS AND OTHER MINOR MIRACLES

Got an old dress that's not quite right? You can update shapes, take seams up, down, in, and out, change buttons and zips, add details like beading, move straps and add sleeves, create hidden corsetry, and even patch together different outfits. The golden rule: Try it on again and walk or dance around before you sign off on alterations. Some problems only come to light with a bit of movement.

OMG, IT'S ALL OVER

What will you do with your dress?

● **Resell:** You'll need to keep your dress in good condition for this.

● **Give to charity:** "You can take the tax write-off and help out a less fortunate bride," says planner Annie Lee.

● **Recycle:** Dresses can be recycled into lots of things big and small, but that normally requires a dressmaker and a vision, not just a pair of scissors.

● **Preserve:** "Preserving a gown protects it so it'll last for a lifetime," says Charlie Tuzzi of NYC's Cameo Cleaners. Even if your dress doesn't have visible stains, there'll be all sorts of invisible stuff that needs to come out, or it'll damage the fabric. NEVER keep your dress in a plastic garment bag. "It'll go yellow if there's no air getting to it," says Tuzzi. "Gowns should be stored in a museum-quality box."

WHERE HAVE ALL THE SLEEVES GONE?

Why are so many wedding dresses strapless? No good reason whatsoever. YOU MUST . . . try on at least one dress with sleeves (or at least straps). Sleeves don't just hide a multitude of sins, they look finished, balanced, and elegant (and a little different from every other bride of the last decade), and you won't be hitching yourself up all day and night.

Dress code Help out your guests and be clear about attire on the invitation. Avoid using phrases that'll leave them calling around going, "WTF do they MEAN?" If there are dress requirements for a religious ceremony, make sure they know that, too.

It's best to spell it out:

black tie, white tie, casual, cocktail, the hobbit.

Q What if a guest turns up on the day and they haven't followed your dress code?

A Don't let anyone make a fuss. Who knows what their reasons are for their getup, but it would be crappy manners to make them feel bad about it.

DRESS CODE DECODED

Black tie: Sharp and formal. Tux and bow tie for men. For women, anything from cocktail dresses to chic modern tuxedoes. "Black tie optional" means tuxes or smart, dark-colored suits for men and pretty much any sort of formalwear for women.

White tie: Normally reserved for state functions and the Queen. Black tail coats and white bow tie for the men, Oscar-style dresses or ball gowns for women.

Semiformal/formal: Men wear a decent suit and tie, but not black tie. Any sort of formalwear for women.

Business casual: No ties or suits necessary, but you'd expect men to wear trousers and a jacket.

Cocktail: Generally accepted to mean knee-length dresses for women, but they're just as likely to turn up in pants. Not necessarily suits for the guys; some may wear jeans.

Casual: This means very different things to different people. Only have a casual dress code if you're really easygoing about what your guests wear.

Beach: This doesn't normally mean swimwear, but your guests might assume shorts are okay.

Drugs

Okay, we know some people like to do drugs at weddings, but it's best if both of you lay off the hard stuff because

- it can mean your marriage isn't legally binding and it's grounds for annulment
- your officiant can flat out refuse to marry you
- it's superembarrassing for your guests unless they're all in the same state.

PROBLEM If any of your friends will be snorting away in the bathrooms or smoking pot, you don't want your granny (or anyone in your family) catching them at it.

SOLUTION Warn the friends in advance. Don't leave it to chance—you don't want your mom finding a powder-encrusted toilet seat or asking if your friends have colds because they all seem to be sniffing a lot. MOST important, kids are often everywhere . . . people aren't guarding purses because they're relaxed around family and friends, and things get dropped.

Dry wedding

Announce a dry wedding, and unless one of you is in AA, all hell will break loose. People who drink one glass of wine a year will suddenly become hardened boozers who can't go ten minutes without a pint of vodka.

DO think about your crowd, because it's a fact of life that people like to drink at celebrations. Unless your crowd are all nondrinkers, have it at a time of day when people won't expect to be drinking: late morning, lunch, or early afternoon tea. See the Cocktails entry on page 87 for a delicious alcohol-free recipe. A dry evening party is a test too far for most people . . . it's inevitable that some people (well, lots) will go searching for the nearest bar. Guests have even been known to come to dry weddings with their own secret stash of booze.

PLANNING AHEAD

- Tell your guests beforehand. If you don't, there'll be uproar. Slip a note into the invitations or highlight it on your wedding website. You don't have to explain why you're doing it.
- Think about going semidry and serving alcohol only between set hours.

Ee

eBay and Etsy These sites have the best of the best and the worst of the worst. But if you're prepared to sift through the complete trash, they are still the places to find anything and everything.

RULES OF ENGAGEMENT FOR EBAY AND ETSY

1. Fakes: If it looks too good to be true, it usually is . . . unless you're buying from a private vendor with excellent feedback.

2. Designers: Christian Louboutin, Jimmy Choo, Vera Wang, Tiffany, Gucci, et al. do not ship from a factory outlet in China.

3. Returns: If you're not prepared to lose the money, don't buy unless there's a return policy.

4. Measurements: Don't take a wild guess in your head. Get out a tape measure and see what the measurements mean in reality.

5. Sizes: For clothes, are the sizes U.S., British, Spanish, French, Italian? Check sites like net-a-porter.com that have conversion charts for everything from underwear to gloves. All European sizes are NOT the same: a French 38 is two sizes larger than an Italian 38, a Russian 38 is smaller than the Italian, and a German or Danish 38 is bigger than all of them.

TOP
5

RULES OF
ENGAGEMENT
FOR EBAY
AND ETSY

ebay and etsy cont

DO check if shipping is guaranteed and trackable, and how long it'll take.

DO verify what it will be delivered in. Will it be ready to use or no good for anyone by the time it passes through customs and lands on your doorstep?

DO read the reviews for similar items; it's no good if someone has a 100 percent track record selling car tires if you're buying custom invitations.

DO check taxes. If you're shipping in from outside the U.S., know what they're likely to be. Sites like www.dutycalculator.com can help you work out costs.

CLOTHING CRITERIA

- fabric
- finishing
- measurements
- lining
- fastenings
- any stains or tears
- if it says "used," how used?

Elope

Running away has so much going for it—cheaper, no fuss, no family snits to contend with (until you get back), no wedding planning eating up your time, money, and life. And it's just the two of you. . . . There's something lovely, sincere, and intimate about skipping off and doing it your way.

IF YOU ARE ELOPING

- Don't tell anyone more than 10 minutes in advance, because they'll try to talk you out of it and make you come home.
- Lay a false trail anyway.
- Make sure you've got up-to-date documentation with you—including divorce certificates if you've been married before—because arriving to find you can't get married takes the romance right out of it.
- Check the residence requirements for a marriage license, because some states (or countries, for that matter) don't do same-day licenses.

PLANNING AHEAD

Don't spring it on children or step-children as a fait accompli afterward. Include them in the planning, even if they won't be at the ceremony itself.

POSTPARTY Consider throwing a party when you get back . . . or having it thrown for you.

HOW ONE BRIDE DID IT . . . Stylist and fashionista Clare Mukherjee eloped with her now-husband (accompanied by their dog). "We eloped because it felt far more intimate, needed less planning, and we didn't want to spend all our hard-earned money on a big wedding. We married on a Friday, which meant only one day off work, and made it a long weekend. Our photographer was our witness and our little Pomeranian was our bridesmaid! It seemed like such an exciting adventure, and the three of us are very much our own little family, so it felt right that it was just us!"

Emergency kit
What do wedding planners never leave home without? (The answer is nothing; they don't travel light.) But you never know what you'll need, so we asked them to compile some small essentials for brides . . . now turn the page and take some cues from the prepared planners and get ready with your own MacGyver moves.

TOP TIP
Take good photos, or you might end up regretting not having memories of the day, plus your mom will want to see SOMETHING.

"I had to SEW a bride into her dress when the zipper broke. I used DENTAL FLOSS because it's really strong!"

PHOTOGRAPHER JULIE SKARRAT

WHAT SHOULD YOU HAVE IN YOUR EMERGENCY KIT?

- **Zip ties** (for anything from hanging chandeliers and mounting florals to draping fabric)
- **Stain remover** (Shout wipes and Tide to Go pens)
- **Lens filter wipes** (perfect for blotting up sweat/humidity on southern outdoor brides)

Tara Guérard

- **Clean makeup sponge** (little-known fact: A clean, dry makeup sponge is one of the best spot remover tools.)

Lindsay Landman

- **Bug spray** (in summer)
- **Static guard** (in winter)
- **Safety pins** (especially if the bride has an American bustle—no way is that thing making it two hours into the wedding)

Annie Lee

- **Scissors** (floral scissors, fabric shears, and plain ol' scissors)
- **Drugs** (Advil, antacid, Pepto)
- **Snack** (granola bar, water, and a piece of gum)

- **Tape** (all kinds! duct tape, floral tape, double-sided)

Melina Schwabinger

- **Lighter** (to light candles, fix frayed shoelaces)
- **Crochet hook** (to button very small buttons on wedding dresses)
- **Sandpaper** (to rub on the bottom of new shoes; it instantly helps break them in)

Angie Nevarez

- **Staple gun**
- **Extra ribbon** (a neutral color, which can be used to replace banding on a cake, hang photos, create an extra nosegay, as a tieback for tent drapery, a bow on a dog's collar . . .)
Lesley Price

- **Superglue**
- **Band-aids**
Sarai Flores and Martha Huerta
- **Baby powder**
- **Blotting paper**
- **Shoe shine**
Cassandra Santor
- **Feminine supplies**
- **Smelling salts**
- **A couple of Valium** (just in case)
David Beahm

- **Cell-phone charger**
- **Glue dots** (carry light, medium, and strong options for anything from fixing the hem in a groomsman's pants to securing escort cards if there's a slight breeze.)
Lisa Vorce

CHILL OUT

No wedding party is complete without someone needing to pop Xanax. So, Lisa Moricoli-Latham, aka wedding blogger the Naughty Bride, kindly answered the question:

"How much Xanax should I put in a nervous bride's Champagne?"

"The answer, of course, is that drugs are dangerous and not to be taken without a prescription—plus it's very fast-acting, so one milligram should do it for about two hours.

"Drugs and alcohol don't mix and drinking before driving is a no-no. As a bride you'll probably be traveling via limo on the big day, so there's room for chemical support if you really, really need it. Go easy.

"Trouble is, Xanax (and any other psychotropic substance, legal and illegal) makes you emotionally labile (that is, mood-swing-y), so if you're usually a sloppy drunk, proceed gingerly. You don't want to spend the entire reception crying (or barfing) into your wedding cake.

"In fact, Xanax is best reserved for the kind of gal who giggles when she's tipsy, so ask your bridesmaids how many times you cried at the bachelorette party first. Any more than twice means a half dose—and ix-nay on any more bubbly. If you take the drug, then have the bartender substitute club soda for you instead—you'll be so blissed-out you won't care what you're drinking, anyway."

Emotion and excitement

Do you want your wedding to be one that you and your guests will remember for all the right reasons? One that everyone will look back on with fondness rather than it having been a feat of endurance for them? It's simple. These are the keys to an excellent wedding, says wedding planner Tara Guérard:

FOR AN EXCELLENT WEDDING

PRESCRIPTION: For an excellent wedding

1. Create a space that's not too big or too small. A filled room makes for an intimate and cozy room.

2. Feel how the room is filled with anticipation and excitement, which creates atmosphere.

3. Have lights always on dimmers to control the mood.

4. Always have comfortable places to sit.

5. Never let the music get so loud you can't have a conversation.

6. Never, ever let your guests wait in line for a drink.

BE KIND: THINK OF THEIR WALLETS

Don't throw the party too near other wedding-related functions. Give everyone a break from money and time commitments for your wedding.

Engagement party

Ignore the daft old etiquette that says an engagement party should be hosted by the bride's parents. Host it yourselves, or share the duties with either or both sets of parents, or anyone else who wants to be involved. If you're having a small wedding, throwing an engagement party is a lovely way to celebrate with all the people you won't be able to have there on the day.

NB . . . Some guests might assume that if they're invited to your engagement party, they're automatically invited to the wedding. If this won't be the case, and you think it'll cause a problem down the road, think about politely letting people know.

Engagement ring

You may already have yours, but if not, are there any "engagement ring" rules? Nope . . . none at all.

1. It doesn't have to be a ring. When he proposed, Eddie Fisher gave Elizabeth Taylor a bracelet. "Engagement 'rings' should be what you want them to be," says jeweler Bec Astley Clarke. "My engagement ring's far from traditional—it is a huge gold ring that I bought for myself."

2. It doesn't have to be a diamond. It's not centuries of tradition that makes us buy diamonds, but a successful 1940s ad campaign for diamond sellers De Beers. "Before the De Beers campaign, engagement rings were simple," says celebrity jeweler Martin Katz. Or people didn't have one at all.

3. It doesn't have to cost a month's salary. It's not about how much an engagement ring costs, either. "An engagement ring should cost as much as you want it to," says Katz. "Decide on your budget, buy the best quality you can, and let the size fall where it may."

Entertainment

Up for something over and above the usual DJ? Entertain your guests with anything from comedy to dancing, magic, showgirls, opera, singing waiters, drag queens, magicians, and fire-eaters to celebrity look-alikes and various circus acts. Before you book any live act or hand over a deposit, run through this checklist:

- Make sure it's appropriate for all of your audience. Will everyone love them? Really?
- Audition them in person. You need to know that they can perform live and hold an audience, not just do their tricks for YouTube in their bedroom.
- Check that your venue has the time, space, capability, and insurance to handle them.

DID YOU KNOW . . .

There are gems more brilliant and beautiful than traditional stones that are just as durable and often cost a fraction of the price . . . Look at these alternatives, says author Antoinette Matlins:

Green: try emerald-green tsavorite or green sapphire

Red: try red garnet or red spinel

Blue: try blue spinel

Diamond: try moissanite

TOP TIP

Use a reputable agency, with contracts, and check the clauses for cancellations, sickness, bad weather, acts of God. . . . In other words, they should offer a plan B.

THE 24-HOUR RULE

Give yourself a 24-hour cooling-off period before you commit to escalating, whether it's over budget, numbers, or minor details like favors.

Escalation Watch out for weddings that spiral out of control, warns a lady who's thrown some weddings in her time, and had a couple of her own: "No matter what you start with, the budget, size of the guest list, the venue . . . all of it grows and grows until you can't stop it." Before you escalate, remind yourself that this is just one 8/10/12-hour period and doesn't represent the rest of your life together. . . .

Escort cards

❝Escort cards and seating plans are a must! You'll have pandemonium if you unleash 200 people into a room to find seating for themselves.❞

WEDDING PLANNER ANNIE LEE

TOP
5
**NEED-TO-KNOWS
ESCORT
CARDS**

NEED TO KNOWS: ESCORT CARDS

1. Have them where people can see them. And make sure guests can get to them easily, especially if everyone will be arriving to spot their names at once.

2. Think three-dimensionally. Hang cards from the ceiling, pin them on walls, or on twine around a tree if you're outside. They don't have to be physical things. "Project seating assignments onto the wall instead of having everyone pick up a card," says planner Angie Nevarez.

3. Tag them. If you've got lots of guests who don't know each other, make your escort cards into name buttons or, suggests Nevarez, "have everyone pick up a paper flower escort card and wear the flower during the cocktail hour."

4. Remember that sometimes the simplest things work best. "Wine corks are a fun stand for escort cards—slit the cork to hold the card, and hot-glue them to trays for stability. Or, tack calligraphied cards to the tops of peaches and it looks amazing—perfect for a summer wedding," says planner Tara Guérard.

5. Double up. "I LOVE having two-in-one details that serve a purpose," she adds. Find things that can be both an escort card and a favor. For example, attach the escort cards to a mini-bottle of bubbly.

ESCORT CARDS VS PLACE CARDS

Use individual escort cards to tell guests which table is theirs. Use place cards if you want to allocate individual places at the tables (see the entry on page 238).

Etiquette When it comes to your wedding, you can do whatever you want. Etiquette is a social guide—it's not necessarily "right" and you're not "wrong" if you do something differently. Use it if it helps you plan, but if you find yourself making decisions based on etiquette rather than what seems logical to you, stop. Everything will work if you use common sense and good manners as a guide.

"Weddings are personal.
Do what feels true to you. "
INTERIOR DESIGNER KELLY WEARSTLER

THE WEDDING PLANNER SAYS "There are no rules when it comes to weddings. N.O.N.E. As long as you are being respectful of friends and family, do what you want. You do not have to follow tradition; write new traditions." —**Melinda Schwabinger**

Exes

Do you invite them? Unless there are zero problems/jealousy issues, why go there? You may be great friends with yours, but does your partner feel the same way? Remember weddings equal alcohol plus emotions plus possible misbehavior.

Expectations

"A lot of couples get stressed out figuring out how to accommodate family members and make the wedding their own as well," says relationship expert and author Dr. Jane Greer. "The most important thing is to be as clear as possible between yourselves about what your expectations are and what you want. It's essential to balance your needs as a couple against everyone else's. Keeping the focus on each other can help alleviate tension; it maintains a feeling of connection. You'll also avoid developing feelings of anger or resentment, and feeling divided against your partner or family."

Expensive

We love a who's who of excess.

- **$26 million:** Not bad, Andrey Melnichenko. At his 2005 Côte d'Azur wedding to Aleksandra Nikolic (after whom he's since named his $500 million superyacht, *A*), Russian oligarch Andrey splashed out millions on entertainment, including Christina Aguilera.
- **$60 million:** Andrey's effort was easily trumped by the five-day, 2004 wedding of Vanisha Mittal, daughter of steel magnate Lakshmi Mittal, to banker Amit Bhatia. The party started at the Palace of Versailles, Kylie sang, and the Eiffel Tower was lit up by fireworks.
- **As an antidote . . .** Facebook billionaire Mark Zuckerberg's wedding to Priscilla Chan had no fanfare whatsoever—apart from the fact that the famously casual Zuckerberg was finally seen in a suit. The ceremony,

which took place in the backyard of the couple's Palo Alto home, was topped off with sushi and Mexican food from two local restaurants. Okay, we did spot a string of fairy lights in the garden.

Experiment

Explore all the avenues for what you're going to wear, eat, and drink.

Start with a cocktail weekend . . . where you sample all the cocktails you can drink. At the end of it, if you can remember what you drank, you'll have some idea of what alcohol to serve at your wedding (and probably some entertaining stories). ENJOY IT. Try things you wouldn't normally, taste different flavors and drinks—open your vision to beyond what you think you have to have. Make it a fun adventure the two of you can share together.

Eyebrows

What's the perfect eyebrow shape? "They should be a consistent thickness and shape from beginning to end (apart from where they naturally taper at the end) with a more angular than rounded feel. Not shaped like punctuation marks or commas!" says eyebrow expert Landy Dean.

SUCK AT DOING YOUR OWN? Get them done professionally, but always take visual references and make sure there's time for your brows to grow back if you don't like the result.

BEEN A LITTLE OVERENTHUSIASTIC? Start growing in over-shaped eyebrows six months before your wedding, says Dean. "Sometimes brows won't grow back; a dermatologist should be able to recommend a product to stimulate regrowth. In the meantime, have a professional tint done to darken lighter hairs and use brow pencil or powder to sketch beneath the existing hairs and enhance the fullness and shape."

Eyelashes

"Long lashes are sexy and feminine, and your number-one friend for emphasizing your eyes, even if you prefer a less-made-up look."

MAKEUP ARTIST AMANDA WRIGHT

STEPS TO LOVELIER LASHES

1. Use essential tools: Mascara and an eyelash curler—we know, curlers feel like you're ripping your lashes out, but they give even short, stubby lashes a nice curl and the illusion of extra length.

2. Do your eye makeup first: If you get watery eyes, you won't ruin the rest of your makeup.

3. Try these mascara tricks of the trade: "Apply from the base of lashes and don't forget inner and outer corners," says Wright. Do top lashes first in black and when they're completely dry, do the bottom lashes in brown. The trick for doing bottom lashes is to put your chin down, fold a clean tissue and place it under the lashes while applying mascara in downward strokes. Slide the tissue out in a downward direction, otherwise you'll stick all your lashes together."

4. Make your lashes look longer: Dot eyeliner right in between your lashes. And try a lash-boosting serum—apply religiously daily for six weeks to see a difference.

5. Remember falsies are your friend: They're the all-time number-one eye enhancers.

INDIVIDUAL FAKE LASHES VS STRIPS "You can't go wrong with individuals," says beauty guru Eden Sassoon. "They're perfect for all eyes and comfortable, look natural, and take a few minutes to apply. Strips are slightly quicker to apply but take time to get used to and can lift off. Both types have to be applied fresh every day; they're NOT meant to last more than that."

EXTENSIONS The best are individual lashes made from silk, mink, or human hair that are professionally woven into your own lashes. You won't need mascara or eyelash curlers, and there's no glue. They need refills at the salon every two to three weeks, so have extensions a few days before your wedding; that should see you through until the end of a two-week honeymoon.

TOP 5

STEPS TO LOVELIER LASHES

TOP TIP

"Use waterproof glue for fake lashes, or they'll come off if you cry." **Amanda Wright**

DIY

Practice with false lashes because the first few times you'll end up with strips glued vertically to your forehead. Don't give up . . . it's worth wrestling with them until you get it right.

Ff

Facials

Regular facials are essential for keeping skin looking its best, says celebrity facialist Amanda Birch. Here, she explains the reasons why:

- **Renewing:** Your skin renews itself every 28 days. From about the age of 25, this slows down, so it's important to speed up the process again using alpha hydroxy acids (AHAs) or other exfoliants and light treatments.
- **Cleansing:** Facials keep your skin clean and free from blocked pores caused by a buildup of pollution, oil, and dead cells.
- **Getting below the surface:** There are many methods (especially LED light therapy) that can work much deeper in the skin and that help to keep collagen and elastin in good shape, leaving your skin well hydrated and plump.
- **Relieving tension:** Facial massage helps release tension in the muscles attached to the skin tissue that are responsible for facial expression. If the muscles are tired and stressed, we see it in our skin as lines, dullness, and drooping. Facial massage can iron out the tension and get circulation back to our cheeks, leaving skin rosy and lifted.

WHICH FACIAL? If you don't know the therapist, Birch says, always choose a basic facial or use these general guidelines:

- **Very sensitive:** Avoid AHA peels and microdermabrasion. Stick to LED red light therapy (Omnilux) and facial massage using gentle products.
- **Congested, oily/acne:** Hydrafacial is very effective for cleansing and LED blue light for healing chronic acne.

TOP TIP

"Try to have at least three or four facials, starting six months before your wedding, timing the final one around a week before."
Amanda Birch

● **Dry:** Hydrafacial or Hydradermie work well.

● **Normal:** Have a Hydrafacial every four weeks, starting six months before your wedding. Light (LED) therapy is relaxing for mind and skin because red light therapy stimulates serotonin release (your happy hormone). Skin will look great after two sessions a week for a course of ten, so start at least six weeks before.

● **Loss of tone:** CACI or microcurrent facials work best.

Fainting
When people faint at weddings it's more often than not when it's hot—because of dehydration and standing still for too long.

TIPS TO AVOID KEELING OVER

AVOID KEELING OVER

1. Drink plenty of water—not just on the day of your wedding, but the day before, too.

2. Pass on the biggest dehydrators, coffee and alcohol (we know most of you won't, but try).

3. Eat.

4. Don't lock your knees when you're standing (it affects blood flow to your brain) and shift your weight every now and again, or at the very least, wiggle your toes.

5. Wear clothes that suit the climate—don't wrap yourself in tight, heavy, or man-made fabrics if it's 100 degrees.

Fall
Do all fall weddings have to have orange flowers and burgundy-clad bridesmaids? No, so don't let color dissuade you from an autumn wedding if the mention of russet, twigs, or pumpkin makes you break out in hives.

THE PROS: Fall is a good value for your guests if they're paying for travel and accommodation.

You're OUT OF HIGH SEASON in most places; DEMAND for venues and vendors FALLS SHARPLY, as do prices.

Temperatures have dropped, so you'll be comfortable dressed up. The best part? It's a time of abundance—all those fruits and vegetables; slightly heavier, spicier wines; richer color schemes; and there's something about a slight nip in the air that has a hint of romance.

> **THE CONS:** You can't rely on the weather. You need a plan B if you want an outdoor wedding.

THINGS TO REMEMBER: Think ahead about your guests' comfort. Have baskets of scarves, gloves, shawls, umbrellas, and even a few pairs of spare wellies to hand out. And the main thing is to keep everyone warm—there's nothing worse than shivering on a freezing patio once the sun goes down.

Fathers A good dad is amazing. He loves and supports you in every way he can. But not all dads always behave well—and especially not when it comes to weddings. Some are completely AWOL, want to bring partners you can't stand, or kick up a stink about stepdads. Or, as in the case of a friend of ours, bring a high-class, cocaine-snorting hooker to his daughter's wedding as his plus one. If any of these apply, the way to deal is to be creative.

ABSENT DADS: If you won't have a dad there on your wedding day, you can have anyone else (and as many of them as you want) take on traditional father roles.

WALK DOWN THE AISLE WITH ANYONE

- your partner (you don't have to meet him or her at the altar)
- your mom
- friends
- your dog/cat/pony
- your stepfather
- your uncles
- your children
- anyone else you want

EXCESS DADS: If you've got multiple dads who are important (stepdad, biological dad, two gay dads), the best thing you can do is give them equal roles in the ceremony. If they can play together nicely, let them share the honor of walking you to the altar; or have one walk you some of the way and pass off to the other. One could get ordained for the day and officiate; the other, give a special reading.

Biological dads can get prickly over stepdads, even if they've been an important part of your life. Do your best to make them understand how you feel about both of them—and make them behave like grown-ups.

Favorite (part of the day) We asked brides and grooms to tell us the favorite part of their wedding day. Wonder what yours will be?

❝Secretly watching my guests arrive. I was so touched that friends and family flew from New York and Los Angeles to meet in Georgia on a farm.❞
PHOTOGRAPHER AMY NEUNSINGER

❝My favorite part of the day was that I was marrying my soul mate.❞
KELLY WEARSTLER

❝Dancing with my father, brother, and husband (not at the same time). Our friends sang a cover of ELO's 'Strange Magic' when I danced with my husband.❞
real bride Daniela

Favors

If favors have become just another thing to check off your list, or budget is even a tiny concern, skip them—no one will notice. If you like the tradition, these are the golden rules:

- **Ask, use it, eat it, drink it. . . .** Give guests something they won't leave on the table or throw away. No matter how cute they looked in *Martha Stewart Living,* those little decorative bits won't go home with your guests. And they don't want stuff with your faces on it, either.
- **Make them personal.** Even if you order your favors, add a personal touch; for example, hand-stamped tags.
- **Avoid favor blunders.** People don't always know what to do with their treats. If it's in a jar, label it; if they can take it home, tell them; if gifts are not on the tables, let guests know where they are. And if you have guests flying in, will your favors fit in suitcases, satisfy carry-on requirements, and survive baggage handlers; or possibly break, spill, or get your guests arrested?

❝ The thing that annoyed me most about planning our wedding was the 'favors.' I still have no idea what they are, what they're for, who cares, and why I had to pay $800." **real groom Mark**

DIY IDEAS
- Lottery tickets
- Candy, cupcake, or cookie buffet with take-away bags
- Fortune cookies
- Mugs with guests' initials
- Saplings, plants, herbs (lavender, basil, parsley, rosemary)
- Books (have a stack and let them choose their own)
- Soaps (watch what you wrap them in, people have been known to mistake them for chocolate)
- Personalized tote bags
- Candles
- Mini-bottles of booze (and a hangover kit)

Films

If planning your own wedding isn't enough for you, work your way through our top 10 wedding films (plus a couple more), chosen by *Empire* magazine's U.S. editor, Aubrey Day.

1. The Godfather (1972)
Ford Coppola's Oscar-winning gangster tale opens with an epic wedding reception, where we meet lots of characters who will go on to bicker or batter each other into submission. Yes, just like a real family wedding.

2. and 3. Father of the Bride (1950)/Giant (1958)

No movie wedding list should omit the eight-times-married Elizabeth Taylor, so here's a double bill. In the first, a charming comedy that was later remade with less charm but more Martin Short, Liz is an innocent young bride. In the second, she's a decidedly less innocent maid of honor who can't keep her eyes off Rock Hudson. Smoldering ensues.

4. The Graduate (1967)

So, the love of your life is marrying someone else because . . . well, okay, you slept with her mother.

Fear not, just burst into the wedding and wield a giant cross at the in-laws. Within minutes you and your loved one will be safely ensconced on a bus heading . . . somewhere.

5. Four Weddings and a Funeral (1994)

Four weddings, Hugh Grant in all his foppish glory, some pretty funny scenes, and a few tearful ones, too . . . what's not to love? And even Andie MacDowell's good.

6. Seven Brides for Seven Brothers (1954)

Four weddings not enough for ya? Try seven in this perennially popular musical that gets remade every few years for TV or stage. The plot (a bunch of brothers kidnap some local girls who all end up falling in love and marrying them) may not stand up to too much scrutiny, but the sunshiny song-and-dance numbers keep the feel-good factor high.

7. Wedding Crashers (2005)

There are lots of weddings in this Owen Wilson and Vince Vaughn romp that thinks it's a gross-out comedy for the

HONORABLE MENTION . . .

● **A Wedding (1978)**
Robert Altman's characteristically ambitious film takes place during a single day at an extravagant wedding. By turns funny and sad, it remains a bit of a minor masterpiece.

boys only to discover it's really a rom-com for the girls (complete with an obligatory sweet ending).

8. The Wedding Singer (1998)

Adam Sandler is a mulleted 80s wedding singer; Drew Barrymore is the girl of his dreams. The soundtrack is like a greatest hits of the 80s and Billy Idol pops up briefly as . . . Billy Idol.

9. Muriel's Wedding (1994)

If you like 70s music (well, ABBA), then this is probably the movie for you. Toni Collette is the "ugly duckling" who dreams of a better life and a glamorous wedding in this surprisingly tart Aussie comedy. (For more ABBA, but less wit, see also: **Mamma Mia!** (2008).)

10. It Happened One Night (1934)

When not running away from weddings, spoiled heiress Claudette Colbert finds time to fall in love with Clark Gable's roguish reporter in one of cinema's greatest rom-coms.

HONORABLE MENTION . . . Kill Bill (2003–2004) Okay, so there isn't actually a wedding in *Kill Bill Volume 1* or *2,* but events do pivot around what happens at a wedding rehearsal. And the main character is called The Bride, so we think that qualifies. Quentin Tarantino's four-hour-plus tribute to lots of films you've never heard of remains remarkably watchable.

Fireworks
Everyone loves fireworks. Man, woman, child, big tough guys, little kids. . . . The only things to remember: If your venue gives you a cut-off time, respect it—fireworks are not much fun for neighbors who get the same show every weekend. And DIY might seem like a good idea, but unless you have a full-on pyromaniac with artistic flair on hand, it'll never match the magic of a professional display, even if it's a fraction of the cost.

WATCH AND LEARN
Should you really take wedding advice from a movie? In this case, yes. . . . Go to the excerpt from *Wedding Crashers* on page 289 for a perfect example of how not to give a speech.

BANG PER BUCK
Expect to pay several thousand dollars per five minutes for a professional display; if fireworks come as part of a package, ask how many you get for your money—$500 seems cool until you find out they're only lighting three fireworks.

Q Does a first dance have to be on the dance floor?

A It makes it easier, but one bride had her first dance in the pool . . . "We made it look like my husband tripped and pushed me in. We had our first (and second!) dance in the pool—my photographer was already underwater with a snorkel!"

Photographer Corey Ann Balazowich

First dance

The first dance is a time-honored tradition and a good photo op. It should always be fun; it doesn't have to be a performance (but see below), or perfect. If it feels hard to dance with guests watching you, invite everyone onto the dance floor with you, or don't do it at all.

- **Like being the center of attention?** Then go ahead, give a performance. Take some lessons if you want to choreograph it, or just for a boost of confidence. Get personal recommendations or take a sample lesson of different styles of dancing. How many lessons? It depends on how many left feet you've got, or how adventurous you want to be.
- **What style of dance can you do?** Anything from a traditional slow dance to the tango or a line dance . . . "We did a fast dance to Travis Tritt's 'TROUBLE.' I changed into my cowboy boots for it," says one real bride.
- **How do you choose the song?** Think about the mood you want. Slow and sentimental, fun, fast, ridiculous? Then make a short list of songs you BOTH love. You don't have to be clever or original; it can be the biggest cliché in the book.

First kiss

The only thing we have to say here . . . please don't make it too passionate or involving wandering hands. Anything longer than a few seconds is probably plenty enough for your audience.

WORLD'S WORST FIRST KISS? Catch Liza Minnelli and David Gest's wedding first kiss on YouTube for the gruesomest example of what not to subject your guests to. Ever. Um, is he trying to chew her face off?

Fitness Do you have energy, focus, and amazing zest for life and, more important, can you walk up a flight of stairs without feeling sick?

All you need to do
TO GET FIT IS: get moving.
Spend more time using your body, walking,
running, doing yoga, riding a bike.

You don't have to do insane workouts to make a difference. Being fit makes life more fun; improves your mood, sex life, and sleep, boosts your metabolism and immune system; and helps you cope with stress.

GETTING STARTED We asked Heidi and Chris Powell, stars of *Extreme Weight Loss,* to share their top three tips for motivating even the most hard-core lazies.

1. Just five minutes. That's it. No more. You don't need to run outside or do burpees. Just walk in place while watching TV. If you do five, you win. If you want to go for more, it's just gravy. The most important aspect of transformation is keeping your commitments, not the duration of exercise.

2. Declare your goals. Write them down EVERYWHERE. Post pictures of what motivates you—your perfect body, your family, the love of your life, or a healthy medical record—around your house, car, workplace, etc. We tend to forget "why" so often, we need constant reminders.

3. Dig down deep and explore your fears. Why don't you exercise? Is it fear of discomfort? Fear of failure? If you understand your fears, they cannot control you.

911!
Are you a die-hard slacker? Get yourself off to bootcamp, which basically means working your ass off in an instructor-led hardcore class. If daily bootcamp won't be strict enough, go for the temptation-free zone of a week-long bootcamp. The only way out is to run away. . . .

TELL NO LIES
Get a fitness tracker. Measure everything from how much you're really moving to heart rate, sleep, diet, and calories burned.

BAG THE BEST SEATS

Want to know which seats on your flight have the most legroom and roomiest seats? Check out www.seatguru.com.

TOP 5

**TIPS:
GOOD
FLIGHT
GUIDE**

*TRIVIA

Who had the most flower girls ever in the history of the universe?

ANSWER
At her 1993 wedding to Tommy Mottola, Mariah Carey had 50 flower girls.

Flights

Is it true that airlines give upgrades to honeymooning couples? Yes (well, sometimes . . .), says an insider, as long as the honeymooners are not too horrible and pushy. It's not automatic and it helps to be a frequent flier with the airline. But the trick is not to wait until you get on the flight. "Crew can't authorize upgrades," says Virgin Atlantic, "but it's always worth asking at check-in."

GOOD FLIGHT GUIDE

1. You need s-t-r-e-t-c-h. Don't travel in anything bulky or stiff or with a tight waistband. Wear lightweight layers of soft fabric and shoes you can slip on and off easily. You don't want to be meddling with laces, zips, or buckles at security or every time you get up to move around.
2. Keep your toiletries and other essentials in an outside pocket of your carry-on. Deep moisturizing face, eye, and hand creams are essential because cabin air will suck your skin dry like a prune.
3. Noise-canceling headphones will be your best friends.
4. Pack a big scarf and lightweight sweater because some airlines just love to turn the temperature down to freezing.
5. Eat light snacks and lay off the vino.

Flower girl

This is the supercute kid who walks before or after you down the aisle, sometimes carries your rings, scatters petals, and charms everyone. One is good . . . but having more than one* helps take the pressure off. Choose kids who won't be completely undone by nerves and aren't so young they can't take in what's expected of them. You could also make them feel special and help them understand what'll be happening by giving them a book. Walk them through everything lots of times and on the day, seat their parents in easy view.

Flowers
Even the simplest or most budget-conscious flower arrangement adds a touch of beauty to your day.

HOW TO CHOOSE YOUR FLORIST

1. Set your budget. Then find a florist whose average job is in your price range, says event designer Lewis Miller.

2. Make sure you like the florist. "Personality, personality, personality," he says. "Talent is fine, it's everywhere, but if you hate the person, the process is going to be hell."

3. Love their work. "A fondness for his or her work along with a nice rapport is the best combination," advises florist Liza Lubell.

WHAT YOUR FLORIST NEEDS FROM YOU

1. Time. "If you're marrying at a busy time of the year or have your heart set on a particular florist, book nine months to a year out. Leaving it until later doesn't mean a florist won't have enough time, it just means you'll have less choice," says Miller.

2. Input. Start collecting images of things that you love. It doesn't have to be flowers or even bridal.

3. Honesty. Don't be scared to say what you like because you think it's not fashionable. It's your choice.

ON A TIGHT BUDGET?

● **Simplify.** "Use more candles, and simplify the arrangements to seasonal elements," advises Lewis Miller.

● **Delete.** "It's better to have several magnificent moments than a lot of diddly things everywhere," Miller adds.

● **Ditch bouquets.** "Think about having corsages or simple hair flowers for the bridesmaids instead of bouquets," recommends Lubell. See Corsages on page 95 and Wreaths on page 317.

"Bring me some pictures NOT from bridal magazines. Try interior tear sheets or paintings you find interesting. Pinterest is helpful, but all the pages look the same."

LEWIS MILLER

HOW TO GET THE MOST FROM YOUR FLORIST It's really important, says Miller, that you ask the right questions. Use these as your starting point:

> **What is in season?** "It's true that with the mass cultivation of many blooms the seasons don't apply, but the best part of using seasonal elements is that you will just get MORE and BETTER. And who doesn't like that? Ask what will be the most beautiful for the time of year."
>
> **What do you suggest?** You're paying for their expertise, so use it! "Ask what they think will look best in the space."
>
> **How can we allocate our budget for the most impact?** Know your own priorities before you ask your florist this—for example, you might prefer more flowers in the church than reception.
>
> **... And please be kind** "The BEST thing a client can do is be appreciative."

THE LANGUAGE OF FLOWERS A beautiful way to add meaning to your bouquet or any floral display is to use the Victorian tradition of the language of flowers. All flowers have an association: Kate Middleton's wedding bouquet included lily of the valley for happiness; white hyacinth for constancy in love; sweet William, which symbolizes gallantry—and an obvious nod to her husband—and myrtle for love and marriage. She even used floral symbolism in the decorations on her wedding cake.

"This is a tradition I love. We often do ceremonial arches using flowers that have specific meanings and print the meanings in the program," says Miller. "White roses for purity, wheat for abundance, rosemary for remembrance, ivy for fidelity, etc."

WHERE CAN YOU FIND THE MEANINGS? Your florist should be able to advise you, or you can search for an online flower dictionary or buy an antique Victorian dictionary for a few dollars on specialist online bookstores.

WHERE CAN YOU USE FLOWERS?

- Your bouquet
- Bridesmaids' bouquets
- Hair wreaths
- Corsages
- Buttonholes
- Ceremony: altar/front seats/pews sides
- Reception: head table guest tables

PLANNING AHEAD

"Make sure your florist knows at the planning stage if your flowers will be out in the heat for any length of time."
Holly Flora

FLOWERS:
Think you may
want to DIY?

Should you even think about doing your own flowers? "Because flowers are perishable, demand a lot of attention, and have such a quick turnaround, I always fear people will be up all night before their wedding stressed and frustrated. Flowers should be left to the pros because of their time-sensitive nature," says florist Liza Lubell. Know your limits—will you still be up at midnight the night before your wedding swigging wine and stuffing flowers into vases?

ONE BRIDE'S DIY STORY

"We bought from a wholesale florist and arranged forty-two flower centerpieces at a barbecue at my parents' house. It was a lot of fun and only took two hours." **Melissa***
*Caveat: She is a graphic designer so it may be easier for her than those of us who are DIY or design challenged.

DON'T WING IT

● **Do a dry run.** You need to find out in plenty of time if you're going to be hopeless or hate flower arranging.

● **Take lessons.** You don't even have to leave the comfort of your own home anymore; there are tutorials on YouTube and online courses, but the best way is hands-on with a teacher at your side. Lots of florists run wedding flower classes. Find one whose style you love.

● **Read.** Books with step-by-step instructions, not just pretty pictures, are best.

● **Grow your own.** If you have green fingers and the time and patience, grow your own plants and flowers to use at your wedding.

**BRIDES HAVE
DONE IT EVERY
WHICH WAY . . .**

- Barefoot
- Sneakers
- Cowboy boots
- Flip-flops
- Uggs
- Sandals
- Platforms and wedges
- Heels

TOP TIP

Don't trail through bad weather, mud, and rain in nice wedding shoes. Get some wellies on. Slip into your shoes once you're on dry land.

Footwear

Getting married doesn't mean you have to wear high heels. Karl Lagerfeld sent model Cara Delevingne down the Chanel catwalk in a bridal gown, train, and white sequined sneakers.

HOW TO BUY SHOES THAT WON'T CRIPPLE YOU Former shoe designer Victor Chu teaches women how to walk in high heels. He explains how to get everything right if you can't do without heels.

> **TIP 1: Forget the shoe size. Keep trying on shoes until you find ones that fit like a lambskin glove.**
> **WHY?** If you buy the wrong size, it will make you shuffle, plus you'll cut and blister your feet. Finding heels that fit perfectly will change your life.
> ● The shoe's heel should be directly under the center of your heel.
> ● The shoe should be strapped or fit around your feet so it feels like it's a sexy, form-fitting walking tool.
>
> **TIP 2: If you're under 5'5" and/or your feet are smaller than size six, DON'T wear heels over four inches high.**
> **WHY?** Five- and six-inch heels are designed for women over 5'11" who wear size nine or higher. Taller women have longer feet that can stretch the distance of the pitch these heels create. If you've got size six feet or under, the pitch is too steep. You'll be in pain and may damage the bones in your feet.

WALKING WITH EASE How can you sashay around in high heels like a model rather than a shuffling hunchback? With practice it can be easier, even effortless. Chu tells us how it's done.

TIP 1: Tighten your abs and walk with your shoulders back.

WHY? High heels pitch the body forward, concentrating the energy of your walk over the balls of the feet and toes, which means pain and blisters, corns and cuts. Engaging your abs brings your upper body back into alignment, and balances your weight over the heels.

TIP 2: Walk heel to toe, heel to toe . . .

WHY? It's the natural mechanics of walking. Most women in heels pitch onto the balls of their feet, dragging the heel tips and causing pain, injury, and ruined shoes—plus it's not sexy. Walking heel to toe seems counterintuitive but with a few minutes practice, you'll hit walking efficiency after about 15 consecutive steps.

TIP 3: Relax your hips and knees.

WHY? It gives you a sexy walk and helps transfer energy outward from the motion of heel to toe, up the legs and out the hips.

> "The look of the shoe is only a tiny part of the sexiness—how a woman controls and walks in heels is really where the sexiness lies."
> **Victor Chu**

Forever, fuck! "Forever is an awesome idea, but any promise about the future's an inherent lie because no one knows what it holds in store," says relationship expert and marriage therapist Eric Paskel. "If you want to be married (and marriage means forever), you have to be interested in what the journey's going to be like with one person—exposing yourself to life's ups and downs with just them. To sum it up, you have to be more into your journey together than any other you can take—that's what keeps you in it."

> "If being together forever scares you, then what the fuck are you doing getting married in the first place?"
> **Author Jason Good**

fun

"Your wedding is the beginning of your life together," says event designer Lewis Miller. "Have fun! You don't have to prove anything, or overemphasize your unique and fabulous personality, or what an adorable couple you are based on your clever and whimsical décor."

Relax, laugh, and enjoy yourself, because your day doesn't have to be perfect, or anything close.

Ron Culberson, author of *Do It Well. Make It Fun* sums it up for us like this: "Our world tells us to 'grow up,' 'act your age,' and 'be serious.' But we need a balance to the seriousness. If you can achieve excellence in your work, your relationships, and your life but make the processes in each more fun, you'll not only be more effective in your role, you'll have a more positive impact on those around you. Remember what Abraham Lincoln said: 'It's not about the days in your life, but the life in your days.'"

Gg

Gg

Garter toss Hmm . . . would you ever normally want family and friends to watch your boyfriend run his hands (or mouth) under your skirt and up your thighs? And then toss pieces of your underwear to his friends? If you're okay with the audience, here's your need-to-know: Traditionally, the groom removes the bride's garter and tosses it out to the single men before the bouquet toss.

Gay weddings Just as with any wedding, a meaningful same-sex wedding starts with the ceremony, says gay wedding expert Bernadette Coveney Smith:

Q: Two brides—who gets to walk down the aisle?
A: I love the idea of two aisles. There's no "who's the bride?" moment and it gives both attention. I also love the two aisles as a unity ritual, a metaphor of two becoming one. Or the couple go down one aisle together holding hands.

> "If the ceremony is thoughtful and personal, where the guests can demonstrate their support for the couple, it sets the stage for one hell of a party."
> **Bernadette Coveney Smith**

TOP TIP

If you are denied services for being gay and live in a state where discrimination on the basis of sexual orientation is banned, file a complaint with the state's commission against discrimination.

ALL ABOARD

"Show your own enthusiasm and ask for advice or input, and eventually that enthusiasm will be contagious. It will 'normalize' the wedding to family members who may not be totally on board." **Bernadette Coveney Smith**

Q: If you're gay, do you need a gay wedding planner?

A: No, what's important is a planner who's willing to be the clients' advocate and let all vendors know it's a same-sex marriage. They'll have a curated list of gay-friendly wedding professionals. They won't make assumptions about roles or traditions. And it would be great if they also had a basic understanding of some of the laws that affect LGBT couples.

Q: Where can you find gay-friendly vendors?

A: There are online directories that can be a great resource. But a couple should still come out every time they reach out to those advertisers—just because someone advertises on a LGBT wedding directory doesn't mean the entire staff is comfortable. It's still important to screen the business.

Q: What are the legal issues specific to gay marriages?

A: LGBT couples need to be aware that their marriage won't be recognized in states where same-sex marriage is not legal. They should hire an attorney who understands LGBT estate planning, so they have the proper wills or trusts, durable powers of attorney, health care proxies, and more, created with their needs in mind.

Q: What's the difference between a legal marriage and a commitment ceremony?

A: I've been to commitment ceremonies, and I've been to legal weddings, and there's a palpable difference. The energy in the room is different when a couple is pronounced legally married. A wedding is a very special rite of passage and emotions are incredibly heightened when it's legal.

SAME-SEX WEDDINGS AND THE CHURCH Not all churches will conduct same-sex weddings, but there are lots that do. The key is to find a church and minister that positively welcome and embrace same-sex marriage. "We celebrate every union because love is love, period," explains Angela Gregory, wedding coordinator at Riverside Church NYC.

HOW THE WEDDING PLANNER DID IT "I married my wife, Jen, in 2009. I wore a white suit and she wore a white dress. It was an amazing day—our friends came from around the world to support our marriage. It was powerful and profound. We had an Irish band, a DJ, and a drag queen . . . exceptionally fun!" says Coveney Smith.

Gifts

No, not for you, for other people. The ones you want to thank for their support, effort, love, and for putting up with you.

The rule of thumb should be to thank anyone who has contributed to making your day special, people who have spent their own time, and maybe money, helping you. It's not about how much you spend, but more about finding the things they'll love. (If you're strapped for cash, most moms will be happy with a posy of flowers or a dedication in the toasts.) That might mean giving everyone something very different. "I gave all my bridesmaids slightly different pieces of aquamarine jewelry because I know their tastes aren't the same," said one March bride. See the Thank-you's entry on page 285 for ideas.

Gift list

It's easy to think you'll remember who gave you what, but unless your circle of friends and family is no bigger than 10 people, trust us, you'll lose track. You need to be organized. . . .

- Make a digital list (get yourself an app).
- Keep track by hand . . . make an Excel document or keep preprinted sheets with the following columns: Who (including address), What, When, Where From, and Thank-you Sent.

Gloves

The icons of the 1950s rocked gloves more than any other decade. For inspiration see Marilyn Monroe in *Gentlemen Prefer Blondes* or just about anything else she ever made.

The only problem with wearing gloves on your wedding day is what do you do with them at the altar when you exchange rings? Leave them on? Take them off? Fling them at the bridesmaids? Well, you could buy a pair with a ready-cut hole in the ring finger (but this will leave you with one finger poking out like a worm). Or take off the glove and hand it to a willing wardrobe assistant/bridesmaid. Remember to put it back on or take the other one off, or you'll look like a one-armed bandit for the rest of your ceremony.

If you want to be traditional, keep gloves on for receiving lines and shaking hands. Take them off for eating, drinking, and having fun.

WHAT SIZE AM I?

Measure around the widest part of your hand at the knuckles (excluding your thumb). If you buy a European brand, sizes equate roughly small: 7, medium: 8, large: 9, and extralarge: 10.

Going-away outfit

If you're changing before you leave, you'll need (a) space set aside, (b) probably a steamer or iron, and (c) somewhere to leave your wedding outfit. Task at least two people with picking it up and collecting everything for you; there's always safety in numbers.

Green weddings

Gg

"The average wedding can generate
400 pounds of garbage
and 63 tons of carbon dioxide."

With 2.5 million weddings each year in the United States, that's one billion pounds of garbage every year," says Kate Harrison, founder of www.greenbrideguide.com. That's a colossal amount, but weddings are all about consumption: the paper and gift wrap; energy spent on travel, shipping, cooking; the flowers grown, sprayed with pesticides, cut, and discarded; the mounds of food.

MAKE YOUR WEDDING GREENER Harrison suggests finding ways to cut down on your carbon footprint and environmental impact, taking into account everything from flowers to favors to what kind of food you serve. "You may not be able to find a green option for every single part of your wedding," says Harrison, "but every green choice you make is a step in the right direction."

KATE HARRISON'S TOP TIPS INCLUDE

- **Jewelry:** Mining gemstones and metals has a huge environmental and human rights impact. Buy a vintage ring or use a family heirloom. Some couples are opting for matching ring tattoos.
- **Invitations:** Wedding invitations can have layers and layers of paper. Simplify to a single sheet or use recycled paper made from postconsumer waste. The greenest invitation is the digital one.

FOOD AND
CAKES
"Always try to
find food that's
sourced locally,
organic, and in
season. Even
for cakes and
dessert. It's the
easy way to
go green."
Kate Harrison

● **Your dress:** Buying something you'll only wear once is inherently wasteful. Get yours from a consignment shop or reuse a dress already in your family. If you want a new gown, many designers offer eco collections made from sustainable fabrics.

● **Bridesmaids' dresses:** Asking your bridal party to wear clothes they already own in the color palette of your wedding is a great way to be completely eco-friendly. Or ask them to buy vintage. Encourage your bridal party to resell or donate their dresses afterward to help promote a culture of recycling.

● **Makeup:** Look for items made with organic or vegan ingredients and try to steer clear of anything containing toluene, dibutyl phthalate, formaldehyde or formaldehyde resin, and camphor, all of which are carcinogenic.

● **Flowers:** Many florists use imported flowers grown under unfair labor practices. Look for flowers that are in season and grown locally and organically.

● **Photography:** Find a photographer who uses digital online proofs to avoid the paper and chemicals in printing. Disposable cameras are fun, but they create a tremendous amount of waste. Encourage guests to use their own digital cameras or cellphones in conjunction with a photo-sharing website.

● **Décor:** Rather than buying new tablecloths and linens, rent them. Reuse the bridal party bouquets as centerpieces at the reception. Use "found" objects like seashells and sea glass (if you happen to be by the shore). On the dance floor, low-energy LEDs or paper lanterns create lighting with low environmental impact.

● **Favors:** These account for a great deal of the waste created by weddings. There are great, more sustainable alternatives—edible favors, like Fair Trade chocolate, organic raw honey, or homemade preserves.

Groom

"It's a revolution! I think a memo went out about five years ago and grooms realized, it's my party, too!"

WEDDING PLANNER ANNIE LEE

Work out what you want together (plus it's better to tackle differences early on).

THE TRADITIONAL GROOM'S TO-DO LIST If you want to go the traditional route, the groom is expected to fulfill other duties apart from party planning. But he doesn't have to go it alone. Some of these, like setting up the honeymoon, you might prefer to do together:

- Buy the engagement ring (probably done if you're holding this book).
- Choose the men in the wedding party and what they'll wear; arrange their accommodation and thank-you gifts.
- Arrange and pay for the honeymoon and get travel documents together.
- Buy a gift for the bride.
- Prepare toasts for the rehearsal dinner and the reception.
- Send out invitations for the rehearsal dinner.
- Pay the officiant and musicians, or arrange for someone else to take responsibility for doing so.
- Bring the marriage license on the day.
- Dance with both mothers and the maid of honor and make them all feel like a million dollars.

PLANNING AHEAD

Give your guests one large canvas to fill in, and you'll get things you'll wish you could cut. Individual notes or cards make editing out the rude stuff easy.

TOP
5

**TIPS:
THE GOOD
GUEST LIST**

EN MASSE

If you have to cut a number of people, uninvite a whole group (for example, work colleagues), rather than singling people out here and there.

Guest book
Want somewhere for your friends and family to write their good wishes on the day? Make it easy and fun:

- Leave out a pile of individual cards and pens.
- Ask them to write messages on photo booth snaps from the wedding.
- Hang pictures, posters, maps, or plain canvas for them to sign (but see sidebar).
- Pass around a guest book filled with old photos.

Guest list
If you're limited by budget or location, putting together the guest list can require a little negotiation. . . .

THE GOOD GUEST LIST

1. Don't play fantasy guest list. Set a budget, then see how many people you can afford to invite. Don't start by creating a wish list of everyone on the planet you'd like to come.

2. But, on the other hand . . . if your guest list is much smaller than you'd like, find ways to cut costs. Far better to have a cheaper party for more people than Champagne and a three-course meal for a few, said one bride. See page 102 for ideas on how to cut costs.

3. Don't invite people out of obligation. Save your guest list for the people you really care about, says event planner Lesley Price. No matter if someone invited you to their wedding: If you haven't spoken in the last year or two or three, you don't have to invite them back.

4. Consider adults only. Children bump up numbers like crazy. If they're eating up your guest list, consider an adults-only wedding. See the Children entry on page 84.

5. Have some rules for plus-ones:

- For guests in long-term relationships, and definitely if they're living together, invite their partners even if you don't know them. See page 239 for more on plus-ones.

- If single guests know next to no one, let them bring someone. If all their closest friends will be there, you don't need to, but it's still a considerate thing to do.

THE PARENT TRAP Parents don't always behave like adults. They can be as sulky and difficult as the next teenager.

PROBLEM: One set of parents is paying more toward the wedding and feels entitled to a major slice of the invites.
SOLUTION: Explain this is a celebration for both families and that you'd like both sides represented equally. Stick to your guns. Point out that dishing out guest numbers according to a family's wealth/available assets stinks. Unless the below applies . . .

PROBLEM: One family is much bigger than the other and your parents are ranting about all your aunties, cousins, and whatnot. How do you decide how many invites both sets of parents get?
SOLUTION: You have to use common sense. If one side of the family has way more relatives, share them out pro rata–ish.

A LITTLE BIT OF controversy

HOW TO UNINVITE A WEDDING GUEST We all know you shouldn't, but sometimes shit happens and you have no choice.

Have they behaved badly? Easy . . . call (if you don't speak, they can swear blind you never rescinded the invite) and tell them. No excuses or groveling on your part needed.

Are they blameless? If you have to uninvite innocents, choose people you see the least or never speak to from one year to the next. Call or talk face to face. Don't bail out by text, e-mail, or Facebook. Apologize sincerely and explain why (have a damn good reason). Be prepared for hurt.

Q What if I can't invite everyone I want?

A Have a B guest list, but handle with care. Chase RSVPs constantly like a rabid dog and send out invitations to the B list the second you get a decline from the A's.

STAY ORGANIZED
Use an app or an online guest list manager, Excel, or typed lists. Things to keep track of:
- When invites go out
- Who has yet to RSVP
- Who's coming
- Who's not

Hh

Haggle

When was the last time you tried to bargain? As a teenager trying to persuade your parents to let you skip off to Tijuana because it was part of your Spanish homework? (If it worked, you're a master and clearly don't need our tips.)

Maybe you don't like haggling because you think it's cheap? All you need is a little mind switch. . . . In business, they call it negotiation. Everyone does it, from the world's richest people downward. Do you think Donald Trump always takes the first price he's quoted? And negotiating can be fun, especially when you knock $$$ off the price.

STRATEGIES TO HELP YOU HAGGLE LIKE A PRO

1. Be charming. Aggression will get you nowhere, and if people like you or you can make them laugh, they'll be more likely to help you. If you're not funny or charming, send in someone who is.

2. Don't haggle with the wrong person. Speak with the person who has the authority to grant your wish. If you're not sure, ask for the manager or owner.

3. Sell what you have to offer. What's in it for them? Will they get referrals and an increase in business? Stress how much guests will be spending or how you'll broadcast what a great vendor they were.

4. Use the salesman's ultimate tool . . . silence. It makes people feel obliged to fill gaps. Shut your mouth and let them gabble until they agree with what you were offering.

5. Practice your poker face. If you really, really want it, don't ever let them see how excited you are.

TOP 5 STRATEGIES TO HELP YOU HAGGLE LIKE A PRO

hair

WHETHER YOU
WANT LOW-KEY
BEDHEAD OR
SOMETHING MORE
FORMAL, THE NEXT
FEW PAGES ARE
ALL YOU NEED
TO KNOW ABOUT
WEDDING HAIR.

EXPERIMENT: Take a few hours or a day or more trying out all the styles you like. Have accessories ready so you can see how they change each look.

TEST-DRIVE: Once you find a style you think you like, take it out for a spin. Do stray bits of hair come poking out after half an hour? At the end of the day do you look like you've gone 10 rounds with Mike Tyson? Do some faux dancing, hug your friends, and move around a lot. Note what styling products you'll need to keep it looking good all day. A slick of gel? A whole can of industrial-strength spray?

Hair.
It's all about the 3 Cs:

cut

Don't get anything daring or drastically new. Think more along the lines of trim and shape about two weeks beforehand, and still being someone your partner will recognize.

TRIED AND TESTED: COCONUT OIL CONDITIONER

Want glossy, soft hair?

● Apply organic coconut oil on dry hair and scalp. Liquify the oil first by running the container under a hot tap.

● Wrap hair in plastic wrap and leave for a couple of hours or overnight if you can.

● Cut the oil by applying shampoo straight onto hair before you wet it. Wet and wash as usual.

condition

How can you get your hair into shiny, glossy condition even if it looks more like a bundle of straw? Like this, says celebrity colorist Marie Robinson, whose clients include Scarlett Johansson.

TIP 1: Don't wash your hair, or blow-dry it, or use other heat styling tools every day.

TIP 2: Use glosses to add shine or texture. They can also help hold your hairstyle because they add pliability. They come in clear and colors, which fade out in 8 to 12 shampoos.

TIP 3: When you're on your honeymoon, prewet your hair with tap water before you swim in chlorine because it stops hair from absorbing too much of the chemical.

color

"Changing your hair color can be very positive. It can really boost your confidence,**"** says celebrity colorist Tracey Cunningham, whose clients include Cameron Diaz and Gwyneth Paltrow.

TRACEY'S KEY COLOR CONSIDERATIONS:

Timing: Leave at least two weeks between color and your wedding to allow time for adjustments.

Lifestyle: Tell your colorist about your personality, lifestyle, and schedule so he/she knows how high or low maintenance your color should be.

Research: Make sure the person you use has experience, knowledge, and skill.

Highlight know-how: Keep slightly more pigment at the root, use finer stitches for more natural blending of color, and create dimension with light and dark patches. Ask your colorist to use these techniques; they'll keep it looking natural.

Photos: Make sure you tell your hairdresser it's for a wedding, because it makes a difference for photos. If you're blonde, be sure the hairline is bright—if your hair is up, there won't be any root to get distorted or look darker in photos. If you're brunette, make sure a slightly lighter formula is used on your hairline so the color doesn't look harsh or inky in photos.

DIY: It's very rare that I see beautiful color that's come from a box. I don't recommend coloring your own hair at home.

THE 3 KEYS TO HOME COLOR

Marcy Cona, Clairol global creative director of color and style, gives these tips:

1. Hair needs dimension: depth, tones, and highlights. Choose a product that has them embedded. Or use two shades within the same shade family, using the slightly darker at your roots, and the lighter on the midshaft and ends.

2. Find your perfect shade. Think about the best color you ever had: Was it a warm or cool tone? Brown, blonde, or reddish? For natural results, your hair should be one half to two shades darker or lighter than your skin tone.

3. Avoid making hair too dark, inky, or harsh. This starts and ends with application and timing. Apply hair color only where you need it, for example, roots only. If you want to refresh midshafts and ends, adjust the timing to only a few minutes, creating less deposit and avoiding over colored, flat, dark results.

hair removal

We've tried every way under the sun to get rid of body hair. Which is best? Take the quiz and find out which solution is right for you.

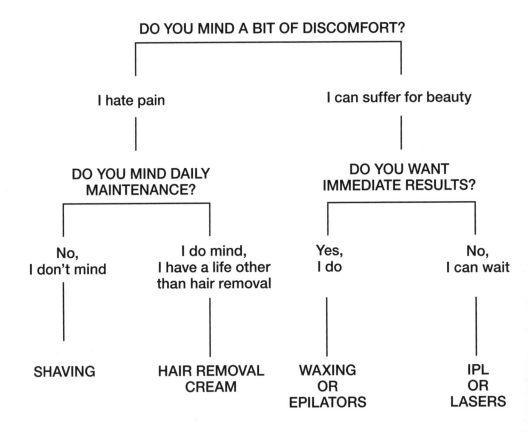

DO YOU MIND A BIT OF DISCOMFORT?

I hate pain

I can suffer for beauty

DO YOU MIND DAILY MAINTENANCE?

DO YOU WANT IMMEDIATE RESULTS?

No, I don't mind

I do mind, I have a life other than hair removal

Yes, I do

No, I can wait

SHAVING

HAIR REMOVAL CREAM

WAXING OR EPILATORS

IPL OR LASERS

SHAVING

PROS Easy and fast anytime for anyone.
CONS Needs daily maintenance to prevent stubble.

WAXING

PROS Can be used anywhere on the body, and lasts for days.
CONS Needs practice, a firm hand, and a highish pain threshold. If you're not up for DIY, head to a professional salon.

LASERS

PROS Fuzz-free skin permanently; some can be used on face.
CONS Not suitable for all skin and hair types, needs repeated treatments, takes months for full results.

IPL

PROS Can treat large areas for permanent hair removal.
CONS Not good for everyone; is s-l-o-w. Allow six months for full results.

EPILATORS

PROS Quick and easy to use, lasts around two weeks.
CONS It tends to be eyewatering on the bikini area.

HAIR REMOVAL CREAM

PROS Easy to apply, supersmooth finish, and lasts longer than shaving.
CONS Noxious and toxic chemicals that stink.

---

and don't forget your . . .
BIKINI LINE

There's NOTHING UNUSUAL left that people can DO WITH THEIR PUBES except GROW THEM BACK; we're back full circle to the VAJUNGLE.

DOWN-UNDER DICTIONARY

● **Hollywood:** absolutely everything removed

● **Brazilian:** leaves a small strip at the front and removes everything at the back and in between

● **Vajazzles:** rhinestones and crystals to give you a sparkly vagina

We've both spent the odd hour hiding under the desk at work trying to sleep off the hangover from hell.

DID YOU KNOW . . .
The liver can only process roughly one alcoholic unit every hour, so the number of drinks you have is pretty much the number of hours it'll take to feel completely normal again.

CURING THE VOMITOUS FEELING

Through trial and error we've got plenty of experience rustling up hangover prevention tips and cures, and we can fully commiserate with anyone who suffers the day after.

PREVENTION: Apart from just not drinking too much, these are the little helpers that can keep a hangover manageable:
- Eat.
- Drink water.
- Take milk thistle tincture (it helps the liver) in water and a homeopathic remedy before you go to bed.

PRESCRIPTION: Curing the vomitous feeling
It's not so much dehydration that makes it painful to move, think, or breathe the day after, but that the body is overwhelmed by the poisonous by-product of alcohol, acetaldehyde. You need to help your body process it as fast as possible.
- More milk thistle
- Homeopathic remedy Nux Vom
- Vitamins C and B (sublingual is best)
- Pedialyte
- If you can stomach it, a banana for the potassium, followed by lots of carbs
- Water (avoid fruit juice, which will be too acidic)
- Go back to bed

Hats

A veil covers and feels private; a hat is much more "look at me, I don't need some tulle pinned to my head to make me a bride."

HOW DO YOU GET IT RIGHT? What's your vision? asks milliner Kelly Christy, whose hats have graced the covers of *Vogue*. Do you want to look feminine, cool, romantic, traditional, glamorous, or a bit Lady Gaga out-there?

HOW TO MEASURE UP: Measure around your head one inch above your ear and across your forehead, leaving an extra finger's width for comfort. Sizes are usually given in inches, or small (21.5 inches), medium (22.5), and large (23).

THINK YOU'RE NOT A HAT PERSON? Milliners are adamant that there's a hat for everyone. If you've tried on fifty hats and still can't find one, try different angles on your head and tilting brims before you give up.

> **DO** stay clear of anything that will block your face. It matters for photos, because you won't want tunnel vision, and because your guests will want to see you say your vows, not look at a hat. . . .
> **DON'T** get hat hair. Leave a finger's width breathing space inside your hat.

WTF IS A FASCINATOR?

It's a *nano*-hat or concoction of tufts of feathers, lace, netting, and beads. Wear (with caution) on the right-hand side of your head or over your part and attach with super-glue strength hairspray and bobby pins. Thin hair? Beware of heavy pieces because they'll slide off your head. For the ultimate fascinator how-to, check out pics of the British royal family.

Help

Ask for it.

Remember . . . you'll attract more flies with honey and all that. . . .

honeymoon

What sort do you want?

SAFARI

Take a safari into the wilds to spot anything from lions and elephants to gorillas, tigers, snow leopards, and rhinos.

- India
- Botswana
- Thailand
- Tanzania
- Rwanda
- Namibia
- South Africa

ESCAPE FROM CIVILIZATION

Do it in five-star style or on a budget. . . .

- In an ecolodge in the Atacama Desert
- In a tree house in Brazil
- In a yurt in Colorado
- In a cabin in Iceland
- In an Airstream in California
- In a tent at Jack's Camp on Botswana's Makgadikgadi salt pans
- Yachting through the Indonesian archipelago

ISLAND ESCAPES

Individual dots of paradise

- Zanzibar
- Bora Bora
- Madagascar
- The Greek islands
- Lizard Island, Australia

WINTER SPORTS AND COZY FIRES

The Northern Lights in Iceland, skiing, snowboarding, log cabins, and *vin chaud.* Wrap up warm for a snuggly holiday.

- Iceland
- Mégève, France
- Aspen
- Jackson Hole
- Telluride
- Montana
- St. Moritz, Switzerland

BEACH PARADISE

Want beach, beach, and more beach? Head for one of these hot spots.

- Maldives
- Brazil
- Corsica
- Thailand
- U.S. Virgin Islands

LUXE AND DECADENCE

Sometimes you just need to be waited on hand and foot. . . .

- One and Only Reethi Rah, Maldives
- Amanpulo, Philippines
- The Oberoi Amarvilas, Agra
- North Island, Seychelles
- Cipriani, Venice

HISTORY LESSONS

All beach and no action not for you? Head to some of the most beautiful and historic cities in the world to take in the sights.

- Rome, Italy
- Luxor, Egypt
- London, England
- Jerusalem, Israel
- Seville, Spain
- Paris, France
- Buenos Aires, Argentina
- Angkor Wat, Cambodia
- Savannah, Georgia, USA
- Prague, Czech Republic
- Siracusa, Sicily, Italy
- Athens, Greece

OLD WORLD BAZAARS

Shopping on your honeymoon? Head for the famous souks and bazaars of these ancient cities. Be ready to haggle.

- Marrakesh, Morocco
- Istanbul, Turkey
- Bangkok, Thailand
- Jaipur, India

ADVENTURE AND EXCITEMENT

Firing up the adrenaline will give you unforgettable memories. But it doesn't have to be all action packed . . . mix and match with some R & R.

- Trek in the Himalayas
- Run with the bulls in Pamplona
- Dive into underwater caldera on the Galápagos
- Bike down active volcanoes in Hawaii (or ski down them in Chile)
- Go white-water rafting in Patagonia
- Build your own igloo at 7,500 feet in the Alps, and sleep in it

Hors d'oeuvres

1 Canapés will kick off your reception.

They're a well-deserved treat for hungry guests who've just sat through your ceremony.

2

3 Bits of yummy food will keep everyone happy while the photographs are being taken.

DO THE MATH

"For 45 minutes to an hour, allow at least five bites per person," says caterer Urban Palate. If canapés are taking the place of a full meal, make sure you don't run out—appetites pick up again after a couple of hours.

INSPIRED IDEAS

Urban Palate suggests these delicious canapés:

● Short-rib empanada with smoked Provolone, heirloom tomato relish, and basil oil

● Yellow and red heirloom tomato tartlet with burrata, arugula oil, and port syrup

● Nueske's bacon maple biscuit, pork cutlet, and scallion pimento cheese

● Mission fig crostini with Humboldt Fog goat cheese, lavender honey, and mint

GAME PLAN: Do a little mental imagery of how things will work. Is there room for waiters to move around or will they be trying not to bodycheck your guests? If space is tight, put canapés on a help-yourself table. Then, follow these simple rules, says Urban Palate:

DO include at least one vegetarian option.

DO make them easy to pick up and to eat (nothing slimy or drippy).

DO have a variety of flavors and temperatures: hot, cold, sweet, sour, spicy, salty, and bitter. How many varieties do you need? For weddings up to 30 guests, plan for five; 30 to 60, about nine varieties; with more guests than this, have a minimum of 10 varieties.

DO serve different textures, colors, and shapes as well as different flavors.

DON'T have everything fried.

Host

Your main job on your wedding day? Apart from getting married, looking after your guests. Don't you love parties where everything's easy? You know from the start what to wear and you're never hungry or thirsty, too hot or cold.

"What makes a wedding special," explains event designer David Beahm, "is a couple who understands what it is to host a fabulous celebration. And I'm not talking about the ability to spend money, but the ability to make each guest feel cared for and welcomed."

Houses of worship

Even within the same religion, houses of worship can vastly differ. All have rules and etiquette, their own style and way of doing things. If you don't have somewhere you go regularly, the biggest question to ask yourself is, Does its style and interpretation of your religion suit you?

Humor, sense of

Laughter triggers feel-good endorphins. It's a stress reliever and pain reliever; it defuses tension instantly and helps create happy memories. If you're having a sense of humor failure, here's our prescription to get it back on track.

PRESCRIPTION: Regaining your sense of humor
Watch a funny film. Top three movies, guaranteed to make you laugh, as prescribed by the editors of film magazine *Empire,* are
- **Monty Python and the Holy Grail** (Terry Gilliam, 1975)
Nev Pierce, editor-at-large
- **What's Up, Doc?** (Peter Bogdanovich, 1972)
Aubrey Day, U.S. editor
- **Better Off Dead** (Savage Steve Holland, 1985)
Mark Dinning, editor-in-chief

"Treat your guests like guests and try to be relaxed. The bride always sets the mood for the entire night."
Wedding planner Tara Guérard

SENSE OF HUMOR

Ii

Ice Does frozen water deserve an entry all to itself? Yes, but we're not talking about the stuff at the back of your freezer studded with frozen peas. We mean crystal clear, sparkling ice made from the purest water.

ICE, ICE BABY Apart from the cubes in your drink, how else can you use ice?

Lanterns: Having a winter wedding? Use hollowed out blocks of ice with electric candles to line pathways and entrances or, if you live somewhere cold enough, make your own knee-high ice lanterns.

Sculptures: Think big, striking, or useful—a bar carved entirely from blocks of ice, a sculpture as part of the raw bar, or a focal point to the reception.

HOW LONG DOES BIG ICE LAST? Outside in hot weather, a sculpture will last about four hours. Inside at room temperature, around six to eight hours. It doesn't mean that they'll disappear, just that they'll be past their best. Ice bars last about 24 hours.

DID YOU KNOW . . .
While we're on the subject of water, all water does NOT taste the same. "Just like wine, waters have a wide divergence in taste," says water sommelier Martin Riese. The best general crowd-pleasers? "Acqua Panna for still water, and for sparkling, San Pellegrino."

GO NATURAL

Try a remedy such as valerian, L-tryptophan, or 5-HTP.

If I'd known then what I know now . . .

There's no handbook to a happy marriage. But there are couples who've stayed happily married for 20, 30, 40, or even 50 years, and they're the ideal people to share the lessons they've learned.

SECRETS OF A HAPPY MARRIAGE

1. "Nothing performs as expected without effort. If something breaks, you don't throw it away, you fix it. The same goes for marriage. Fix it!" —Bob, married to Carolyn for 50 years

2. "Always try to give more to the relationship than you take out of it. It took me about ten years to figure that out, and I still regress frequently, but I'm trying!" —John, married to Carol for 37 years

3. "The secret to a happy marriage is to laugh, listen, and talk. It took me a few years to get there." —George, married to Sonya for 25 years

4. "Treat each day like it's the last day you'll have together." —Tanis, married to Jim for 44 years

5. "When your spouse says something's wrong, listen. When they get angry about something, not necessarily at you, give them time to cool off. This isn't the time to talk. That comes later." —Fay, married to Bob for 40 years

Insomnia Are you waking up at 4:00 a.m.? Lying there for a couple of hours with general crap churning through your head? Here's how to fall into deep sleep, and stay there.

LESS STIMULATION Cut down caffeine, nicotine, and alcohol. No caffeine less than six hours before you go to bed. Alcohol might help knock you out but it's a diuretic, so you'll need the bathroom in the night, and it interferes with deep sleep. Same for other drugs—they're not the friend of healthy, restorative sleep.

SCREEN FREE Stop looking at ALL screens at least three hours before you go to bed. Blue light, which all screens including phones, iPads, computers, and TVs, emit, interferes with the production of the sleep hormone melatonin. "Exposing the eyes to light, especially blue light, during the hours before bedtime is a major cause of insomnia," says Dr. Richard Hansler of the Lighting Innovations Institute at John Carroll University. If going cold turkey is too much, download a blue-light filter for computers, or invest in a smartphone, iPad, computer screen, or TV filter, or blue-light blocking glasses, which trick the brain into thinking it's dark.

THESE, TOO:
- Exercise every day.
- Get more magnesium in your system.
- Consider acupuncture and acupressure.
- Be consistent with bedtime and waking, even on weekends.

Try this:

Get some natural sunlight every day (lunchtime sunlight is best) because it resets your circadian rhythms. And make your bedroom a refuge from chaos. Take out anything related to work or weddings.

Insurance

You've got it for your car, house, and health—any asset worth protecting. A wedding is just one more asset to look after. Once you've paid deposits, you've probably committed to some big sums of money. Wedding insurance is there to protect that money if anything goes wrong. Let's just say you have to postpone because someone's sick, a vendor fails, or a storm causes chaos. Insurance can't wave a magic wand and bake you a cake in place of your baker who went bust, but you will get your money back. Expect to pay several hundred dollars for a no-frills policy that will cover photos, clothes, wedding gifts, rings, and deposits.

WHAT SHOULD BE COVERED
- Cancellations due to bad weather
- Sick bride or groom
- Vendors not turning up, going bankrupt, or double booking
- Death or illness in the family
- Theft
- Military duty
- Having to move because of a job

INSURANCE NEED-TO-KNOWS

● Make sure you're comparing like for like when you're deciding which policy to take out. Do they have similar benefits or the same deductible?

● Check if a policy pays up in the event of cancellation or postponement.

● What is covered and what isn't? If you're having a destination wedding, check that the policy covers all your belongings in transit. Do items over a certain value (for example, your engagement ring or expensive designer clothes) need an additional policy?

WHEN?

Take out insurance as soon as you've paid deposits anywhere, although most insurance companies won't insure until the wedding is two years or less away.

Interfaith This is a merger. A bringing together of two families and faiths, blending beliefs to create your happy union, even though, at times, it might feel more like you need a UN peace negotiator. You might be starting from two views that feel oceans apart, but these are a few ways to get the love flowing, or at least get everyone in the same room.

TOP
5
**WAYS
TO MAKE
IT A HAPPY
MERGER**

WAYS TO MAKE IT A HAPPY MERGER

1. Be open to compromise. A little give-and-take on both sides goes a long way.

2. Find the common ground. Start with the things you have in common, not the differences. "For example, choose readings that are common to you both," says Lindsey Silken of InterfaithFamily.

3. Celebrate a tradition from each faith.

4. Let your guests know what to do. "Some rituals and traditions might be unfamiliar, so put notes in the program and ask your officiant to explain during the ceremony."

5. Speak the same language. "Be sure that anything said in Hebrew, or any other language, is translated or explained for guests who aren't familiar with it."

Invitations

What should an invitation look like? As plain, colorful, simple, or formal as you like. Just make sure that the style and tone of the event are reflected in some way and the dress code noted. "Use graphics, colors, and textures—above all, have fun!" says Ming Thompson, creative director of Pounding Mill Press.

THE WHO, WHAT, WHERE OF INVITES

- **Who's invited:** List all names individually, including children's.
- **To what:** Tell them what the event is—the wedding, a shower, or the rehearsal dinner.
- **Where:** Include the address.
- **When:** Give a time and, if necessary, specify a start time for the ceremony.
- **Dress code:** Be clear what it is.
- **RSVP:** Include an e-mail or postal address, telephone number or wedding website, with a deadline.

"Get your ducks in a row before you begin searching for invitations. Have your venue and wedding date booked."
Luxury invitation designer Ceci Johnson

FURTHER READING
Go to the Stationery entry on page 274.

It's (not) just your day

Is your wedding all about you, or everyone else, too? Well, the marriage is yours but a wedding is a family rite of passage that everyone loves to share; it creates memories across generations. Sometimes, consider doing things not because you want to, but because it's important to someone else in your families. "The day was for my parents who'd dreamed of throwing a party; for my grandparents because I was the first grandchild to get married; and for my cousins who were flower girls," said real bride Camilla.

"Remember that this day will hold special meaning long after the wedding is over. For example, the groom may want to forgo the mother/son dance, but if this is something that will mean the world to his mother for years to come, it is worth creating the memory," says event designer Jung Lee.

Jj

Jj

Jealousy

Jealousy can swirl around every which way when it comes to weddings . . . brides get jealous; friends and family get jealous . . . the day can be one giant mess of emotions.

DEAR GOD, I'M INSANE WITH ENVY . . . Are you jealous of what other brides have? Honestly, there is no easy way to just switch it off; you have to suck it up and move on. Jealous of money? More money doesn't always make for better weddings, but yes, it can make planning them easier. Go to the Cheap and chic entry on page 82. Jealous of their jewelry? See the celebs that rocked costume jewelry on page 97. Jealous of their loving family? See the Parents entry on page 228 and Arguments, squabbles, and fights on page 28 for how to bring peace to family friction.

DEAR GOD, I'M GETTING SOME CRAP THROWN AT ME . . . "Be aware that deeper feelings can be at the heart of jealousy," says psychologist and relationship expert Yvonne Thomas. "Try to be compassionate and think about why they might be feeling jealous about such an important time in your life."

WAYS TO HEAD OFF JEALOUSY

Thomas offers these tips for dealing with jealousy:

1. Make the people who are jealous feel included. Ask them to help planning or use one of their ideas for something wedding-related. They'll feel a part of, as opposed to outside of, the experience.

2. Commit some time to talk on the phone or see each other at least once a week. Don't e-mail or text.

TOP 5

WAYS TO HEAD OFF JEALOUSY

And don't only talk or see each other for wedding-related reasons—you had a relationship before you were planning a wedding.

3. Balance the attention so that it's not just "all about me," but also "all about you." Give them center stage.

4. When you're around friends who are single or in unhappy romantic relationships, don't gush too much about finding "the one." Instead, spend time encouraging and being supportive.

5. Make them feel important and valued by asking for their advice and words of wisdom. This can let them know that you take your relationship with them seriously at this significant time in your life.

Jewelry

"Jewelry transcends time. Small pieces like rings and bracelets may seem insignificant, but they're time capsules that open the door to memories and emotions," explains celebrity jeweler Martin Katz.

ADD MEANING TO YOUR WEDDING JEWELRY

● **Engraving:** Add a date, initials, a name, numbers, words, a message or code, a line from a poem or song, a symbol, or anything from a fingerprint to an image if you use laser engraving.

● **Monograms:** You can create your own monogram in anything from brass and rhinestones to gold or diamonds, on pendants, rings, bracelets, and earrings.

● **Gemstones:** They could remind you of a place, a time, or someone in your family, or they could be a birthstone.

● **Charms:** No one needs to know exactly what it means except you.

TOP TIP

Buying online? If there's no picture of the piece on a model, ask how the piece sits on the hand or the wrist, says jeweler Bec Astley Clarke. Some online jewelers will happily send extra pictures.

THE ULTIMATE IN MAKING IT YOUR OWN "Bespoke jewelry takes time and communication, but you'll end up with a piece that is so personal and unique you'll love it forever," says jeweler Hattie Rickards, who recommends these steps:

BESPOKE JEWELRY

1. Budget: Tell the designer what it is—jewelers can often produce far more on a tight budget than you could ever imagine, using tricks of design and production.

2. Design: Establish what you want—is it for occasional wear or everyday? We can make you a "showstopper," but it might not be versatile enough to be worn alongside the rest of your jewelry.

3. Style: Are you flamboyant or subtle, do you prefer contemporary or traditional, do you like large pieces or do smaller pieces suit you better? It helps if you have an opinion from the start.

4. Sentiment: Search for family heirlooms or old pieces of jewelry. Incorporating metals or stones into newly designed commissions enhances the sentimental value and keeps costs down.

5. Communication: Research and talk to the designer. You'll quickly establish whether he or she is someone you can trust to understand and translate your desires.

TOP
5
TIPS FOR BESPOKE JEWELRY

Just one thing What's the single most important thing you need to know about weddings?

"If you're having fun, EVERYONE around you will be having fun."

EVENT DESIGNER DAVID BEAHM

Kk

Keepsakes Make a time capsule and a plan to open it on your tenth anniversary. Include all the little things that went into planning your wedding—notes and reminders, cards, swatches, stationery. . . .

Ketubah "The very first ketubah, which was written by rabbis over two thousand years ago, was innovative for its time because it was intended to protect the bride financially if her husband died or divorced her, as well as spelling out her rights in the marriage," explains Arielle Angel, cofounder of Ketuv: Fine Art Ketubahs.

"Because it's two thousand years old, the traditional text can be problematic for those looking for a more egalitarian arrangement to define their marriage. If you're not from a strict, Orthodox, or traditional community, you do have other options," says Angel. These also include modern texts for same-sex, interfaith, and nondenominational couples. "I'd always suggest that a couple consults with their rabbi before choosing a text."

Q Can I have a ketubah if I'm not Jewish?

A Yes, they're a symbol of commitment and anyone can have one made up. Look online; there are literally thousands of choices.

Kneeling Will you be kneeling at the altar? Ask yourself . . .
- Have I removed price stickers from the soles of my shoes?
- Can I actually kneel in my wedding dress without help?
- Have I checked my shoes for rude messages from friends?
- Do I want my bridesmaids to sign the bottom of my shoes (it's tradition that whoever's name is left at the end of the day will be the next married)?

Ll

L

Legal issues Getting married goes hand in hand with legal practicalities. Use this as a guide:

- **Marriage license:** You can't get married without it. See the entry on page 208 for more information.
- **Ceremony:** See the Ceremony entry on page 80.
- **Divorce:** A divorce needs to be final and the courts need to sign off before you can apply for a new marriage license.
- **Children:** Check with your lawyer or the courts before taking any steps involving children.
- **Taxes:** As a married couple, you'll be able to file joint tax returns or continue to file separately.
- **Debts:** Will you be responsible for your partner's debts when you marry? It depends where you live. In community property states (Arizona, California, Idaho, Louisiana, Nevada, New Mexico, Texas, Washington, and Wisconsin), debts incurred by either of you during the marriage (not before) will be owed by both of you even if only one of you signs the papers.
- **Changing your name:** If you want to, you can do this easily when you marry (see the entry on page 219).
- **Workplace benefits:** Getting married may give you automatic access to your partner's health care or pension benefits. Get documents to providers as soon as possible after your marriage.

● **Prenups:** Whether you want to draw one up or have been asked to sign one, prenups always need a lawyer (see the Prenups entry on page 240).

● **Wills:** Get legal advice—especially if you have complex arrangements.

● **Next of kin:** You'll automatically be considered next of kin once you're married. Decisions about, for example, medical issues will defer directly to you.

Lighting How much thought have you given to lighting?

"Imagine TRYING TO SEE all the things you've chosen for your wedding WITHOUT LIGHTING.

You need basic lighting, candle lighting, or dramatic lighting."

LIGHTING DESIGNER IRA LEVY

USING THE PROFESSIONALS

How expensive is it? Fees vary, but it's set-up time that pushes up prices, so ask the engineer for ways to cut staff-hours if you're on a budget.

It's important not just so you can see what you're doing, but because it sets the mood. "One of my favorite lighting teams has a great way of explaining this," says planner Cassandra Santor. "When you go out for dinner you often choose your restaurant based on how it feels—and, in most cases, that's to do with the lighting. Bright and cheery, soft and romantic, funky and festive . . . lighting holds the key."

WHAT MOOD DO I WANT TO CREATE WITH LIGHTING?

ceremony

_____

cocktail hour

_____

reception

_____

dancing/partying

_____

COLOR ME HAPPY
Use color psychology to help plan your lighting.
- **Orange:** energizing, happy, stimulates the appetite
- **Red:** energizing, passionate, can speed the pulse and breathing
- **Blue:** relaxing and peaceful
- **Yellow:** warm, happy, and cheerful

DIY It's not as complicated as those professionals make it sound, but ask when you rent what would suit your space best.
- **Large spaces and high ceilings** need big, dramatic touches. "Darkness is just as important as light when it comes to creating drama; you need highs and lows," says Levy.
- **Smaller spaces** should feel cozy, and you can get away with strings of lights and clusters of candles. You need a bit more light in areas where people are eating and drinking, entrances, exits, and bathrooms, and less where they're relaxing.

COLOR THEORY "If you use LED color-change lighting, guests can walk into a cheerful lavender cocktail hour, transition to warm amber for dinner, and finish off with a cool 'loungey' blue for dancing," says Levy.

LET THERE BE LIGHT
Use any of these light sources to start setting the mood:
- tealights
- candles
- chandeliers
- bonfires
- strings of fairy lights
- paper lanterns
- rent-your-own LED projectors
- uplighters
- single illuminated words

Linens Tablecloths, runners, and napkins are basic linens you might need at your reception. The only real questions are:

Do they come supplied by your venue or caterer?
AND
If you're responsible, do you want to rent or buy?

YOUR LINENS COME SUPPLIED

PRO: One less thing to think about. The venue is responsible for everything.
CON: Color choice can be limited.

RENTING YOUR OWN

PRO: Huge choice—every size, shape, and color under the rainbow, with every permutation of added decoration known to man—and you're not responsible for cleaning, collecting, etc.
CON: It can end up costing as much as buying.

BUYING YOUR OWN LINENS

PRO: If you're prepared to buy secondhand, you can get real value for money. Check online bridal forums and eBay for used-once wedding linens.
CON: You'll be stuck with shedloads of linen.

Lineup This is the order in which your wedding party will go down the aisle. You can do it by height or age, line them up alphabetically, or simply pair up people who will be comfortable walking together. If all else fails, throw their names in a hat and let them draw for who walks in what order—it makes it fun and removes any doubts about why anyone's where they are in the lineup.

> **DON'T:** line up anyone according to how important they are to you. That's a recipe for so much bad feeling you won't know what to do with it. Would you want to be the one at the back?
>
> **DO:** use common sense for this, not strict rules.

SLIP 'N' SLIDE
Hiring chair backs? Steer clear of polyester and shiny, slippery fabrics that will have everyone sweating or sliding off their seats.

Lingerie What's the difference between lacy, flimsy bits of not much and some plain everyday bras? One's about making you feel good/sexy and the other's about keeping you in place, says author of *The Lingerie Handbook,* Rebecca Apsan . . .

LINGERIE

"Lingerie is something carefully chosen to set a mood."

UNDERWEAR

"Underwear is an everyday necessity that's grabbed from a drawer with no thought."

INSIDER TIPS FOR GETTING LINGERIE RIGHT Buying lingerie's not as easy as grabbing a plain bra and undies off the rack. It's flimsy, lacy, and doesn't hold you in but, says Apsan, you just need the right pieces:

● Make sure that no matter what you wear, you feel comfortable and confident—if not, it'll show. Keep looking until you find something perfect.

● If you're more low-key, don't feel pressured to pull out all the stops just because it's your wedding or honeymoon.

● The right piece of lingerie will play up your best assets while drawing attention away from any parts you're not happy with. Don't like your tummy? Try a babydoll nightie. Worried about your thighs? A silky chemise will cover them. If you have great breasts, go for a demicup and no one will notice any other minor flaws.

Liposuction

Lipo isn't the way to drop a few dress sizes. "It's a contouring or sculpting procedure, not a weight-loss procedure," reminds Dr. Robert Gotkin. But if you've got some stubborn areas of fat to shift, it's one route you could take.

WHAT ARE YOUR CHOICES?

● Classic surgical lipo, where tubes are inserted under the skin to suction out fat.

● Newer-generation noninvasive procedures that use everything from radio waves to lasers to melt and disperse fat internally.

INVASIVE SURGICAL LIPO

PROS: Very effective. Sucks out lots of fat at once (although legal maximum is usually 5 liters in one go) for visible results. Newer techniques include using ultrasound, laser, and water before fat is suctioned out.

CONS: Minimum one-week downtime; pain; swelling for a few weeks; can take up to six months for final results; need to wear compression garments for a long time; side effects include scarring, rippled skin, and stray lumps of fat or holes. Expensive.

TREATABLE AREAS: Upper thighs, butt, knees, back, stomach, arms, and, at a real push, ankles.

NONSURGICAL LIPO

PROS: "The best part is that you don't need anesthesia, there are no incision marks or scars, and no downtime," says dermatologist Dr. Debra Jaliman.

CONS: Expensive, repeated treatments are sometimes necessary; two to four months for final results. Can't get the same results as invasive lipo. "I'm not aware of any procedures that come close to achieving the same results as surgical lipo," says Dr. Mitchell Schwartz.

TREATABLE AREAS: Chin, thighs, butt, knees, back, stomach, hips, arms.

love

Here's our favorite gesture of love:

British farmer Winston Howes planted a six-acre field with thousands of oak trees—leaving a perfect heart-shaped meadow in the center—after his wife of 33 years, Janet, died suddenly. Not visible from any roads and known only to the family, his memorial to his wife stayed a secret for almost two decades until it was spotted from the air by a hot air balloonist flying over the land. The tip of the heart points toward Janet's childhood home.

TOP 10 LOVE SONGS

Chosen by Film and television music supervisor Ann Kline

1 **Song for Zula,** Phosphorescent
2 **This Love,** Bryan Ferry
3 **When the Stars Go Blue,** The Corrs featuring Bono
4 **At Last,** Etta James
5 **Nothing Compares 2 U,** Sinéad O'Connor
6 **Wonderwall,** Ryan Adams
7 **Can't Help Falling in Love,** UB40
8 **Lovefool,** The Cardigans
9 **In My Life,** The Beatles
10 **Broken Arrow,** Rod Stewart

Mm

Mm

Made-to-measure

Unless all your parts (arms, legs, boobs, butt, waist) are a completely average size, there are a hundred different reasons off-the-rack clothes will never be a perfect fit. Made-to-measure, on the other hand, will fit like a glove even if your top and bottom halves have three sizes difference between them because they're created from your personal measurements.

Are most wedding dresses made-to-measure? Nope. In a lot of cases (even expensive ones) they're ordered in your nearest size and then a seamstress pins, tucks, and alters. The best way of getting real made-to-measure is through a dressmaker rather than buying from a store.

THE NEXT STEP UP?
Couture. This is where something is designed especially for you. See the Couture entry on page 101.

Maid of honor

What does the maid of honor do? EVERYTHING. Except marry the groom. The poor woman has to look after you, sometimes dress you, advise you on your underpants, wrangle the bridesmaids to the right place at the right time for months on end, throw parties, control impending crises, and act as unofficial hostess, caregiver, and Xanax doler-outer. Don't ask a major flake to be your maid of honor; ask yourself who you can rely on the most.

Who is unflappable,

can make you laugh in the middle of a disaster, isn't prone to bitchy/drunken/uptight outbursts, and is superorganized?

Answer this and you have your maid of honor.

DON'T BE ECONOMICAL WITH THE TRUTH Be honest about what you really want her to do, because it can be a big job and a drain on her time and wallet. Do you want someone who'll take everything off your hands or are you happy to work together? Are you asking someone who already works 16-hour days?

TRADITIONAL DUTIES If she does all this, she deserves your endless gratitude.

A LITTLE BIT OF CONTROVERSY

Who should pay for the maid of honor's dress, shoes, and accessories? Traditionally she pays for them herself. But we think it's time to move this tradition on. If you can afford to pay for some or all of the costs, you should. See also the Bridesmaids entry on page 54 for more on this.

Before the wedding:
- organizes a bachelorette party
- organizes a bridal shower
- helps the bridesmaids sort out their outfits and accessories
- makes sure they get to fittings
- helps you choose what you wear
- attends fittings
- gives a second opinion on anything.

On the day:
- makes sure that you're 100 percent ready to go
- possibly carries the groom's ring to the altar
- signs as a witness
- dances with the best man at the reception
- packs up your wedding dress if you're changing and takes it home if you're heading straight off on honeymoon.

Makeup and makeup artists

Makeup should make you look and feel better. If it doesn't, or you think there's a thing or two you haven't quite come to grips with, read on. . . .

THINK ABOUT HAVING SOME LESSONS Lots of celebs are famous for doing their own makeup for the red carpet, including Kate Winslet, Kate Middleton, and Gwen Stefani. You can bet there are a few insider tips you don't know. Book a free consultation or makeover with a brand you like (Bobbi Brown does famously good ones and also has heaps of how-to videos online), or use a professional makeup artist for one session. Then practice, practice, practice.

ALL MAKEUP ARTISTS ARE NOT THE SAME They have different techniques, looks, and favorite products. When you're hiring one, run through this checklist:

- Always ask to see their portfolio. Don't book them unless you like their style. One person's light makeup is another one's hooker.
- ALWAYS have a practice session beforehand.
- Be honest before they start about how much makeup and what sort of colors you feel comfortable wearing. You don't have to end up sporting every product in their case.
- Don't be scared to speak up if you feel they're going off track or if the finished result isn't quite right. Say what you don't like and ask them to make some changes. If you still don't feel comfortable, it's OK to walk away.
- Ask if they can incorporate your favorite products.

Male grooming

We know that most men aren't familiar with being primped to within an inch of their lives, and we don't think many will wear makeup even if it is by Tom Ford,

WHO ARE YOU, WHO WHO WHO WHO

"The most important thing to remember with wedding makeup is to stay true to who you are. You should recognize yourself."

Makeup and beauty salon Blushington

TOP TIP
Ask your makeup artist to teach you some touch-up tips for the day.

but a little bit of grooming can go a long way here. "What is it that makes a man well groomed? If a man does not have inner confidence, he won't look his best. Part of men's grooming is making a man feel confident," says male grooming expert Diana Schmidtke, who works with stars such as George Clooney.

"The bits that men should pay attention to are
their hair, skin, and body."
DIANA SCHMIDTKE

HER TIPS FOR THE PERFECTLY GROOMED MAN

HAIR: Never get your hair cut the day of your wedding. Go a week before and have a neck trim the day before for a cleanup.

- All men look a little better in photos with some product in their hair. Apply from front to back, and then back to front—it needs to be even. If you don't like product, leave a little conditioner in to help weigh hair down.

SKIN: Moisturize using nothing less than an SPF 15 in the daytime. If you don't, it'll show as you get older; you'll get what I call "alligator nose." The skin turns dry, bumpy, and rigid instead of looking smooth.

- Take it further with monthly facials and use a face scrub two or three times a week to remove dead skin cells. Get a facial a week before the wedding so skin has time to heal from extractions.
- Apply eye cream to smooth out crow's feet, using serums for more advanced skin care needs.

EYEBROWS: The quickest way to make a man's face look feminine is to trim or tweeze away too many eyebrow hairs. Remove from the top, but easy does it on anything under the brow. Trim away stray hairs one by one—never cut straight across.

INSIDER SECRET

Want to groom Hollywood style? Well-known actors tint their eyebrows and eyelashes before each big project.

TEETH TOO

Get his smile brightened. It's no good if you have a pearly white smile and he has teeth like an old donkey. See the Teeth entry on page 283 for more.

Manicure

"Color can only look beautiful on beautiful nails," says red-carpet manicurist Jenna Hipp. First, you need to see to the health and condition of your nails.

> **"Make your hands a priority, spend time daily keeping up moisture levels, the shape of nails, and hydrated cuticles."**
>
> JENNA HIPP

NAIL HEALTH TIPS Want to know how to get long, strong, healthy nails? Follow these steps for daily TLC.

DO leave off the polish, gel, and acrylics. "Don't apply polish all the time. Your nails need to breathe," says podiatrist Bastien Gonzalez. If bare nails feel naked, buff them up to a natural gloss, but no more than once every three or four months or you'll thin the nails.

DO massage cuticles every day with a natural cuticle oil. "It moisturizes the nail plates, and increases blood flow to the bed of the nail," says health and beauty guru Eden Sassoon.

DO wear rubber gloves when you're doing housework or cleaning and moisturize every time you wash your hands.

DO make sure you're getting enough B vitamins, especially biotin, which is found in bananas, peanuts, cauliflower, salmon, soy, oatmeal, and mushrooms. If you take a biotin supplement, it'll take three to six months to see noticeable improvements, says Hipp.

DO keep nails groomed and snags and tears in check. If you bite or pick nails to the bone, try hypnotherapy.

DON'T put anything on your nails containing formaldehyde, formaldehyde resin, dibutyl phthalates

DID YOU KNOW . . .
Using nail polish remover to clean nails before polishing is the worst thing you can do. Swipe nails with rubbing alcohol instead, says Hipp.

Q Are gel manicures a lazy girl's best friend or too good to be true?

A "Too good to be true," says Hipp. "The process can cause months of damage to the natural nail."

(DBP), toluene, or camphor. Toxin-free brands are sometimes called "three-free" or "five-free."

WHICH COLOR? (And yes, red is officially neutral) If pale pink or nude polish isn't your thing, don't wear it just because it's "bridal." "Classic shades like nude, red, or deep burgundy go with everything and every skin tone. Short nails can pull off deep, dark, vampy shades—almost black, but not. Consider deep navy, eggplant, and oxblood for drama that's not so direct," says Hipp. "But be careful that you don't detract from your dress or ring."

DIY MANICURE Prefer to do your own nails? Follow Hipp's five easy steps to a manicure good enough to see you through the honeymoon, too:

1. Remove old nail polish without killing your nostrils, nails, and skin. Look for a chemical-free remover made for sensitive skin.
2. After scrubbing nails, push back cuticles with a warm, damp washcloth. This is gentler than a wooden orange stick and will prevent hangnails. If your cuticles are hardened or overgrown, soak nails in a bowl of warm whole milk. The lactic acid will help remove dead skin cells and soften cuticles while the fats replenish dry skin.
3. File and shape. Play up a short and simple nail shape by slightly rounding the corners, making nails appear a touch longer. Clipping can be just as precise as filing.
4. Don't forget a clear basecoat; it will ensure a chip-free, long-lasting manicure straight through your honeymoon. Don't forget a thin swipe over the tips to seal the edges! I recommend using the same basecoat as brand of polish.
5. Paint two coats of polish for even coverage, allowing three to five minutes for each coat to dry before applying the next. Then apply a clear topcoat, which will seal your color and add high shine.

TOP
5
**TIPS FOR
A DIY
MANICURE**

DID YOU KNOW . . .
"If your nails are yellow from previous polish, scrub them with whitening toothpaste and an old toothbrush. Add a little peroxide and baking soda to the mix for deep stains and to make tips extra white."
Jenna Hipp

marriage

How to have a great marriage, straight from the experts.

DR. LAURA BERMAN

The *New York Times* bestselling author has this advice. . . .

- **Communication:** "Nothing is more important. If you can't tell your partner what you are feeling AND hear what he or she's feeling, you're going to have a tough road ahead."

- **Fidelity:** "It's so hard to rebuild trust and intimacy after an affair. The damage can last for years, and sometimes it's impossible to undo."

- **A willingness to work at it:** "People think that great sex and happily ever after are supposed to come easily, so when it takes work and patience, they think there's something wrong with their relationship. But the truth is great relationships (and great sex) take effort and planning and communication."

DR. JANE GREER

Relationship expert, author, and creator of *Shrink Wrap with Dr. Jane Greer* offers this advice. . . .

- **Empathy:** One of the most important things is when your partner is able to put him- or herself in your shoes and really understand what you are experiencing emotionally.

- **Tolerance:** Rather than taking his or her behavior personally and getting locked into anger, tolerance allows you to accept who he or she is and live compatibly without getting into power struggles.

- **A sense of humor:** It's essential because it means you can neutralize those millions of little moments where you are going to get angry, annoyed, and irritated on any given day.

RABBI DR. JONATHAN ROMAIN

Author Rabbi Jonathan Romain has been counseling couples for many years and has this advice. . . .

- **An attentive attitude:** "Keep talking; do things together. It's very easy to take each other for granted, to slip away unconsciously and do less and less together. Successful marriages should not be an uphill task, but the little things need nurturing."

"If you're married to the right person, it makes all the good things in life twice as good and all the bad things half as bad." real groom Josh

Marriage certificate
Not to be confused with your marriage license (see below), which gives you permission to marry, the certificate is the official, certified, and legally binding proof of your wedding that you'll receive afterward. You'll need it to claim spousal workplace benefits like health care or insurance or if you want to change your name on official documents.

Marriage license
Here's the what, where, when, and how of a marriage license. It may not be glamorous, but it's important.

THINGS YOU NEED TO KNOW
1. You can't get married without a license.
2. As a couple you need to go together to the county clerk's office with all your documents and apply for it. Check the county's exact requirements before you go.
3. Turn up sober or they can refuse to give you one.
4. Have your license with you on your wedding day. It's normally the responsibility of your officiant to return it to the authorities.
5. Once it's processed, you'll receive your marriage certificate (see above).

MARRIAGE LICENSE 101
● **ID:** All states will ask to see at least one form of photo ID.
● **Marriageable age:** If you're younger than 18, most states will ask for written consent from your parents or guardian. Under 16 is normally only by permission of the courts.
● **Divorced or widowed:** You'll need to provide details or official proof of a divorce or death of a spouse. Some states require you to have been divorced for a certain period of time before they'll issue a new marriage license—the longest wait is six months.

TOP
5
THINGS YOU NEED TO KNOW

- **Degree of relation:** The marriage of close relatives is not allowed in most states. Some will allow first cousins to marry if the woman is over a certain age—i.e., too old to have children.
- **Same sex:** Not all states allow same-sex marriage. Check first.
- **Residency:** If you're having a destination wedding, check how long you need to be a resident before a license can be issued.

Massage

The Swedes say they have invented a cow massager that makes the cows calmer, happier, healthier, and more productive. Couldn't you do with something similar? Massage has been proven to reduce stress hormone cortisol and increase levels of feel-good serotonin and endorphins. It increases blood and lymph circulation, unknots muscles, and gives you a sense of calmness and well-being.

Rock 'n' roll massage therapist Dr. Dot, who perfected her craft backstage on tour with the world's best rock bands ("the Rolling Stones' Charlie Watts was my first paying client"), has been practicing massage since walking on her parents' backs at five years old.

DR. DOT'S TIPS FOR ENJOYING A MASSAGE

1. Don't wash your hair beforehand. Worrying about it getting oily will stop you from fully relaxing. Plus, having your scalp massaged is one of the wonders of the world.

2. You need to disconnect and enjoy each and every minute. Don't waste time worrying about what the therapist thinks of your body, and turn off your cell phone.

3. Avoid ALL conversation. If your therapist is chatty, tell him, "I prefer to speak afterward." Only speak up if the pressure isn't right for you.

HOW OFTEN? "I think you should never go more than a month without getting a massage because it's beneficial for your body, mind, and immune system." **Dr. Dot**

Do anything that relaxes you. Walk, dance, play with your dog. Or plug yourself into decent stereo headphones and use binaural beats aimed at relaxation, which influence the brain in the same way as deep meditation. Buy online or from iTunes.

Meditation It makes us saner, calmer, and more creative

and generally helps us keep our shit together. Supersuccessful people, from CEOs to musicians and world leaders, do it because they know it gives them an edge.

"We all have a response within us that's opposite to the stress response," explains Dr. Herbert Benson, director emeritus of the Benson-Henry Institute for Mind Body Medicine. "And that's the relaxation response. There are scores of techniques that elicit it, including meditation, yoga, and tai chi. They all lead to a change on a genetic level, to counter the harmful effects of stress."

CROSS YOUR LEGS AND OOOHMMM A LOT? No, it's really easy, all you have to do is breathe.

❝You only need to do this once or twice a day

for five to ten minutes

to elicit your body's relaxation response. ❞

DR. HERBERT BENSON

1. Put yourself somewhere peaceful, even if that means locking yourself in the car. Breathe in through your nose and imagine taking the breath down into your abdomen. Hold it there for a couple of seconds before breathing out slowly. "On each out breath, repeat a prayer, a positive word, short mantra, an ohhhmm, peace, love—anything that's uplifting," says Dr. Benson.
2. "Ignore any thoughts that pop into your head while you're doing it. They invariably will, so when they do, say, 'oh well,' and come back to the repetition."

Midnight snack

Drunk, hungry, needing a coffee or three . . . yup, that's wedding guests come midnight. We know they ate only a few hours ago, but weddings are hard work, so line up some snacks and coffee at the end of the night. An accommodating venue can serve up piles of BLTs, grilled cheese, mini burgers, and fries. Greasy food is the answer to everything at this time of night. "It's the only way to stop a hangover dead in its tracks," says Cory Murphy of Roaming Hunger food trucks.

Mile-high club

A successful mile-high venture needs planning. Cabin staff are very wise to it: "We often see passengers getting overamorous, especially after a few drinks," says Laura Hutcheson of Virgin Atlantic. No lewd acts in public, boys and girls.

WHEN You'll have the best luck on a night flight where everyone's asleep and lights are dimmed. There's also less likely to be a postmeal line of annoyed people building up outside the bathroom.

WHERE The bank of bathrooms at the back of economy has so many people going in and out that no one will notice if one bathroom's jammed up for a bit longer than it normally takes to freshen up. If you head for the marginally bigger bathrooms in business, be warned. It'll be far more obvious to the far fewer passengers what you're up to and you'll likely be doing a walk of shame when you both exit.

PLANNING AHEAD
Don't wrap yourselves in tight, inaccessible, buttoned-up layers and belts. You'll give up before you even get going.

Mood board

The idea of a mood board is to create something that captures, via lots of images layered together, everything you love, feel attracted to, or that inspires you but would be impossible to explain with words alone.

"The internet's a boundless resource for inspiration. Collect and archive imagery and ideas and create a mood board. It's a simple (and free) way to find out what works and what doesn't."

Kelly Wearstler

DID YOU KNOW . . .

You can print a Pinterest board by saving it as a PDF and selecting Print to Adobe PDF in the print option.

OLD SCHOOL Every time you see a photo that makes you look twice or affects your mood in a good way, keep it. Put the images on a large board or just taped to a wall. Choose big central images and group smaller ones along the same themes around them.

ONLINE You can do the same thing using Pinterest—which is basically the biggest online mood board in the universe. "There's limitless inspiration from fellow brides, blogs, wedding planners, and wedding photographers, whose inspiration you can tap into," says Pinterest's communications manager Malorie Lucich.

HOW TO MASTER PINTEREST Want to know how to get the most from Pinterest? Lucich explains how.

- Stay organized by creating multiple boards devoted to different parts of the day: what you're wearing, flowers, the food, and the location, plus one for your honeymoon.
- Follow blogs and wedding boards you love. Click Follow All to get updates from all boards in your home feed.
- You can add a Pin It button to your browser bookmarks, so you can pin items from websites you visit.
- For an easy way to keep everyone involved in the planning, create a group board and invite friends and family to comment and like their favorite picks.
- Interested in seeing all of the pins from a specific source, such as a wedding blog or vendor? Just edit the URL and add the website: http://pinterest.com/source/NameOfWebsite.com/.
- Make out-of-town guests feel welcomed with a "things to do" board. Fill it with recommendations for great restaurants, weather tips, and sites to visit.
- You can make Pinterest settings private so you're the only one to see the inspiration, or invite a select few, like your mom, wedding planner, or bridesmaids, to view the board.

Mother

How much does your mom want to be involved? A little, a lot . . . she'd rather roll up on the day, drink Champagne, and enjoy the party? Know thy mother and assign tasks accordingly.

IF YOU NEED TIPS ON . . .

- **Getting more (money, emotional support) from your mom,** go to the Parents entry on page 228.
- **Putting her skills to the best use,** see above.
- **Saying no,** go to the Pushy people entry on page 241.
- **Stopping blowups and snarky comments:** Go to the Arguments, squabbles, and fights entry on page 28.
- **Showing your love and appreciation,** go to the Thank-you's entry on page 285.

Mother-in-law

We're not here to give you advice about your relationship with your mother-in-law. We're only concerned with her and your wedding, because, let's face it, the groom's mom can get a bit sidelined. But a happy family celebration is one where everyone's on an equal footing, so here's how to include your mother-in-law (if it's what she wants . . .).

WAYS TO INCLUDE YOUR MIL

1. Talk to her; see if there's any part of the wedding planning in particular that interests her. She no more wants to do the boring stuff than anyone else.

2. If you get on and value each other's advice, ask her opinion on your choices. Shop together for the wedding so it's not all about your mom.

3. Consider what would make her happy to have included in the ceremony or on the day—her family is as much part of this celebration as yours.

4. Give her the same gifts and treats that you give your mom.

5. If you're doing a father-daughter dance, arrange a mother-son dance, too.

TOP
5
**WAYS TO
INCLUDE
YOUR MIL**

Music "We all know how strongly music can affect our emotions. You hear a certain piece of music and suddenly you feel relaxed or happy or sad or lonely," says music supervisor Ann Kline, who has worked on soundtracks for shows such as *ER,* the *West Wing,* and *Shameless.*

"Music is such an amazing tool for transforming the atmosphere."

ANN KLINE

TOP
5

**WAYS TO
WORK THE
MUSIC**

WAYS TO WORK THE MUSIC

It doesn't matter what sort of music you prefer; follow Ann Kline's five tips for creating a soundtrack for your day:

1. Split your day into sections and create playlists. Think about the different parts of your wedding, from when people arrive to the ceremony, cocktails to dinner and dancing, and maybe even a late-night wild party, and choose music that suits the mood and the venue.

2. Think about the size of the room and how high the ceilings are. Big bands in tiny rooms will blow everyone's ears out; a string quartet will get lost in a ballroom.

3. Consider whether your venue has any restrictions on numbers or types of musician. Ask the venue or the musicians for advice.

4. Try not to alienate people with your music choices—keep your guests in mind. You don't want your guests leaving or talking and you want them to feel comfortable.

5. Add personal touches. You can personalize the music even if your day is very traditional. For example, if you're having a string quartet, include arrangements of modern songs. "One of the favorite moments of my wedding was the start. At sundown we had the quartet play The Police's 'Bring on the Night.'" Start with picking a vibe that you want to create and a few songs that really speak to you.

HOW TO HIRE LIVE MUSIC You want music that rocks, right? Don't book anyone without a little due diligence. . . .

- Before you hire them, go to see them play. It's the only way to know if they can carry a party.
- Agree on the playlist and make requests for must-play songs well in advance.
- Check how organized they are. Do they have their own transport or will they be calling for a lift?
- Get written confirmation of all agreements and check the cancellation policy. What's included in the price they quote you? What will be charged as extras?
- Check when they need access to the venue to set up.
- Always have backup, even if it's just the venue's sound system.

GET INSPIRED

Playing with music is fun and there are so many tools to help you; just keep making playlists.

- Use Spotify and create different folders like Ceremony, Reception, and Party; drag different songs in.
- Search wedding playlists online or on iTunes.
- Take the playlists with you and listen while you drive, or work out, or when friends are over. It's great to let your guests be involved.

Ask your guests to jot down three songs they'd love to hear at the reception when they RSVP, and create a playlist everyone will love.

myths

How much do you think wedding myths have affected the way you're planning your wedding? A little? Not at all? You might be surprised. Some myths are buried so deep we don't even know we're buying into them.

MYTH: My wedding day must be perfect.
BUSTED: No—and really, where did that come from? It's about throwing a celebration and having fun whatever happens.

MYTH: Every single detail has to mean something or reflect our personalities.
BUSTED: Gahhhhhhhhhhhhhh. No, it doesn't. A napkin can just be a napkin. A favor can just be . . . a cookie. You don't have to tell your life story.

MYTH: I'll cry when I say my vows.
BUSTED: You might be the only dry eye in the house, having a fit of giggles, or trying to remember what to do next. (We know brides who did all three.)

MYTH: I have to book everything a year in advance or there'll be no venues/cakes/flowers/photographers available.
BUSTED: It's true that booking way in advance might give you more choice, but closer to the date you have huge negotiating power over vendors with slots to fill.

MYTH: I have to follow etiquette or I'm wrong.
BUSTED: Etiquette isn't "right"; it's just an old-fashioned guide that sometimes mistakenly gets taken as the word of God. Use common sense and good manners and do what you want.

MYTH: My vendors can copy everything they see on my Pinterest board.
BUSTED: A lot of those pictures, especially if they're taken from magazines or professional blogs, have been styled to within an inch of their lives. A bit like airbrushed models, they're not always representative of real life. And lots of vendors don't want to copy; they want to do their own work.

AND THE AWARD FOR THE BIGGEST MYTH OF ALL GOES TO . . .
I have to wear white.
BUSTED: You can wear whatever color you like. It doesn't equal virginity or being a bride. See the White entry on page 313.

Nn

Names, to change or not Suffragette and women's rights campaigner Lucy Stone fought long and hard to give American women the right to KEEP their names after marriage. She fought so that we'd have the choices we do today. . . .

WHEN YOU GET MARRIED YOU CAN
- **keep your own name**
- **take your partner's**
- **create a hybrid.**

Do you think you want to change your name?

NO, I DON'T THINK I DO . . . Then you have nothing to do. You'll automatically keep your maiden name unless you request a change on your marriage license. Although many women don't change their names anymore, you might still get some who ask you why not.

YES, I THINK I WOULD LIKE TO CHANGE MY NAME . . . If you want to change your name, here's how:

1. Fill in your new name on your marriage license on the day, which your officiant returns to the authorities.
2. You'll be sent your certified marriage certificate (ask for a few copies) with your new name on it.
3. Now you can start changing your name on official documents. Do your social security card first.

DID YOU KNOW . . .
In some countries, for example Greece, women have to keep their birth name for life. In Spain, women keep their own name on marriage and tack their husband's at the end.

Officiant

Do you have a choice of who performs your wedding ceremony? If you're planning a religious service, or one performed by a state official, you may not have any say. Otherwise, use these tips for sorting the really good from the bad and the ugly.

MY VENUE COMES WITH AN OFFICIANT Okay, so you can't pick and choose the person, but you can talk with them to see if you can add any personal touches.

I CAN USE MY OWN Great . . . here's how to find the right person.
- **Ask around for recommendations.** It's always the best place to start and beats cold calling hands down.
- **Interview the candidates.** If you can't meet face to face, use Skype or FaceTime to chat. Talk through a sample service, and see how far they're prepared to go to make it personal to you. Don't leave it to e-mail. Can they offer advice on readings and vows?
- **Trust your gut.** If you don't like them on first impression, don't have them perform your ceremony.

I'D LIKE A FRIEND OR FAMILY MEMBER TO DO IT There's nothing lovelier than having someone marry you who actually knows you.
- **By the state:** Some states are very supportive. California, for example, gives people the power to perform marriages for a day. Check with your state marriage bureau to see if they run a similar program.

MAKING IT LEGAL AND GRAY AREAS

Check with the county clerk's office if your ordained-online officiant is legally allowed to perform weddings and if he or she needs to be registered. Triple-check the rules in the county, not just the state.

officiant cont

● **Online ministers:** In less than five minutes you can get friends or family ordained online—they're then officially a minister and can perform your ceremony. The Universal Life Church Monastery, for example, asks for your name, address, e-mail contact, and consent. Celebrities ordained online as ULC ministers include Sharon Stone, Johnny Carson, and Joan Rivers.

Open bar

It's gracious and lovely of you, but an open bar means your guests can drink like fish all night and you pick up the bill. They'll likely not only drink more, but put drinks down and forget about them, or drink only half before getting a new one. If you're having an open bar, you need to be fairly relaxed.

WHAT SHOULD YOU OFFER? Know your crowd. Always give people a good choice, including beer, wine, spirits, and mixers, but weight it with what works best for your group.

HOW ARE OPEN BARS CHARGED? Depending on your venue it could be either of the following:

Prices fixed in advance: good if you have lots of heavy drinkers

● per person, e.g., $40 a head for drinks

● a fixed all-inclusive price

Open-ended prices: better if you have more nondrinkers in the party

● by the bottle

● by the drink (a consumption bar)

CUTTING COSTS On a strict budget? You don't have to go bankrupt by the end of the night, just play clever:

1. Limit the hours. There's no need for an open bar for the whole evening.

PACKAGE OR PER PERSON? If the venue is asking you to choose in advance between a per-person package or paying per drink, you may as well roll a dice—it's guesswork. Ask them to write into your contract that you'll pay whichever is the lower at the end of the night.

2. Have a ceiling: Let your guests spend up to an amount that you agree with the venue and, after that, they buy their own.

3. Negotiate a better deal. Ask the bar manager to use cheaper generic brands for some spirits such as vodka, rum, and American whiskey.

4. Bring your own. If the venue allows it, supply your own alcohol. You'll need to factor in the cost of corkage if applicable (see the entry on page 94).

LAST BUT NOT LEAST Open bar + drinking = taxis. Print out a list of taxi numbers and stick it up where it can't be missed, or have them ordered and lined up in advance at the end of the evening.

ARE YOU PAYING PER DRINK? For a rough estimate of what your total bill might be, allow two to three drinks per person for the first hour and one drink per person for every hour after that.

Order of service
Who, what, where, when, how . . . your guests are going to see a performance. They need to know what to expect, who the principal figures are, if there's an interval, and when there's an end in sight. Help them out by giving them a program, even if it's just a slip you print off at home.

TRADITIONAL ORDER OF CEREMONY
- Background music while guests are milling about
- Processional: if you're walking down an aisle, this is when the wedding party enters
- Opening introduction by the officiant
- Readings/prayer/song
- Promises, vows
- Exchange of rings
- Unity candle/sand ceremony/hand fasting/music/other rituals
- Pronouncement: "I now pronounce you . . . "
- Kiss
- Closing words
- Recessional: wedding party leaves

Organization

Want to know how to fit in all your wedding planning (and the rest of your life) without collapsing into a heap of red wine by 8:00 p.m.? Here are our top tips for kicking some bridal organizational butt.

ZZZZZ . . . .

If your early-to-rise approach is hurting, have a power nap. Famous nappers include Leonardo da Vinci and Bill Clinton. It never hurts to just switch off and drift for 20 minutes.

BE AN EARLY BIRD: We hate to say it, but the most organized people get up early. *Vogue* editor Anna Wintour has, allegedly, already had a game of tennis by 6:00 a.m. every day. Michelle Obama's up at 4:30 a.m. It's not because they love getting up in the dark; it's just sheer determination to fit in everything they need to do in a day, whether that's an essential outing in your tennis whites or planning a menu.

MAKE A LIST: It's been proven that if you write down a list of things to do, you're far more likely to complete them than if you keep them floating around in your head. First do the ones you'd rather ignore; then they're not lurking at the edge of your thoughts all day. If you have a task that feels overwhelming, break it into steps and check them off one by one.

FIRST THINGS FIRST

Choose what needs to be done in order of importance, not what's most fun. You can while away hours finalizing cake fillings, but if you haven't got a venue, you'll have nowhere to put it. If your wedding planner gives you homework, do it in the order asked. Prioritize your tasks daily and weekly and methodically schedule them in.

VISUALIZE: It seems like anyone who runs a successful global corporation credits visualization for helping them succeed. As broadcaster and author Dr. Joseph Murphy explained in his best-selling book, *The Power of Your Subconscious Mind,* the time to tap into your unconscious and fix your visualization is just before you drop off to sleep. As you feel yourself nodding off, picture yourself completing your tasks and feel how happy you are. When you wake up, take a few moments to get clear in your head exactly what you're going to achieve that day.

KEEP LEARNING: Recognize what hasn't worked for you so far and make changes. Lists not working because you just ignore them? Stick them everywhere until they annoy you so much you pay attention. Keep changing until you find something that makes you complete your chores.

Outdoor weddings

Even if there's not a cloud, wisp of wind, or ice-storm predicted within 2,000 miles of your venue in the next decade, you will need a plan B for an outdoor wedding. Even the Sahara gets rain at least once a year.

OUTDOOR NEED-TO-KNOWS

1. Preparation: Will you need power and water mains? If there are none, do your vendors have the right equipment to make up for it?

2. Access: Can everyone get to your site? If caterers, tent vendors, or musicians are coming with trucks, is there an access road? And the same for guests—can they get there and back easily, or should you arrange transport?

3. Bathrooms: You can never have enough . . . see the entry on page 38 for more information. Keep them out of sight but not too far from the party.

4. Lighting: Your guests need to see where they're going and, up to a point, what they're doing. Light entrances, exits, pathways, steps, and anywhere there'll be eating, drinking, and dancing.

5. Bugs: Have the site sprayed 24 hours in advance or have individual insect repellents or citronella bands available, including some kid-friendly formulations. Don't do a giant spray just before your guests arrive—it'll reek.

TOP
5

**OUTDOOR
NEED-TO-
KNOWS**

❝ If the venue can't hold the whole group inside for all the festivities in a pinch, I put up a tent regardless of the forecast. ❞

WEDDING PLANNER SANDY MALONE

Pp

Page boys

If you want a full wedding contingent, you need a couple of cute pages rolling down the aisle with the flower girls. Traditionally they carried your train, but now they're just a chance to include the young boys in the family.

WHO SHOULD YOU CHOOSE? Children who won't be uncomfortable or scared by the attention. Under 10 and over toddler age works best.

WHAT DO THEY WEAR? If you want to be very traditional, miniuniforms—knickerbockers or short trousers and Nehru-collared or military-style jackets with patent leather shoes. But let them feel comfortable; trussing little kids up in unfamiliar stiff shoes and suits doesn't help them relax—unless, of course, they love dressing up.

WHO PAYS FOR THE OUTFITS? If you can pay for some or all of it, do. Otherwise, choose outfits that won't break the bank for their parents.

> **DO** make sure children can see their parents or someone very familiar as they go down the aisle; it makes that walk far less daunting.
> **DON'T** buy or make outfits too far in advance, or they'll be outgrown by the wedding day.

HOW TO TRAIN THEM
It's like puppy training . . . make it fun, with a reward and a cuddle, over and over again, until they're completely at ease with what they have to do. No pressure, no getting mad even if they don't get it on the hundredth try. Do as many rehearsals as you can where the ceremony will take place so that the surroundings are familiar.

Try to get both sets of
parents together before
the wedding. If they are
wildly different, have
a short, sweet get-
together like a meal.
Divorced parents on
either side? Ask them if
they mind spending an
evening with their ex. If
they'd rather stick pins
in their eyes, arrange
separate gatherings.

Parents
Caution: Dealing with parental units is tricky and should be treated with care. It's all about compromise.

WHAT KIND OF PARENTS DO YOU HAVE? Are they nice and normal, and did your mom bake cakes, feed you nourishing meals, and fill you with confidence-building advice? Or was their parenting a bit off the mark?

Wherever your parents fall on the spectrum of present and loving to difficult or absent, only you can know how much you want them involved in your day. Anyone you love, who's had an important part in your upbringing, can be involved in the same way as a biological parent—whether it's a stepparent, long-term partner of one of your parents, grandparent, or family friend.

HOW TO ASK FOR WHAT YOU NEED

I want my parents to..

. . . KINDLY BUTT OUT
You want to get on with planning your wedding and you want your parents to have zero input into the details.

SOLUTION: See our list on page 230 as to how to easily include your parents without letting them launch a hostile takeover of the big decisions.

. . . GIVE ME MORE HUGS

You need more emotional support. We hear you: You could use some kind words to keep you going, even if you know they think your wedding planning leaves a bit to be desired.

SOLUTION: Your parents might not be the tender types, but you can always ask for what you want straight up. I need a hug . . . or, Mom, can I just bitch to you about what so-and-so did? Honestly, asking works wonders—your parents can't always read your mind.

. . . GIVE ME SOME MONEY

The wedding you want isn't going to happen without an aid package.

SOLUTION: Ask nicely without playing each set of parents against each other. Never make assumptions about how much they're going to give (it's not their job to fund you). Create wedding plans after donations are finalized, not before. Be super-discreet if one set of parents has much deeper pockets than the other—that means no telling anyone who gave what. If either set of parents is giving a lot of money and wants some say in the proceedings, compromise.

. . . HELP ME GET SHIT DONE

You want some help with your to-do list.

SOLUTION: First figure out their strengths. Play to them. What are they good at, and what would they enjoy doing? If your mom is the kind who thinks a spa is hard work, don't put her on guest list duty. And if you are desperate to offload the boring stuff like seating plans, give them to someone with an analytical mind who enjoys a puzzle.

HOW TO SAY YOUR THANK-YOU'S Give your parents a special wedding photo album with tons more photos of them and their friends and immediate family than you'll have in yours. Before the wedding, point out the right people to your photographer so he can get extra shots.

DIVORCED PARENTS
Got divorced parents who still can't be civil? Keep them apart, even if it's only by a few feet. At hotels, the reception, receiving lines, the ceremony, anywhere their paths might cross, put them on opposite sides of the room/ building/table and put someone else between them as a buffer.

Parents:
Top 10 ways to include them
from painless to not-for-the-faint-of-heart

PAINLESS

1. Duplicate your mother or mother-in-law's wedding bouquet. If it's too dated, out of season, or she didn't have one, just include her favorite flowers.

2. Ask them to do a reading.

3. Invite them to officiate.

4. Ask for help choosing or making outfits for flower girls and page boys.

5. Include a tradition that's particularly special to them.

6. Wear your mother's wedding dress or veil. A nip and tuck, change of hemline, or deft alteration can make the world of difference to even the most gruesome outfit.

7. Allocate a portion of the guest list to your parents and ask their advice on the more distant relatives.

8. Invite parents to the bachelor and bachelorette parties. If you like to party on the wild side, fingers crossed that they'll be busy that night.

9. Turn over whole areas for them to plan. Cake? Flowers? Or even honeymoon?

10. They plan the whole thing. You just turn up on the day. To wherever they tell you to. We know one bride who found this really liberating and stress-free.

NOT FOR THE FAINT OF HEART

Peeing ... with a wedding dress on

Has anyone ever told you how hard this is? Ever thought about how big and heavy some of those skirts and trains are? Most of them won't even fit in the average bathroom cubicle (TIP: Always head for the handicapped bathroom; there's lots more space).

Be prepared for bathroom visits to be a social activity. You'll need good friends to help you get that dress off and on.

"Peeing in a wedding dress can be challenging, but Spanx are your bladder's enemy," says wedding planner Annie Lee. "Some of that underwear has that little tiny slit that they made for baby vaginas but for the most part the Spanx have gotta come off. So either be prepared to derobe every time you want to go to the bathroom or cut that hole large enough to pee out of. I had a bride who didn't precut the hole and had to go urgently. She had a corset, laced-up dress and there was just no time to get her out of it. There was only one thing to do. 'Don't move,' I told her as I crept closer with a sharp pair of scissors."

Permits

Heavy fines or plugs being pulled are what you get for trying to do things without the right paperwork. Follow our rough guide for where and when you might need a permit:

OUTDOOR WEDDINGS

Special events permit: If you want to get married on public land—let's say, on a beach, in a park, or standing on top of the Grand Canyon—you'll probably need a special events permit from whoever is responsible for the land. These permits sometimes limit the number of guests and restrict timings—you

RIDE 'EM COWBOY

If you don't have anyone to help, you might want to come at the toilet from a different angle. To stop long trains, skirts, and whatnot trailing down the bowl, straddle the seat back to front. Feels weird, but it'll stop you from peeing on your dress, too.

might be hard pushed to get a permit for a major holiday somewhere that attracts lots of visitors.

MUSIC
Music permit: If there's going to be music, like a band or DJ, you might also need a PA or amplified sound permit. If you don't have one, the police can come along and turn off your wedding.

DRINKS
Alcohol permit: If your venue doesn't have a special events liquor or banquet license, you'll probably need to arrange one yourself. Check with your state authorities; most are set up to issue them quickly and cheaply online.

Personal trainer
Are you a bit challenged on the motivation front? Need a nudge (or kick in the butt) to get going? Personal trainers can be a godsend. They're like your very own bootcamp.

TOP
5
**PERSONAL
TRAINING
MYTHS**

FACT OR FICTION? PERSONAL TRAINING MYTHS
MYTH 1: Personal trainers only work with superfit hotties.
BUSTED: There are personal trainers for everyone, from complete couch potatoes and upward. The key is to find the trainer who suits you and what you want to achieve. No one's going to ask you to jog for three miles, followed by 100 push-ups, unless you've lied about how fit you are.

MYTH 2: I can't afford one.
BUSTED: They're never going to be as cheap as a group class, but some trainers will work with small groups, so share the costs with your bridesmaids or a group of friends with a similar level of fitness.

MYTH 3: They'll shout at me.
BUSTED: That's army training you're thinking of. Or maybe actual bootcamp. Some trainers might use aggression as a motivator, but interview them and ask them about their style and personality. Find one that won't have you cowering.

MYTH 4: The higher level of certs, the better the trainer.
BUSTED: Not always, no. Certification tells you that they've studied, but it doesn't tell you how good a teacher or motivator they are, or if they can really change lives. Ask to speak to their existing clients, see before-and-after pictures, and, even better, see their clients in person.

MYTH 5: I'll get fit just by looking at my personal trainer.
BUSTED: We really wish that one were true, but having a personal trainer turn up once a week won't make you fit. You have to take responsibility for your own fitness, including what you eat.

WHAT'S THE GOLD STANDARD FOR A TRAINER? We asked Chris and Heidi Powell, stars of ABC's *Extreme Weight Loss,* to highlight the five most important things a personal trainer should do for you:

- Declare a SMART goal. It will be Specific, Measureable, Attainable, Realistic, and Time-Sensitive.
- Create a structured path toward reaching your goal.
- Hold you accountable, and make sure you are keeping your commitments to yourself.
- Work around any injuries.
- Have a positive attitude and be excited about your health and fitness.

photography TOP 10:
tips from seasoned photographers

> "It's unrealistic to believe that EVERY situation can be documented. A photographer can't be in all places at all times and some situations might fall between the cracks." **Miguel Fairbanks**

1 SET YOUR BUDGET. "Accept what funds you have and work within them," advises Thayer Allyson Gowdy.

2 LOOK AT AS MANY PHOTOGRAPHERS IN YOUR BUDGET AS YOU CAN. To help you choose, think if you can picture yourselves in the photos you see on the website, says Liz Banfield. "Is there a breezy, effortless feel? Or very romantic, or even sexy? Or does it all look a bit forced?"

3 NARROW YOUR CHOICES DOWN TO TWO OR THREE. Chat in person, or by Skype at the least, to see if you click. Compare quotes. Before you confirm, ask if they'll be the principal photographer, advises Michael Simon. "If not, who will? Can you meet them?" Made a choice? Book straightaway.

4 FIND SOMEONE THAT SUITS YOUR STYLE. "Choose the right photographer that matches your personality," advises Gowdy.

5 FIND OUT WHEN AND HOW YOUR IMAGES WILL BE DELIVERED AFTER THE WEDDING. "Get it in writing," says Simon. "And ask how long they'll keep the whole wedding on their system."

6

ON THE DAY, JUST RELAX.
"Everyone likes the amazing candid shots of themselves! You don't need to pose all the time," says Gowdy.

7

TIME IT RIGHT. Between noon and 2 p.m. the sun's directly overhead and causes dark shadows on the face. Try to schedule photos for late afternoon or the "golden hour" just before sunset.

8

MAKE A LIST OF ESSENTIAL SHOTS.
Don't assume your photographer will automatically take them. Include a few old-school posed shots, even if that's not your style, says Brian Dorsey.

9

HOW DO YOU SORT THE GOOD FROM THE CLEVERLY BRANDED? "Do they produce quality work all the time or are they showing 'best of' galleries from lots of different weddings?" asks Aaron Delesie. "Anyone can cherry-pick their best shots. Around fifty images per event is ideal."

10

CAMERA SHY? "Have one drink. It usually does the trick! DO NOT HAVE TWO OR MORE BECAUSE THEN YOU LOOK SLOPPY," says Delesie.

WHAT BRIEF?
If your photographer doesn't follow your brief on the day? "Ask someone in your family to gently emphasize that certain images are really important, and you want those to take priority."
Corbin Gurkin

"Make sure you own personal usage rights to your images immediately after your wedding so you are not stuck paying for prints if you don't want to."
Aaron Delesie

PHOTO BOOTHS

Are all photo booths the same? No. They come in all sorts of shapes and sizes, from retro old-school to glammed-up jobs that can fit half a football team inside and have a live monitor outside broadcasting what's going on . . .

● Can you DIY a photo booth?

Yes. Set up a laptop with webcam running a photo booth application, a photo-grade printer, and a space where guests can be silly to their hearts' content. Backdrop and dressing-up props optional, but you might need an extra light source if the room's dark.

photography cont

GET SPECIFIC "When choosing your photographer, ask yourself what makes you like that photo. Is it the composition, is it the way the men's outfits match the women's? Look at everything in it so that you can determine what you'd like to see in your own."
—male grooming expert Diana Schmidtke

TRIMMING THE BUDGET . . . CAUTION: "I have only one suggestion," says Fairbanks. "Don't trim your photography budget. I have only ever seen this false economy come back to haunt otherwise happy newlyweds. Remember, the guests have left and flowers, wilted; only the photos will endure for generations, so be sure they're amazing. Some years ago I read an article that posed the question to newlyweds: If you had it all to do over again, what would you do differently? The number-one response: Budget more for the photography."

If you've got to trim your budget, start here . . .
● "Look for talented up-and-comers. Ask for referrals from people in the industry." —photographer Liz Banfield
● "Set the principal photographer free earlier in the event and have only the second photographer." —Simon

THE FINAL SELECTION "Do an edit, then ask the photographer to weigh in. Mix landscapes and still life for breathing room and to get the whole picture. It will bring back the memories in different ways and keep anyone else looking at your album from falling asleep." —Thayer Allyson Gowdy

❝Less is more.
Think of your wedding album as a piece of art.❞
JUSTIN LEE

Photography
Should you or shouldn't you?

ENGAGEMENT PHOTOS

A set of casual-ish shots taken to mark your engagement

YES

"Doing an engagement session is a way for a couple to learn how to feel comfortable," says photographer Mel Barlow. "It doesn't happen during the shoot so much as after when you get the pics back and realize there are a hundred you'd frame."

NO

"I truly believe that engagement photos are for the most part a waste of time and money," says Delesie. "Most people don't realize that they're just a way for the photographer to sell them stuff."

PHOTOSHOP

The digital alteration of your pics, and the people in them . . .

YES

"Most people understand that overmanipulating a photo will be embarrassing when they show it to people who know what they really look like," says Delesie. Approach with extreme caution, a very light touch, and realistic expectations. The photographer isn't always the best person for the job; ask to see before-and-after shots of other couples' images.

NO

"I prefer that images remain true and realistic," says Fairbanks. Aside from that, Photoshop fails include missing limbs, Barbie proportions, and skin so artificially smooth plastic comes to mind.

FIRST LOOK

Photographs taken alone as a couple with the photographer, just before the ceremony

YES

"I did a first look and it was a beautiful, private moment where the images reflect a palpable emotion. I didn't feel the ceremony was any less meaningful having already seen my husband," says photographer Corbin Gurkin.

NO

"I didn't do it, because I wanted the first look to be the moment I came down the aisle—it was much more emotional and spontaneous that way," says real bride Melissa.

Place cards

If want your guests to sit in designated seats, rather than choosing their own spots at the table, you'll need these.

DID YOU KNOW . . .

Caterers can use place cards as a way of indicating who's having what meal choice, without having to disturb guests. Ask your caterer if this would be helpful.

RULES OF PLACE CARDS

1. Have place cards in place. Each guest's name should be written out individually and legibly, and should already be at the tables before they sit down.

2. No anonymous guests. If you have any mystery plus-ones coming, pin down their names before the day so the place cards can be written out.

3. They don't have to be fancy. Place cards can just be pieces of card with handwritten names or, if you want to step up, get a calligrapher to write them (see the Calligraphy entry on page 67).

4. Don't forget a seating chart. If you're having place cards, you'll still need a seating chart or escort cards to tell your guests which table they're at.

5. Accept with grace that people switch places. "I've seen some of society's finest move a place card because they weren't happy with where they were assigned to sit," says event designer David Beahm. On the whole, people want to sit with whomever they're most comfortable. Don't be upset if your hours of laboring over who goes where are gamely reinterpreted by your guests.

Planning

"Plan, plan, and plan and then twenty-four to forty-eight hours before the wedding, let it all go. It's the only way to have fun!" says photographer Aaron Delesie.

HOW TO KEEP YOUR PLANNING UNDER CONTROL . . .
with a little science called Parkinson's Law: Projects or work expand to fill whatever time you have available. Give yourself a

day to complete a half-hour task and that's how long it'll take. Limit the time you give to wedding planning to an hour or two at once, or go away for the weekend and do a big chunk.

Plus-ones

To allow or not to allow.
Which will it be?
Yes

Don't you want your guests to have fun and be comfortable with someone THEY want to be with? We know that the fear of random dates can make you want to stick a ban on plus-ones. Or maybe you just don't like your friend's partner. But whether it's a long-term lover, short-term fling, or someone they met last week on their arm, wouldn't you rather your guests enjoyed themselves?

No

It's my party and I don't want to share it with anyone I don't know well. Only extend plus-ones to long-term partners you've met before and name them on invitations. People don't love being singles at weddings—so be prepared for tussles with guests you've invited on their own, and see the Guest list entry on page 164.

It's my party and I can't afford to share it. See above. If it's down to pure numbers, find somewhere to draw the line that seems fair across the board. Rather than picking randomly, give them to, for example, those in live-in relationships or relationships longer than one month/six months/18 months, etc.

Q What if someone isn't invited with a plus-one, but asks to bring one?

A It depends on your situation. Can you squeeze in the plus-one? Do you want to? If you just don't want them there, say no again and blame it on venue or budget restrictions.

Pregnancy

How do you do weddings with style if you're pregnant? Easily. There's no fashion compromise necessary.

WAYS TO ROCK PREGNANCY

● **Think fitted.** An empire waistline (just under the boobs) is the standard for pregnant women, but body-conscious, silhouette hugging or slim-fitting clothes can look amazing and still be comfortable if the fabric's got some give in it.

● **Find alternatives to long dresses.** If you've got good legs, show them off in shorter dresses or sharp-fitting skinny cigarette pants.

● **Don't stick to maternity wear.** It can be so frumpy you'll age thirty years just looking at it.

Prenuptial agreement

Billionaire Donald Trump is famously vocal about prenups. And not just his own. He advised Facebook founder and fellow billionaire Mark Zuckerberg not to let his now-wife Priscilla Chan "hit the jackpot."

Trump's "Don't ever get married without one" advice might seem relevant only if one of you is fabulously wealthy or brings heaps more assets to the marriage than the other, but a frank conversation about how you would divide your financial assets in the event of a divorce is far more useful than hoping for the best. Having a prenup doesn't mean your marriage will fail, or that you don't love each other; it means that you're mature enough not to put your head in the sand.

HERE'S WHAT YOU NEED TO KNOW:

● Prenups need to be watertight. Trump's first wife, Ivana, challenged theirs in court and won.

● Both sides must have legal representation for it to be valid.

● Neither party can be under the influence of alcohol or drugs when it's signed.

- Both parties must be honest about the extent of assets (try to hide them and your prenup can be legitimately challenged in court).
- There can be no hint of coercion—for example, asking for a prenup to be signed close to the wedding.
- A prenup can stipulate things other than financial terms. For example, not to drink/do drugs, be unfaithful, or watch crappy TV 24/7.

Pushy people
Are you good at saying no, or are you what salespeople politely call a complete pushover? Here's how to stop yourself from falling into the "yes" trap.

SALESPEOPLE (that's most of your vendors) are trained to use tried and tested psychological techniques to get you to say yes to things you never knew you wanted. You need to reverse-engineer their tricky little traps.

- **The oldest trick in the book:** They ask a question they know you'll say yes to ("You want a beautiful wedding, don't you?"), then tack on the real question they want you to say yes to ("That's a yes to the $8,000 dress then?"). Saying yes once makes your brain more likely to repeat it. Don't be embarrassed to backtrack if you've said yes to something you really don't want.
- **No means no.** Never explain why you're saying no or offer excuses. They've honed their skills until they can wear down every objection in the book. Can't afford it? How about credit? Don't love it? How about this one? A polite and confident "No, thank you," and then silence signals no pushovers here.
- **Don't feel guilty, sad, or sorry for them.** They can spot easy pickings from twenty miles away, and your soft heart is flashing like a beacon for wily salespeople.

PLANNING AHEAD
Start having a prenup drawn up a few months before your wedding. If you move states, get it reviewed there, too.

PUSHY FRIENDS AND RELATIVES
They are old masters because they know your weak spots. Whether they want your time or to bring twenty extra guests, the key is to say no without making it personal.

- **It's out of your control.** Make sure saying "no" isn't about them but external forces. Extra guests? So sorry, but there's a cap on numbers at the venue.
- **Offer an alternative.** Sorry, I can't do this, but how about this? And remember, no one will stop liking you if you say no.

Qq

Questions To get the right answers, you need to ask the right questions. We've highlighted what you need from every vendor in individual entries, but you can use this as your basic checklist no matter who you're quizzing.

1 Are you available on this date?

2 Can I see the most recent examples of work that you've done on a similar budget and in a similar setting?

3 How much do you charge?

4 What's included in the price?

5 What's not included—what do you charge extra for?

6 What's your cancellation policy?

7 Do you require a deposit? How much and when?

8 Can I see some references and recommendations from recent clients and can I speak to them personally?

9 Do you have insurance? What does it cover?

10 How long have you been in business?

Rr

Rain It's okay if it rains on your wedding day. It's probably not what you want, but you have to embrace it like a 20-year-old at a music festival waiting for the headline act in pouring rain—in other words, it's part of the fun.

BUT DON'T LEAVE IT TO CHANCE . . .

1. Have a rain plan. Run through your day and see where you might need a plan B. Where will you take photos, where will your guests shelter, will they get soaked walking from one area to another?

2. Plan with your photographer where you'll shoot and decide what sort of shots will work best if it's raining.

3. We can see that if yours was supposed to be a sun-soaked outdoor wedding, a rainstorm can be hard to love. But think of the symbolism—fertility, fresh starts, an unbreakable bond, and good luck.

DID YOU KNOW?

Rain doesn't ruin photos. The light is softer and flattering (once you're inside), and the focus turns to people and emotion, not blue skies. "If the rain stops for even a moment, brave the mist for a few playful photos outside," says photographer Mariah Ashley.

PLANNING AHEAD

We've been at way too many functions where people looked like they were eating the microphone. If you'll be using one, have everyone practice.

UNDER PRESSURE

Do those giving a reading need to know it by heart? No, it's not a test.

Readings It's such a personal thing, the only rule is to choose something that has meaning for you.

WHO GIVES THEM? Anyone. It doesn't matter how old they are, but they need confidence, so don't ask the painfully shy.

HOW TO CHOOSE A READING

1. Talk to your officiant to see what is allowed. As a rule, houses of worship like you to stay godly; everyone else is probably fine with anything except sex, drugs, and rock 'n' roll.

2. Remember that officiants are a great resource. Ask them for suggestions.

3. Use the internet. There are so many sites dedicated to readings; add a search term to narrow down the results—funny, poetic, spiritual, silly, religious, etc.

Receiving line

Do you want to line up and greet your guests formally, rather than wafting around at the reception?

Then you'll need a receiving line. This is where you, and the hosts of the wedding (or basically all your parents and wedding party), line up and greet every guest in turn just after the ceremony or before the reception.

PRO: You get to thank everyone personally for coming.
CON: If you have anything more than 50 guests the momentum of the day grinds to a halt. And the people at the back of the line are desperate.

THE ALTERNATIVE: You can just as easily chat with guests at your reception without feeling like a sheepdog who has to get his flock rounded up in time. Or go to every table during the meal or at cocktail hour, thanking them individually.

WANT TO DO IT THE TRADITIONAL WAY? Here's how . . .

1. Hosts at the head of the line. If that's just you and your partner, you can do it on your own.

- If both families are hosts, don't line up according to how much everyone paid; mix it up.
- Divorced parents? If they hate each other, separate them by as many bodies as possible.
- Stepparents: If they've been part of your life and the day, include them.
- Include the whole wedding party if you want, but bear in mind how much time it'll take to get through everyone.

2. Do the introductions. You and your partner introduce guests neither knows to each other and to parents. Shake hands, hug or kiss, thank them for coming, and then move on to the next person.

3. Location, location, location. Position the receiving line out of strong sun, wind, or rain.

FEED AND WATER PEOPLE We've learned a few tricks from spending far too much time in lines for sample sales: when you're waiting in a LONG line, nothing makes you happier than being plied with Champagne and snacks. Have someone move up and down offering Champagne, soft drinks, and something to munch on.

DO THE MATH
To get 100 guests through a receiving line in a little over 30 minutes, you need to herd them along at a swift clip—no more than 20 seconds of hugging, kissing, handshaking or chatting each. There is nothing nice about standing in a line for 30 minutes, whether you're at the bank, the store, or a wedding.

I HAVE _____

GUESTS AT _____

SECONDS EACH

THAT'S _____

MINUTES

reception

This is where the party starts, where you gather everyone together and celebrate your marriage.

TRIED AND TESTED

The heart of a good reception has these. Take your pick:

- Alcohol
- Canapés
- Catering
- Champagne
- Cocktail hour
- Cocktails
- Décor
- Entertainment
- First dance
- Dessert
- Cake
- Midnight snacks
- Music
- Speeches and toasts
- Wine

See specific entries for more tips.

You can do that whatever way you want, whether it's a formal black tie dinner, a quiet lunch, or a BBQ in the yard with your family, but we think all celebrations need some music, food, fun, dancing, and laughing.

START WITH A TIME LINE. A schedule will help you visualize what you want to include and how to structure it. Break down the time and allocate chunks for cocktails, food, toasts, and dancing or anything else you want to throw in. Then move on to the finer details like the food, drink, décor, music, and dancing.

These are a couple of examples of skeleton time lines.

Evening reception
6:00 p.m. cocktail hour
7:00 p.m. dinner
8:00 p.m. Champagne and speeches
8:30 p.m. cake cutting, first dance, bouquet toss
9:00 p.m. party and dancing
12:00 a.m. midnight snacks

Morning or lunch
1:30 p.m. cocktail hour
2:30 p.m. lunch
3:00 p.m. Champagne and speeches
3:30 p.m. first dance
5:00 p.m. cake
6:00 p.m. everyone leaves

RECEPTION NEED-TO-KNOWS

1. All together now: Let your guests know what's happening when. Depending on the style of your wedding, you could chalk it up on a board, pin up a notice, or put a fun time line on your wedding website.

2. Beat the clock: Leave enough time at the end for vendors to do a breakdown (or for you to do it yourself) before your time's up. You'll probably need about an hour.

3. The eleventh hour: Want to stop everyone from drifting off too early? Plan something for the end of the evening, and let your guests know about it: midnight snacks, sky lanterns, fireworks, food trucks, or a late cake cutting.

4. Small is beautiful: The secret to a packed dance floor is a small dance floor. A big space will always look empty unless you have every guest getting down at the same time. People are more likely to join a dance floor when it's already packed, so keep it intimate with the lights turned down. No one wants to dance under a floodlight.

5. Exit strategy: If you don't want the party to grind to a halt, don't say good night to people on your rounds or hang around by the exit—they're both an unconscious signal that it's all over.

REMEMBER . . . A little perfection goes a long way. Parties designed down to the microlevel can be intimidating unless all your guests feel most at home at the Met Ball. "Don't force perfect," says Melina Schwabinger.

RECEPTION NEED-TO-KNOWS

PARTY ZONING

Want to know how planners keep a party flowing? It's all about intimate spaces for mingling, a lounge area for relaxing, a packed dance floor, upbeat music, and closed doors so guests don't feel like leaving.

Recycling

Recycling your wedding isn't just about being green and separating out the glass, paper, and plastic; it's about spreading a little happiness, too. "From one average-sized wedding we can repurpose around thirty to forty single bouquets for hospital and hospice patients. That's a lot of people to positively impact with a smile, bouquet, and pulse of positive mental health," says Larsen Jay of Random Acts of Flowers.

GO GREEN Here's how to share some goodness.

● **Flowers:** A simple bouquet can be a ray of sunshine if you're stuck in a hospital or nursing home. Check on the internet for local charity organizations that accept floral donations. If there are none, call local facilities to see if they can accept donations.

● **Food:** Donate leftovers to a local food rescue program, which will get perishable food out to the hungry and homeless shelters the same day. "Start by talking to your caterer or chef; they may already be working with a community food program," advises Lisa Sposato of City Harvest. "If not, the Feeding America website lists emergency food programs nationwide."

Registry

Why have one? It makes life easier for your guests. It doesn't imply you expect presents; you're acknowledging that 99.9 percent of guests give gifts at weddings, and most love direction.

This is as close to an adult Christmas list as you're ever going to get, so spend time on it and enjoy it.

WHAT YOU SHOULD REGISTER FOR: Is there a sliding scale of what's okay? Kitchenware, a honeymoon, money, tickets to the Lakers, liposuction? It depends on your friends and family and what you feel comfortable asking them for.

"Most of our couples register for a trip, and many for home down payments or DIY projects," says Sara Margulis, cofounder of registry www.honeyfund.com. "We've seen a lot of requests for cars, tuition, pet care, and general savings—the most interesting was a couple who added fertility treatments."

REGISTRY DO'S AND DON'TS

DO register for things you really want. "There are no rules; just think about all the items you've always wanted to have," says Susan Bertelsen, group vice president of Macy's wedding and gift registry.

DO register across lots of different departments if your registry's at a big store.

DO register for individual pieces, not sets, which can push price tags out of people's reach.

DO give plenty of choice at all price points. "Aim to have at least twice as many items as guests," advises Bertelsen.

DO a touch-and-feel test. "If you have a store registry, go in at least once to feel your towels and hold the cookware to make sure it's comfortable to use," she adds.

DON'T just register for things; register for experiences. "But don't forgo the department store list completely," says Margulis. "Guests who balk at alternative registries will be pleased to have a familiar choice."

WHERE CAN I REGISTER? At a department store, your favorite specialist store or website (anything from travel to sport, food or wine), or on universal registries that allow you to make up your list from lots of different stores or websites, and in some cases even add cash. For example, myregistry.com comes with an app that lets you scan in barcodes from any store using your phone.

> **TOP TIP**
> "Think about what will be meaningful to you in ten or twenty years. Is it a set of china that becomes an heirloom, the memories you made on your honeymoon, or a donation to charity?" says Sara Margulis.

GET CREATIVE

Why not ask for:
- the taxi ride to and from the airport
- dinner and a bottle of wine
- tickets for your gondola ride up Venice's Grand Canal
- a room upgrade
- new luggage.

HONEYMOON HELP Registering for a honeymoon?
- Create individual minipackages that people can buy into as gifts. "Couples who offer a rich list of experiences receive more than couples who don't," says Margulis.
- Link your registry to a website where you share pictures of your dream trip to get guests excited, too.
- Take pictures of you both doing all these things that people have contributed to and send as a thank-you note when you get home.

QUESTIONS TO ASK . . . REGISTRIES

1. How long after the wedding do I have to return unwanted gifts? It can vary from 30 days to 12 months or more.

2. What's your return policy? Will they give you cash or gift cards? Do you have to pay return shipping?

3. How long after my wedding will my registry account be closed? If you're going to use it as the only way to remember who gave you what, get your thank-yous off before it closes or make a printout.

THE AGE-OLD QUESTION

How do you tell people where your registry is?
There are two ways to go here.

BE DIRECT: Wedding websites are a great place to let everyone know. The alternative is to print off a slip of paper and put it in with your invitations. This is nice and simple and easy, but some people don't like it.

BE COY: Let people call around until they find the answer. If you think that telling people you have a gift registry will offend them, or you don't like being direct, you'll need to use word of mouth to get the information to the people who want it. Having friends and family do this is fine, but it only works if your guests all know each other, have each other's contact details, and know where to start. Otherwise it's just annoying.

Rehearsal dinner

This is a prewedding get-together—a sit-down meal, buffet, BBQ, or just drinks and snacks. You can hold it anywhere you want: at home, a relative's home, in a restaurant or bar, on the beach. Traditionally it's the night before the wedding, but two nights before is better—or get everyone to bed early. You don't want everyone partied out at your wedding.

WHO PAYS? You do, unless someone else has offered to host it. It was traditionally the groom's family's responsibility, but don't assume someone else will foot the bill.

WHO DO I INVITE? Your immediate families—it's a chance for them to socialize before the wedding. You could also invite the wedding party or out-of-town guests, but you can keep it as small and intimate as you want.

WHO GIVES THE TOASTS? The host or hosts normally give the first toast, then anyone can follow.

COME JOIN US

If you're having a destination wedding or lots of out-of-town guests, hosting rehearsal drinks rather than dinner is a good way to make everyone welcome. If not, look after guests by putting together lists of restaurants, or ask them to join you for dessert, coffee, and liqueurs.

If the relative is a bad drunk, likely to start fights, grope anything with a pulse, or start a cocaine racket from the bathrooms (and any of those make you twitchy), you can leave them off the invitation list—they'll know why.

PARENT PROOF

To put a stop to out-of-control-relative inviting, give each set of parents a fixed number of guests. Warn them that if they invite more than that, they'll be the ones telling invitees they're uninvited.

Relatives

Ah, the joy and the pain of relatives—some you love, some you cannot believe you share a single strand of DNA with, and some you'll now be tied to by marriage. How do you bring them all together for a wedding and keep everyone happy?

DON'T get into a dialogue with relatives who disagree with your choices. You don't always have to justify your decisions to other people, and manipulation and emotional blackmail should be cut off early.

DO tell everyone when the guest list is final, closed, not open to random invites of cousins three times removed.

DO be united with your partner on all decisions when you deal with relatives on either side.

DO realize it's not possible to please everyone no matter how hard you try, so do the best you can and leave them to get on with it.

DO choose your battles. Know who or what will cause the most drama and put the most effort into running interference there.

WHO GETS AN INVITE? If you can't invite all the relatives you want, how do you decide who comes and who doesn't? If it's important to have everyone there, cut your budget in other areas and allow for more guests. If the problem is a cap on numbers at your venue, you have to be pragmatic.

Use this equation: Have you had any contact with them in the last year?

No? Put them at the bottom of the list.

DO YOU HAVE TO INVITE RELATIVES YOU DON'T LIKE? Sometimes, to keep family relations smoothed over, yes. A personality clash isn't a good enough reason for kick-starting family friction. If the rest of the family hates them, too, and you don't care if you ever speak to them again, go ahead and scrub them from the guest list.

Religion

Even if you didn't grow up with it, religion can give meaning. It makes us feel connected to something bigger, wider, and more significant—which is why it becomes important at weddings. If you don't have a religion you already follow but want it to be part of your day, here's how you can approach it:

EXPLORE: America is culturally diverse, with many very different religions to explore. If you want to bring spirituality into your ceremony, look for religions that really suit your feelings and thoughts about life. And the people are superimportant, too. The way the same religion is interpreted can vary wildly. Find the officiant whose style is right for you.

PRESSURE TO BE RELIGIOUS . . . when you don't feel like it: Do your parents want you to have a religious ceremony, but you don't? You're building your own family, which possibly includes children. You have to do what's right for your new family, not your parents. But, can you find ways to compromise—are there elements of your parents' religion you could incorporate without it being an empty gesture?

FURTHER READING

If you're having an interfaith wedding, see the entry on page 184 for tips on how to bring everyone together peacefully.

Reluctant brides (and grooms)

This isn't a reluctance to get married, it's a reluctance to plan your wedding. Organizing a wedding does not come naturally to lots of people.

DON'T think you have to be interested in cakes, dresses, hair, and makeup and invest time in every wedding decision. It's OK to feel complete indifference and it does not make you abnormal.

DO get help. If you're reluctant but still want a big party, invest in a planner. You can just turn up on the day and enjoy.

DON'T feel you have to like or relate to any single thing in wedding magazines or blogs.

DO elope if your reluctance extends to not wanting anyone else involved. Sneak off for a fuss-free ceremony. See the Elope entry on page 126.

DON'T think you have to have traditional dresses, cakes, catering, or venues. You can get married in shorts and flip-flops and polish off your ceremony with a burrito and a beer if it helps.

Remembering loved ones Is there a friend or a member of your family you'd like to honor on the day?

WAYS TO REMEMBER LOVED ONES

1. Put a bottle of their favorite drink on a table, with a photo, and a sign to your guests to help themselves in his or her honor.

2. Make something that belonged to them an integral part of the day. "On my table at the reception we had my gran's china," says one real bride.

3. Tie a simple tag with a dedication to them around your ceremony program, or set side a page in the program with their names, photos, quotes, and readings.

4. Use pictures. Slip their photo in your pocket, hang pictures, or have a photo wall at the reception. "I had my favorite pic of my grandfather at the front of the church so he didn't miss anything. One of our ushers moved it into the bar after the service—I think he was the last one in the bar, too, as he would have been!" says real bride Caz.

5. Raise a glass during the toasts. It's short and sweet and never fails to bring a tear to the eye.

THINK TWICE

If your first reaction when you hear their name is to sob, don't do something public, like have the officiant talk about them. Keep your ceremony upbeat and your tribute out of the spotlight.

Renting

Diamonds, tuxes, dresses, cake, linens, guests, flower girls (yes, you read that right) . . . they can all be rented for the day. Renting can stretch your budget further, broaden your choices, and make life easier all round.

WHY RENT? It's easier. Someone drops it off where it's needed, then takes it away again. You don't have to look after it, clean it, or store it ever after. Also . . .

Some things you just don't need to own—25 tablecloths, 150 chair backs, a tux . . . If there are things you can be pretty sure you're unlikely to ever need or use again, rent, don't buy.

It's cheaper. For a one-off piece like a designer dress or diamond jewelry, you can have it for a day at a fraction of the normal purchase price.

More choice. Rental options can give you more colors, more designs, more sizes.

WHAT DO YOU NEED TO KNOW?

● **Quantity:** You'll need to know how many in advance so they can be sourced and reserved for you.

● **Timing:** When do you need it? Check that their delivery and pickup fit with your schedule. You might need friends and family to help with returns.

● **What's included in the price:** Will there be any extras on top of the price you're quoted?

● **What you see is what you get:** Are there guarantees that what you've reserved is what you'll get on the day? Is there a substitution policy?

● **Insurance:** Is it insured and what are you covered for? How much is the deductible?

● **Deposits:** How much is it, when do you have to pay it, and how soon after the item's returned do you get it back?

● **Damage or breakages policy:** What's the procedure for signing off on returns?

DO THE MATH
Before you rent, do some addition. Once you factor in delivery, shipping, cleaning, insurance, and deposits, renting can be a false economy. Sometimes it's cheaper to buy what you need and recoup your money by reselling.

DID YOU KNOW . . .
You can also rent:
● **Guests** (yes, really): Got no friends? Flesh out your guest list with a handful of model-actor types.
● **Flower girls and page boys:** If the potentials in your family don't make the cut, hire a gaggle of supernaturally good looking kids from a model agency.
● **Celebrities:** fake or the real thing, depending on your budget . . .
● **Paparazzi:** for the above

rice

If my guests throw rice as confetti, will it make the pigeons explode? NO.

Neither will the sparrows, swifts, robins, or anything else with wings drop dead. Not only will it not make their stomachs explode, they'll probably be happy for the meal. It's an urban wedding myth that throwing rice confetti will kill the birds. Your guests can throw this symbol of fertility and abundance with a clear conscience. "Rice is just like any other grain or seed, and lots of birds eat them," says Dr. Kevin McGowan of the Cornell Lab of Ornithology. "In fact, some birds specialize in eating seeds. Rice is easily digested by birds and won't cause them to explode." See also the Confetti entry on page 92.

Ring bearer

Anyone or anything that can make it up the aisle on command and be trusted with your rings can be your ring bearer. It's a job that normally falls to children and pets: if you think it's not a good idea to let a five-year-old or an animal loose with your fine jewelry, give them fakes.

WILDLIFE CAN BE UNPREDICTABLE Birds might seem inspired, but unless they're riding on your shoulder like a parrot they can literally fly away, as one couple found. "The plan was for the couple to say their vows, then the owl would fly down the aisle with the rings," said the reverend Christopher Bryan. "But she flew straight past our heads up into the roof and went to sleep. You might ask why I allowed it. Lots of people think a church wedding is off the shelf, take it or leave it. Of course there are legal parts that must be done a certain way, but I believe that God made us individual with our own creativity and it's good to reflect the interests and character of a bride and groom in their service."

FURTHER READING
Go to the Animals and Page boys entries on pages 20 and 227 for more info, and see the Ring pillows entry below for ways to present your jewelry on its journey up the aisle.

Rings

Did you know that neither of you has to wear a ring? It doesn't mean you're any less married, or slacking in the commitment department. Lots of people, for lots of different reasons, decide not to, and rings on men were almost unheard of before WWII. Just tell the officiant if you'd like to skip this part.

WHO LOOKS AFTER THEM ON THE DAY?
Usually the best man and maid of honor keep them safe until you're at the altar.

Ring pillows

Whether you're having two- or four-legged ring bearers, they don't literally have to carry a pillow. Use ribbons, dishes, muslin or burlap pouches embroidered with the date and your initials, dishes, platters, or special dog collars (that one's not for the kids). Look to your surroundings. For a beach wedding, put your rings in a shell or tied to a tiny piece of driftwood. Will you be in the garden? Twist some flowers and tie the rings to them.

Ss

Sales

To buy successfully at sales, you need a plan. That's the only way you won't be beaten by more talented shoppers. And because stores slash prices by up to 70 percent, competition can be fierce.

STEPS TO BE SALE-READY

1. Make a list. Be armed and prepared. List every single thing you want and where it's on sale. If it's online, make a wishlist. The minute the sales start, flip straight to your wishlist and buy.

2. Try before you buy. Before the sales start, go into stores and see items in the flesh. If you're buying clothes, try them on so you know exactly what size you want, and what the actual fit is.

3. Know your size. Measure yourself (waist, hips, bust, shoulder to waist) so you can head straight for the right size and, if you're buying clothes online, know in advance what you are in European sizes.

4. Get the inside scoop. Sign up for mailing lists, newsletters, and social media for retailers and stores you're interested in. Lots of them give subscribers advance notice of sales and a 24-hour head start online before they open to the public. Opt out again once the sales are over.

5. Act quickly. We've had many sad moments where big bargains have disappeared from our online baskets because we got sidetracked and were beaten to the checkout. If you see what you really want, buy it, then go back to browse for more.

TOP 5

STEPS TO BE SALE-READY

PLANNING AHEAD

Find out what sample sizes the sale will include. Most range from a size 6 to 10. If you're not a sample size, be realistic about what alterations can achieve.

SAMPLE SALES There are sales and then there are sample sales. These are where boutiques and designers sell off the previous season's sample garments they've kept in stock for customers to look at and try on.

TOP 5

TIPS FOR SAMPLE SALE SUCCESS

SAMPLE SALE SUCCESS

1. Know if it's appointment only. To avoid a scrum on their doorstep, some stores and designers do sample sales on an appointment-only basis or hand out slots on a first-come first-served basis.

2. Be prepared. Wear the right underwear for the type of dresses you'll want to try on.

3. Take a friend (or two). As well as giving advice, they can grab things off racks and hold your handbag, coat, and any layers you have to strip off to try things on.

4. Be fighting fit. Eat very lightly, drink plenty of water, and go to the bathroom before you walk through the door.

5. Travel light. Make that handbag a small one. Carry a snack, water, and cash AND credit cards.

DO'S AND DON'TS: SAMPLE SALE STRATEGY

DO your research. Don't be lured by the promise of low prices. Only go to the sales of designers or stores you love.

DO be prepared to get up before the sun. If you want choices, you'll need to be through the doors early—for some big sales, the line can be a couple of hours long.

DON'T feel that just because you stood in line for what feels like six weeks to get in you have to buy something. Some trips you just have to write off.

PLAY CLEVER

Human psychology at a sale is not complicated. We want what we can't have—i.e., what someone else has found. If that's you, show zero interest and walk away, but silently stalk them until they lose interest and put it down or have you arrested.

Save the date It doesn't matter if the nitty-gritty isn't finalized; as soon as your wedding date is set in stone you can send out save-the-dates. There are no rules for your STD except letting people know the date (of course) and where they should plan to be. See the Stationery entry on page 274 for more ideas.

WHY ARE THEY A GOOD IDEA? They give people time to make travel arrangements and get the best deals, block off vacation time, arrange child care, and fix the date in their calendars so they don't double book.

DO YOU HAVE TO SEND THEM? No, if none of these above reasons apply. And if you're on a tight budget, send a simple e-mail or a written note. But only send them out to people you are 100 percent sure will be invited to the wedding.

THE STD ESSENTIALS
- Who is getting married
- The date
- The venue if you know it, otherwise the general location
- Wedding website if you have one
- Invitation to follow

Scent

"Smells speak directly to our emotional brain, bypassing conscious thought. They interact with buried emotions and hidden memories," explains French perfumer Francis Kurkdjian. In short, the scent you wear on your wedding day will always take you back there.

"When I got married I made a fragrance for my husband and gave a sample to everyone at the wedding. Every time I smell it I remember the day," says bespoke natural perfumer Mandy Aftel. And the plus is that unlike almost everything to do with a wedding, perfume doesn't require fittings, negotiations, or planning sessions, and you don't need anyone else's permission to choose one you love. It's about pure pleasure, says Alyssa Harad, author of *Coming to My Senses*.

NEED TO KNOW
- **Try before you buy.** "Wear a scent for at least an hour, ideally a day, because it's the only way you'll know how it'll unfold," says Robert Gerstner of perfume boutique Aedes de Venustas.
- **Be aware of your location.** "Behind closed doors, in a church for example, don't go overboard," he adds.

"Scent is a PRIMAL SENSE. It's the most archaic of our senses, the most instinctive."** FRANCIS KURKDJIAN

"For weddings, I always recommend a sunny and bright scent no matter the time of year— it's a beautiful day, full of love and joy." **Francis Kurkdjian**

HOW DO YOU WEAR YOUR PERFUME?
MYTH: Easy . . . on your wrists and then rub them together, right?
BUSTED: "I don't hold with the accepted wisdom about pulse points," says Aftel. "Most people aren't smelling the backs of your knees. You talk with your hands so put your fragrance on the back of them, then you can smell it, too."

MYTH: Perfume should only be used on your skin.
BUSTED: "You can spray your hair, the inside of a jacket, or the bottom of your dress, which works very well," says Kurkdjian. This is good to do when it's hot, because heat can intensify perfume on the skin, making it too strong.

Seating plan Seating plans have a bad reputation. They take time, they're fiddly, and everyone switches places anyway. Still, there are plenty of reasons you should have one. They make your guests relaxed, because they know where they'll be sitting and with whom. That feeling you get when you board a flight with no assigned seats, and everyone lines up because they're worried they won't be sitting with their spouse/friends/ children? It's similar at a wedding without a seating plan.

TIPS FOR THE (NEAR) PERFECT SEATING PLAN
1. Keep people together. "Guests appreciate being near people they know," says planner Melina Schwabinger. "They want to celebrate with their friends, not network."
2. "Keep your family closest to the best part of the room and near the wedding party," says wedding planner Annie Lee. "But seat the elderly near aisles and exits, so they can go to the bathroom easily. And keep them away from the band or the speakers."

TOP
5
**TIPS FOR
A SEATING
PLAN**

3. Put together tables of guests with similar interests or lifestyles. "Seat people together who you think will enjoy getting to know each other," says Lee.

4. Don't have a singles table. "It's mean. People don't have something in common just because they're single," says Schwabinger.

5. Mix up personalities so that all the talkative or fun people aren't at one table. "Try not to seat shy folks all together," says event planner Tara Guérard.

AVOIDING A CLUSTER**
Keep in mind that people may show up who didn't RSVP. To keep this from ruffling your feathers, consider in advance how you might deal with it.

Try this:

Assign your guests to tables but not seats, and let everyone choose who they sit next to. "I want my guests to have a good time," says event designer David Beahm, "so I don't use rigid social seating rules unless the event calls for strict protocol."

PLANNING IT THE OLD-FASHIONED WAY: Use different-colored Post-It notes for both sets of family and different groups of friends and colleagues.

PLANNING IT THE TECHIE WAY: Apps make shifting your seats for the hundredth time only a second's work. There are other benefits, too, says Dan Berger, CEO of www.socialtables .com. "If you use web-based software, collaborating is as easy as sharing the URL, and software that has 3D rendering helps you visualize your event."

AND FINALLY . . . "The bottom line is, seating is only for a portion of the evening. Guests can and will get up and move around. Do the best you can and then let it go," says wedding planner Cassandra Santor.

YOU DON'T NEED A SEATING PLAN IF . . .
● You're having a small wedding where everyone knows each other really well.
● You're not having a sit-down meal. If people are grazing and socializing, there's no need to assign seats.

Second, third, or more, marriages

Are there rules about second weddings? Do they have to be smaller, more discreet, not "white?"

NO.

A wedding is a wedding, whether it's your first or fourth.

Service options

A great meal is as much about *how* you serve your guests as *what* you serve them. Think about the size of your venue, your budget, how many guests you have, and how formal or casual you want to be. You don't have to stick to one style of service for the whole meal—you could have a passed starter, stations for the main course, and a buffet-style dessert.

What will work best for you?

BUFFET: Can be casual or sophisticated. There's lots of choice for your guests, even picky ones, and no one should leave hungry. Great if you want a menu from two different cultures, cater for special diets, or mix traditional and more adventurous dishes.

- **Planning ahead:** Have bread and condiments on individual tables so the line isn't held up by 150 people buttering their bread.
- **Downside:** It's a myth that buffets are always the cheapest option. Caterers need to prepare more food and people eat for longer, which means more labor. And then there are the lines. . . . To avoid them, have more than one serving table and position them so guests can move down either side at the same time. If you do this, you can serve up to 200 people in 20 minutes.

STATIONS: Guests love having a choice and you can offer variety and cater to very different tastes.

- **Planning ahead:** Have more than one or lines will build up quickly. Mix up the choices so there's something for everyone. Four choices for 100 guests work well.
- **Downside:** Stations need more equipment and staff than a buffet, which equals higher costs.

SEATED DINNER: Easy to timetable an evening around. Guests don't have to do anything for themselves, and wastage is minimal because you know in advance exactly how much food you'll need.

- **Planning ahead:** Have enough staff so that all the tables are served at the same time. Decide with your caterer how guests will choose their entrée and how you'll cater for special diets.
- **Downside:** It's one of the most expensive options, and formal dining tables take up a lot of space, so you might need a bigger venue. Choices are limited and portion sizes are controlled so guests sometimes leave hungry.

FAMILY STYLE: Still a seated dinner but guests choose what and how much they want to eat from communal platters, which gives choice, a sense of abundance, and a more relaxed and social feeling.

- **Planning ahead:** You'll need plenty of space for platters, so that may affect the size of tables.
- **Downside:** It's less formal than a plated dinner and heavy plates can be difficult to pass around. Portion sizes aren't controlled, so caterers have to make more food than for a plated meal, sometimes making it a more expensive option.

KEEP ON TRUCKING

- Go-anywhere food trucks are the ninja caterers of weddings. Hire them to serve anything from gourmet entrees to burgers, coffee, and dessert.
- **How many can they serve?** "Roughly seventy-five people per hour on a cook-to-order basis," explains Roaming Hunger. "But if you're looking to serve three hundred tacos in one hour, trucks are fully capable of prepping for that type of event."
- **How does a truck compare on price?** "To knock your wedding out of the ballpark, set a $15 to $25 per-person budget."

COCKTAIL PARTY AND CANAPÉS: Everyone's socializing and you can offer lots of choice and cater to special diets. You can fit more guests into a smaller space than if you have a seated dinner.

- **Planning ahead:** Factor servers into your costs—food needs to be circulating all the time.
- **Downside:** Not everyone likes standing and eating, and bite-size canapés feel too piddly for some. People tend to drink more, raising the bar bill.

Sex

How do you feel about committing
to having sex with the same person
for the rest of your life?
Happy . . . secure . . . or already bored
and one step away from a fling?

We asked world-renowned sex and relationship expert Dr. Laura Berman, who hosts *In the Bedroom with Dr. Laura Berman,* how married couples can keep their sexual spark going.

TIPS: KEEPING YOUR SEXUAL SPARK

TIPS: KEEPING THE SEXUAL SPARK
1. Be proactive. If you're bored in the bedroom, don't sit back and wait for your partner to fix it. I always tell couples to be the change they want to see in their relationship. In other words, if you want more spontaneity, be more spontaneous. If you want more romance, be more romantic.

2. Talk about what you want. Your partner isn't a mind-reader. If you need more foreplay, don't be afraid to ask for it. You don't have to do so in a mean or demanding way.

3. Don't be afraid of fantasy. Sometimes couples think that fantasies have to die once they are in a monogamous relationship. Not so! It's okay to fantasize and think about people other than your partner (if you don't act on it), and it's even better to think of fantasies that you can act out with each other.

4. Self-stimulate more. Sounds counterintuitive, but masturbation is actually good for your relationship. It increases circulation to your genitals and helps to improve your sexual response. It also allows you to get in touch with your own desires.

5. Don't use the word "should" when it comes to sex. In other words, don't think things like "I should be able to orgasm without so much effort" or "We should be having more wild sex." If you want to work on improving your sexual response, that's great! But don't put pressure and expectations on the way your body "should" work or what you think a "normal" sex life looks like.

Shirts, suits, and tuxes
Okay, grooms: think personal style, not uniform. You're under no obligation to wear a full suit or a tuxedo. Figure out what suits your individual style and venue, and voilà, you'll have your outfit. Maybe it's a shirt and suit pants, a full tux, or a suit, no tie. Maybe it'll be, like Robert Downey, Jr., a suit and lilac tennis shoes.

DO try on lots of different styles, cuts, and fabrics, whether you're renting or buying a suit or a tux. You shouldn't feel trussed up or look like a stuffed sausage.

DO tailor off-the-rack suits to get an exact fit.

UNLIKELY ADVICE
They say that the wisest people are those who keep on learning. Daniel Stern, author of *Swingland*, undertook sex research by taking part in swinging parties. What did he learn? "The most important lesson I learned is that sex is fun. It was demystified and the myriad experiences to be had were revealed. Ever since, I've done everything in my power to try as many of them as possible."

BEING CUTE WITH CUFFLINKS . . . Is it a style crime? Only if you lead a very dull life. Menswear has so much less opportunity for fun and individuality than womenswear, so if the groom loves novelty cufflinks, great.

DON'T button a suit jacket all the way and don't ever fasten the bottom button.

DO leave a finger's width between your neck and collar to get the correct shirt size.

Skin

"If your skin looks great, you can get away with a lot!" says Erin Flaherty, *Marie Claire* health and beauty director. If yours leaves a bit to be desired (tired, gray, dried out, pimply, or blotchy), start preparing early, because there's a lot that can be done. Acne and spots can be blitzed, old scars and sun damage lasered away, wrinkles replumped or Botoxed, your whole face firmed up, and, with a diet and exercise overhaul, you can look dramatically better from the inside out.

Skin tips: straight from the experts

THE DERMATOLOGIST: "Use a serum or lotion containing retinol every night—get an inexpensive one in the drugstore. Buy one containing hyaluronic acid so it doesn't dry your skin out." **Dr. Deborah Jaliman, author of *Skin Rules***

THE NUTRITIONIST: Avoid alcohol, cigarettes, and caffeine. "Stimulants like alcohol increase puffiness. They also interfere with sleep, lack of which is one of the main causes of puffy, bloodshot eyes and black circles. Avoid caffeine the whole day before your wedding." **Amanda Griggs, nutritionist**

THE BEAUTY EDITOR: "Wear sunscreen every day. If you don't, it doesn't matter what you do to treat sun damage, it'll just keep coming back." **Erin Flaherty, *Marie Claire* health and beauty director**

"If you wake up on the day of your wedding with puffy skin, drink a glass of hot water and lemon as soon as you get up," says Amanda Griggs.

WHAT ARE THE INGREDIENTS THAT REALLY WORK? A face cream can't turn back time, but there are ingredients proven to help improve the look of your skin. Look for these key ingredients, says Dr. Debra Jaliman:

- **Moisturizers:** hyaluronic acid
- **Cleanser:** ceramides and glycerin for mildness
- **Wrinkles and antiaging:** peptides and vitamin C

HOW LONG DO YOU HAVE UNTIL YOUR WEDDING? Here's what the experts advise for brides on these time frames:

1 month: "You could have a facial, microdermabrasion, some Botox, and some filler. Do them two weeks before the wedding in case there's swelling or bruising, or you need to touch up the treatment." —Dr. Debra Jaliman

6 months: "Have a Clear and Brilliant laser every six weeks, filler, and Botox." —Erin Flaherty

12 months: "If you've got more than a year to go before your wedding, use topical antioxidants, sunscreen, and exfoliate regularly—either using a gentle scrub or retinoid cream." —Erin Flaherty

Smokers Don't forget your smokers. You might not want people smoking, but they'll do it anyway, so give them ashtrays or sand buckets and somewhere to puff away to their hearts' contents. If not, you'll have a doorway littered with cigarette butts or someone setting off the alarms because they've snuck off for a ciggy in the bathrooms, like the groom who caused a full-scale building shutdown in the center of Manhattan. "He lit up a cigarette in the bridal suite of The Rainbow Room on the top floor of the Rockefeller Center and set off the smoke alarms— the elevators shut down and no one was allowed to leave," said photographer Julie Skarrat.

DID YOU KNOW . . .

"The number one beauty myth is that anti-aging creams can erase wrinkles. They can't!"
Erin Flaherty

SALLOW SKIN

If you smoke, you know it's doing a number on your skin. Can anything help brighten up smoker's complexion? "Vitamin C serum makes dull skin glow instantly," says Flaherty.

A vintage condom and a shoplifted blue sweater may not be what you had in mind . . .

but as Monica and Chandler's old, new, borrowed, and blue contributions to the tradition in an episode of *Friends* proved, anything goes, really.

SOMETHING OLD is a piece of your past going into the future with you.

1. Tuck an old love note somewhere. (Inside your bra will do.)

2. Put a penny from the year you were born in your shoe.

3. Has your mom saved any of your baby clothes? Pin a piece inside your dress.

SOMETHING NEW symbolizes your new life together.

1. A pair of new shoes.

2. A new fragrance.

3. Your wedding bouquet.

SOMETHING BORROWED should come from a happily married woman (hopefully some of her happiness will rub off on you).

1. Get married on the same date as your parents or grandparents.

2. Wear jewelry belonging to anyone special.

3. Wear your mom's or mother-in-law's veil or dress.

SOMETHING BLUE is the color of purity in Christianity.

1. Have a tiny blue temporary tattoo.

2. If you're wearing functional undies, sew a tiny blue bow on your bra.

3. Sew a tag with the date of your wedding written in blue ink, or a secret blue button, into your dress.

DID YOU KNOW . . .
"Something old, something new, something borrowed, something blue" is only the beginning of a rhyme that ends "And a silver sixpence in her shoe." If you want the real thing, you can order one from Britain's Royal Mint, who will ship a genuine, gift-boxed silver sixpence, struck between 1920 and 1946.

Spring

Winter's over and everything's coming to life again—what better time for a wedding? There are deals to be had before the high-season rush kicks in. Colors are fresh, the weather's warming up, and days are long (spring gives great light for photographs). Fewer guests will be AWOL on vacation.

CONS: Late spring equals high season in some places. Weather can be unstable and rainy. Some religions restrict weddings at certain times—Jewish couples can't marry between Passover and Shavuot, and Christian churches don't usually carry out weddings during Lent.

MONEY-SAVING TIPS: Seasonal flowers are the best way to get the most for your $ and spring flowers include everyone's favorites—peonies, freesias, lilies of the valley, and sweet peas.

Stains

Plenty of brides get alcohol poured over them in the excitement, smear makeup down their dress, or have children's chocolate hands tugging at their skirts. Most stains can be removed by professionals, but if you need to DIY or for on-the-spot emergencies—e.g., you haven't taken your pics yet and you're drenched in red wine—here's how to minimize the damage.

INSIDER TIPS: HOW TO REMOVE STAINS "You can use these techniques on all fabrics," says Charlie Tuzzi of Cameo Cleaners.

- **Lipstick:** Soak a Q-tip with nail polish remover and lightly brush the stain. Any kind of remover will work.
- **Red wine:** Blot the stain and then dab with a capful of over-the-counter (3 percent solution or less) hydrogen peroxide. Wait, and then repeat if you need to. The peroxide won't leave any kind of rings.
- **Mud:** First, blot the mud; at this stage don't rub it or it'll get worse—try to use a sponge if you can. After the heavy mud is gone, use the same sponge with soap and water—rub it back and forth and a majority of the mud should come off.
- **Chocolate:** Use exactly the same technique as for mud.

SHOUT, SHOUT, GET IT ALL OUT "Shout wipes are my most treasured discovery as a stylist. They're literally magic—the lightest swipe and the stain's gone." **Stylist Clare Mukherjee**

OVERKILL?

"One of the most common mistakes people make is looking at too many options and getting confused. Just go with the design that makes your heart skip a beat." **Luxury stationer Ceci Johnson**

Stationery

Will you go electronic or use traditional paper? It doesn't have to be one or the other—you can mix it up and use both.

LET'S HEAR IT FOR ELECTRONIC! "Whether you opt for paper or online is a matter of choice, because neither is inherently more polite. Good etiquette is about the intention with which you craft your message. A carefully considered, well-designed online invitation can feel more special than a perfunctory paper one," says Alexa Hirschfeld, cofounder of Paperless Post.

LET'S HEAR IT FOR PAPER! "There's something beautiful about a slow and old-fashioned method of communication. There's a magical feeling when I open my mailbox and find a hand-addressed envelope," says Ming Thompson, creative director of Pounding Mill Press.

❝ I don't believe there are any rights or wrongs when it comes to stationery. Traditions don't need to be followed blindly. **❞**

MING THOMPSON

DO THE MATH

You don't need as many invitations as you have guests. Divide the number in half and add roughly an extra 10–30, depending on the size of your wedding and whether you're having a B guest list.

THE WHERE AND HOW OF WEDDING STATIONERY: There are lots of different ways to make or buy your wedding stationery:

1. DIY: It can be much cheaper and still look fantastic, but it's not always quicker. Download free templates online or buy DIY designs for home printing from online stationers.

● **Word of warning:** Look out for tricky things like double-sided designs and too many layers of detail that will have to be repeated 100-plus times, say stationers Eunice and Sabrina Moyle.

274

2. BUYING ONLINE: There are endless possibilities, from what-you-see-is-what-you-get to completely customizable, interactive, and paperless options.

3. STATIONERY SHOPS: This one has obvious appeal if you like to see things in the flesh. Rifle through samples of paper, cardstock, and colors on the spot.

4. DESIGNER/BESPOKE: "Choose someone who shares your aesthetic, and who will be easy to work with," advises Thompson.
- **Where do you start?** "Find things that speak to you and work them into a personalized design," says Ceci Johnson. "Obvious sources are your wedding location, the time of year, or colors, but even pets have made an appearance!"
- **How long does it take?** Allow three to six months. "Custom design always takes twice as long as you think," says Thompson.
- **How much does it cost?** It depends whether they're charging by the hour or on a fee basis, where you are in the country, or whether they're also sourcing paper and printing, but an individual graphic designer doesn't always cost as much as you might think.

5. PAPERLESS/ELECTRONIC: They're instant, can have minimal or no cost, and are completely green. And gone are the days of supercrappy e-vites; some of the most prestigious stationery companies, photo agencies, and famous designers now produce ranges. Alternatives are to create your own or have a graphic designer do one for you.

❝What annoyed me the most about planning our wedding was taking more than a week to choose the font and paper for the invitations. Women want to discuss things. Men want to decide. Meet halfway . . .**❞ real groom Jason**

STATIONERY CHECKLIST
What might you want? The only essential is the invitation.

Before your wedding:
- Save the date (see page 262)
- Rehearsal dinner invite
- Invitation (see page 185)
- Thank-you's

Send with the invite:
- RSVP
- Envelopes
- Transportation cards
- Accommodation cards
- Map cards

Use on the day:
- Escort cards
- Place cards
- Menus
- Ceremony program

Stationery
It's all in the detail:

ASK YOURSELF . . .

Is your font too small? Will old people (or the over 25's) be using magnifying glasses?

Is your font too close together?

Is the color too light?

Is evrythng spellled croectly, with the rite time and dayte?

THE FINAL WORD

It's your job to read through proofs and spot any problems. If the error isn't yours, the stationery should be reprinted for free.

STATIONERY TIME LINE

● **12 months:** If you want something bespoke, start researching companies or designers.

● **8 months**: Start working with your stationer so you have time to play around, get creative, and love the end result. Order save-the-date stationery.

● **6 months:** Send out save-the-date cards, and start finalizing bespoke paper stationery, reply cards, and any other enclosures you're sending out.

● **4 months:** A calligrapher will need time to write out all those envelopes, so drop them off ASAP. If you're ordering from an online store, start shortlisting your favorite designs.

● **3 months:** Order online stationery, making sure you've got enough turnaround time for proofs and corrections.

● **6–8 weeks:** Send out your invitations, whether they're paper or electronic.

● **1 month:** For last-minute weddings, you still have plenty of time to proof and print a customized design online, but send them out as soon as you can.

TOP 5: questions to ask your stationer

These are the key things to know before you place an order, say stationers Eunice and Sabrina Moyle, cofounders of Hello Lucky.

1 What type of paper do you use? "Thicker paper and cotton papers tend to feel more luxurious."

2 What can I customize for free? Do you have to pay extra to make changes to fonts, colors, and motifs?

3 Are there coordinating items if I want them?

4 Which ink colors look good together? Will they be legible? What looks great on a computer screen doesn't always work well on paper.

5 What's the turnaround time, and when does it start? For example, does it begin when you sign off the proof and does it include transit time?

LOOKING PAST PAPER

Stationery doesn't have to be an old-fashioned paper invite. These are our favorite things you can print or write on.

1. Tote bags
2. Stickers
3. Leaves
4. A bar of chocolate
5. Record labels

PLANNING AHEAD

Be letter perfect.

● **Postage:** Don't guess. Have everything you're sending out weighed.

● **Stamps:** Add customized wedding stamps with your photo, names, dates, or a cute design.

Stepchildren

Are there stepchildren in the mix of your wedding? We asked psychologist Yvonne Thomas how to tackle common problems.

DON'T LIKE YOUR STEPCHILDREN? Remember that these kids are an extension of the person you love enough to marry. Treat them with respect and warmth because it'll make your partner happy and keep you operating at a mature level.

If you can identify why you don't feel good about them, find a healthy way to remedy it. For example, if you feel you have to compete for time with their dad, arrange events all of you can share together.

THEY DON'T LIKE YOU? Have your partner ask them (not in your presence) how they feel. If they really don't like you, he needs to ask why, and what they think will make them feel better about you. Try to stay respectful and warm, setting a good example of how to treat each other that perhaps the stepkids may emulate. Find a way to experience positiveness together—set up something around a common interest (e.g., go to a sporting event or concert everyone would enjoy).

At bare minimum, try out a special interest of the stepchildren as a way to bond and understand them better. It's also really important to let them have alone time with your partner.

IS THE EX BEING DIFFICULT?

"You and your partner need to draw boundaries. The stepkids (unless they're under six years old) can be given the chance to speak for themselves and decide if they feel comfortable being at the wedding. If the ex tries to make the children feel guilty for wanting to be there, you or your partner needs to try and reason with them."

Yvonne Thomas

Stress

Feeling under pressure can trigger a whole range of crappy symptoms, from snappiness to insomnia and depression. If you can't remove the cause of stress, help your body turn off or manage its response to it. Acupuncture, massage, and hypnotherapy are all proven to increase levels of happy hormone serotonin. Do some of the deep breathing we keep going on about (see the Meditation entry on page 210). Get physical, have sex. Tune out all of your electronic devices for 10 minutes, half an

DE-STRESS THE NATURAL WAY

"Spray magnesium under your feet before you go to bed."

Amanda Griggs

hour, a day. "Also, if you're under stress, take vitamin C," says nutritional therapist Amanda Griggs. Failing that, try rhodiola, the adaptogenic herb given to Russian cosmonauts to help them cope with the pressures of deep space.

Style

Some people just have their own style nailed. They know who they are and how they want to look. And then there are the rest of us, who are a bit more schizophrenic. How do you pin down your style so you don't end up looking like a Frankenbride mishmash?

"Go to your closet; your design style is there. Look for silhouettes and necklines that make you feel great," says interior and fashion designer Kelly Wearstler. Translate those ideas into what you wear on your wedding day. How do you know when you've got it right? You'll feel comfortable and at ease.

FIND YOUR STYLE
- You can only rescue one item in your wardrobe from a fire . . . what is it? Why?
- How would you dress on your wedding day if no one else was looking, if it was just you and your partner?

STYLE IS NOT: being in fashion, following trends, spending a lot of money, or buying only designer labels or status symbols.

Summer

The biggest pro of a summer wedding is choice—all those locations, from beaches to parks, vineyards to the backyard. Good weather is almost guaranteed, and you don't have to travel for honeymoon sun.

CONS: Prices. They're are at their highest for you and your guests. Venues, vendors, accommodation, travel, and honeymoons are in peak season. Guests need lots of notice because it's family vacation time. As for the weather . . . high summer can be just too much, bugs take over the world, and late-summer scenery can look done and tired.

MONEY-SAVING TIP
Get more for your money with in-season flowers: stock, sunflowers, roses, poppies, freesia, and hydrangea.

Table names Naming your tables is much more fun than numbers—plus, it's more egalitarian and no one can take offense. Tie table names into something that's important to you and enjoy brainstorming. To get you started, think about special dates, places you've been to or plan to visit, pets, bands, songs, colors, sports teams, flowers, books, films, or even your favorite ice cream flavors.

Tanning

Don't stray too far from your natural skin tone . . . aim for a natural glow.

Whichever way you're tanning, always exfoliate to get the most even cover, paying special attention to knees, elbows, hands, and feet. If you're tanning naturally or on a bed, get out of the rays a week before your wedding to give your skin time to settle. Undecided which is best for you?

BEDS, BOTTLES, AND THE SUN
Tanning bed
DO wear the goggles and limit yourself to very short exposures suitable for your skin type—not the maximum some crazy behind the desk will allow.

Self-tan DIY

DO leave at least four days before your wedding to allow color to develop and have time to put mistakes right.

DO mix tanner with moisturizer on knees and elbows.

Spray tan

DON'T spray tan less than two days before your wedding, says celebrity beauty therapist Nichola Joss. "That way you're guaranteed no transfer onto your clothes because the tan has developed, set, and calmed. A spray tan's optimum color is on day two—so if you're getting married on a Saturday, have your tan on the Thursday."

DON'T moisturize the day you have it. "It'll act as a barrier and your color won't be as rich."

Tanning the old-fashioned way

This happens to be our favorite. A natural glow from the sun can't be beat. Just avoid using the dregs of last summer's lotion. Always buy a new bottle, and use sunscreen with a minimum of SPF 30 for the face and body.

JUST SAY NO

"Spray tan ruins photos. Stay away from it. In real life you may look sun-kissed but in photos you look like you were left under a heat lamp. Use the sun to tan or don't tan at all. It's not a human skin tone and can be near impossible to correct out of images." **Aaron Delesie**

Tattoos

Want to wear your heart on your sleeve . . . or your chest, or your fingers? Health and fitness expert Heidi Powell and her husband, Chris, star of *Extreme Weight Loss,* each tattooed "my best friend" around their ring fingers when they married. "We have it written in the other's handwriting," says Heidi. "It's a constant reminder that being together is a CHOICE, not an obligation. We always treat each other like a best friend."

TATTOO REMOVAL Got a tattoo you'd like to cover on the day, or have removed completely? Here's what you need to know.

- **Cover it with makeup:** "Use the opposite color on the color wheel to cancel out colored areas before you apply concealer. For example, for red, you need a green cream. Wipe skin with alcohol or a toner first, then finish with a waterproof sealer to keep it covered all day," says makeup artist Mizzie Logan.

- **Remove it with laser:** The only way to permanently remove a tattoo, aside from cutting off the offending skin, is by laser. "How effective it is depends on what color and how old the tattoo is, and on you because the ink's broken down inside your body," says removal specialist Ken Saler. "Factor in nine to twelve months because you need to leave four to six weeks between treatments and no one can predict how many you'll need."

Teeth
A little bit of teeth whitening goes a long way. It's one of the easiest ways to make you look fresher and younger. And if you don't love a trip to the dentist, you can do it at home. We asked Dr. Jonathan Levine, associate professor at NYU College of Dentistry and founder of GLO Science, to give us the essential need-to-knows on the best DIY solutions.

- **Over-the-counter tray and gels.** "You heat a tray, fill it with gel, and place it in your mouth. It takes weeks to deliver results, and eighty percent of users report sensitivity because of the breakdown of the carbamide peroxide gel." **Results: weeks**
- **Whitening strips.** "The efficacy is excellent for an OTC product. If you're patient and compliant, you'll see results in a few weeks. Be cautious not to rest the strip on the gums." **Results: two weeks**
- **Paint-ons.** "User-friendly and convenient, paint-ons avoid contact with the soft tissue that often results in sensitivity and irritation. Look for a gel that does not migrate from the tooth. It requires commitment, and

A LAST RESORT
Cover it with a patch: Experiment to see if you can get the result you want— patches don't give as close a match as make-up. Clean skin with alcohol to remove all oils and residue before you apply.

MAINTENANCE
You've bleached them to within an inch of their life . . . here's how to keep your white teeth white.
- Avoid coffee, red wine, tea, cola, etc. for a few hours after whitening.
- Chew whitening gum after you eat stuff that can stain.
- Use whitening toothpaste and finish with a whitening rinse to reach anywhere you've missed.

and is another good option if you have two weeks."

Results: two weeks

● **Whitening devices.** "They bring elements of professional lightening to the user at home. If you are short on time, it will begin to whiten your teeth in two days, with clinical studies showing five shades lighter in five days."

Results: two days

Tents

Big or small, summer or winter, for formal or informal weddings, tents are the ultimate all-purpose blank canvas.

WILL A TENT KEEP THE WEATHER OUT? Yes, tents protect you from rain or snow, and you can heat or air-condition them.

HOW BIG? "There's no formula based on the number of guests," says Andrew Partridge of Sperry Tents. "The factors are what style you like, whether you're having food stations versus a plated meal, band versus DJ, farm-style tables versus round tables, etc. Your caterer is usually a great addition to the discussion of how much space you'll need."

HOW DO YOU DECORATE? "Lighting and décor are the two most effective things for transforming a tent into an atmosphere for celebration. Also, think about furnishings that offer a departure from rows of tables lined up around a dance floor," says Partridge.

PLANNING AHEAD

Workers will need access at least one or two days before your wedding, and the morning after to take it down.

Thank-you's

Whole books are written around the proper etiquette of thank-you's, but really it's simple. A sincere thank-you given from the heart, in any form, is always the right way. It can be as simple as a hug and verbal praise, a handwritten note, or something more extravagant. How can you express appreciation to the people who've invested a lot of time and effort in your day?

PROCRASTINATION IS NOT YOUR FRIEND Is there a cut-off point for saying thank-you? If you're thanking people for wedding gifts, straight after the honeymoon is ideal. If it's for their help and contributions, try to do it on the day. Get all thank-you's out to everyone by two months after your wedding. Otherwise (a) it's becoming pretty pointless because it's obvious you couldn't be bothered and (b) you'll have constant nagging guilt hanging over you because you know you should have done it.

WAYS TO THINK BEYOND THE CARD

1. Have a personalized gift made—anything from initial or monogrammed jewelry to diaries, key rings, or wallets.

2. Give them an experience—Is there a band or sports team or singer they've always wanted to see, or something they've always wanted to do, like take a helicopter ride over the Grand Canyon?

3. Are they a foodie or wine buff? Give them wine from a year that's special to them or just their favorite kind. Champagne, cheese, and cupcakes always go down well, or buy a meal at their favorite restaurant.

4. For book lovers, track down a first-edition favorite from an online site.

5. Grand gestures . . . such as spa days, weekends away, and fine jewelry are never, ever tacky and always gratefully received (in our homes, at least).

A CARD

The simplest thank-you is a note.

● Address the person by name.

● Mention what you're thanking them for.

● Sign off personally.

● Be yourself; no superformal stuff or following formulas if you're usually very laid back.

TOP 5 WAYS TO THINK BEYOND THE CARD

Themes Before you embark on a themed wedding (Star Trek/hobbits/Halloween . . .) and get overcome with excitement, ask yourself if ALL your guests, whatever age they are, will enjoy it.

Do your MOM AND DAD really want to dress up as the Borg Queen and Spock or SONNY AND CHER?

Themes are like formalwear—some people embrace it like their life depends on it, others can't wait to go home. Think about your guests before you commit.

Tiaras Tiaras equal an updo, right? Not necessarily. If you want to avoid looking like Honey Boo Boo on a pageant day or something out of the 1980s, you need to keep hair fairly simple, that's all. The British royals, who have access to more tiaras than most, wear theirs with hair up or down. If you can, try out a few different styles with your hairdresser beforehand.

Time out "Take a few minutes after the ceremony to be alone," says wedding planner Cassandra Santor. "Jewish tradition has *yehud*—it's a time for the couple to be alone and take in the commitment they've just made. I wish every couple would do it, regardless of their own tradition. Even if it's just a limo ride alone somewhere; take a minute to hold each other before all the reception festivity begins, really soak in what just happened, and celebrate it!"

Tipping There are no hard and fast rules about tipping, no matter what anyone says. How much and to whom you give is up to you. If the hair and make-up was awful or the waitstaff stank of cigarettes, you don't have to hand over an extra 15 percent bonus because everyone says you should.

Tipping is a reward for good service.

Not poor or mediocre service. Great service where someone goes the extra mile.

The only rule of thumb should be to tip the people who deserve it and give what feels comfortable to you, not according to a pre-designated tip chart of what you "have" to give.

A FEW POINTERS

DO budget for tips from the beginning, but don't take them as a given.

DON'T hand out tips if what you got was subpar or you were unhappy in any way.

DON'T tip waitstaff, bartenders, and anyone else who works your reception individually—it'll take all night. Give a lump sum to the manager to split. You could allocate around 15 percent of the total bill, or do a flat sum for each member of staff.

TIP INCLUDED? Check your contracts because many vendors include a service charge of 15 to 20 percent or a gratuity fee. You don't want to be double tipping . . . but make sure the money will go to workers, not line the pockets of the owners.

DID YOU KNOW . . .
Photographers, florists, and planners: "You don't have to tip anyone who is a business owner, but it's a nice way to show your appreciation if you feel they've done an excellent job," says planner Annie Lee.

NO TIP INCLUDED?
Give tips to people on the day. Designate the best man or a family member to be responsible for it.

WHO AND IN WHAT ORDER?

This is a very traditional order; mix it up however you want:

- Best man (speech)
- Maid of honor (toast)
- Father of the bride (plus Mom if she wants to) (speech)
- Groom's parents (toast)
- Groom (speech)
- Bride (toast)
- Anyone else who wants to have a go

FEAR OF PUBLIC SPEAKING

Toasts and speeches

"You can't celebrate without speeches," says one real bride. But what's the difference between a speech and a toast? A toast is all about saying congrats or thank-you (very briefly), and raising a glass. A speech is slightly longer and might include some personal stories. If you've asked people to do either, make sure it's clear which you want. And give people a (short) time limit for speeches. A few minutes is plenty.

DO break up the toasts. Have some before you start the reception and then in between courses.

DO thank your guests for being there. "That's the only rule I always insist couples follow," says event planner Angie Nevarez.

DON'T assume that just because someone's in your wedding party they'll be happy to stand up and speak.

DON'T ask people who are deathly afraid of public speaking.

DON'T ask too many people—everyone will get bored.

PRESCIPTION: Fear of public speaking

Can you stand up and make a toast without being overcome by a cold sweat? If the thought of public speaking makes you want to throw up, run through these tricks.

1. All those physical symptoms are a by-product of adrenaline. Learn how to turn off your body's fight-or-flight response in five minutes by reading the Meditation entry on page 210.

2. Be prepared. Practice what you're going to say and visualize it going perfectly.

3. Realize that everyone wants you to do well. They'll clap and laugh in all the right places.

4. Take a homeopathic remedy containing Argent Nic.

WHAT NOT TO DO WHEN GIVING A SPEECH
It may be fiction, but it's spot-on advice.

From the 2005 hit film *Wedding Crashers . . .* read, laugh, and learn.

John Beckwith: Are you going to give a toast?

Claire Cleary: Yes.

John Beckwith: Nervous?

Claire Cleary: A little bit.

John Beckwith: What are you going to say?

[Claire pulls a piece of paper from inside her dress]

John Beckwith: You keep it in your cleavage.

Claire Cleary: Nowhere else to put it. Normally I'm not very good at these things, but I think this one's pretty good. [John reads from Claire's notes]

John Beckwith: "I never thought my sister would find someone who cared about what other people thought as much as she did—until I met Craig?"!

Claire Cleary: Yes, that's funny. It's funny because it's true. People like funny.

John Beckwith: I know, but the whole funny-because-it's-true bit only works if the truth is a *small* thing like "everyone knows Jennifer likes to shop, ha ha ha." I think you're better off going with something from the heart. Honestly.

Claire Cleary: I think people are going to like this.

John Beckwith: I think you're going to hear crickets.

Claire Cleary: I think you're wrong.

John Beckwith: Sounds of silence. Go walk the plank.

Claire Cleary: Uh-uh. I'm sticking to it.

John Beckwith: Okay, meet me at the back of the room. I'll be the guy waiting to say I told you so.

Q **Does a long speech = better speech?**

A No. "Anyone giving a speech should write it out and then cut two-thirds. Length and ad-libbing work against you unless you're a toastmaster or Jon Stewart."
Brian Dorsey, Photographer

A LITTLE HOMEWORK

"Always explore your heritage and find out why certain details are symbolic or meaningful. Then you'll understand why they should be incorporated in your wedding." **Jung Lee**

Traditions

Wedding traditions range from sacred, somber, and serious to fun and downright strange. The great thing is that, apart from the religious ones, they're not set in stone. You can pick and choose the ones you want to include. Have no idea why you're tossing a garter? Lose it. Hate the idea of being "given away" by a man? Walk down the aisle with your partner. Want a wedding canopy even though you're not Jewish? Fine!

Trains

Ever tried turning a corner with six feet of fabric trailing behind you? A train is great if you've got lots of help behind you (i.e., plenty of well-trained bridesmaids to pick up the slack), but if not, it can end up wrapped around your ankles in a knot. Approach with caution, and keep friends in spiky high heels at a safe distance. Choose a detachable train; bustles always tear after a couple of hours.

Transportation

Anything that moves, from a horse and carriage to a rickshaw, taxi, boat, helicopter, vintage convertible, motorbike, bus, your dad's station wagon, or a limo, can be used as transportation.

GET MOVING: What you need to know
● **Numbers:** Traditionally, you're responsible for getting the wedding party to and from the ceremony and to the reception, but if it's an out-of-the-way location, think about providing transport for all your guests.
● **Timing:** You might only need transportation for two hours but ask the most economical way to hire—it's sometimes cheaper for longer chunks of time.
● **Extras:** Is there unlimited mileage?

FURTHER READING

For details on carriages and horsey things, turn to page 71.

Trends
In everything from clothes to food and décor, even photography, wedding fashions date. But does it matter? Is being timeless better than following trends?

TIMELESS

"Aim for timeless," advises wedding planner Annie Lee. "You might want people to be able to guess what decade you got married in, but not which month and year." In other words, you won't look back and go, WTF were we thinking?

TRENDS

Photography captures a moment in time—fashions, mood, the absolute essence. When you look through old photos, it's the things that date them that make them interesting, fun, and sometimes really embarrassing. If you want to follow wedding trends, these details will paint a thousand words about your day.

Tripping and slipping
"Rub the bottom of new leather shoes with sandpaper to give them a grip and make them less slippery," advises event planner Angie Nevarez. It should prevent around 99 percent of slips. Alternatively, stick cute sandpaper hearts to the bottom of new shoes.

Trousseau
The Brits call it a bottom drawer. In America it's a hope chest. But the French *trousseau* sounds so much more romantic for the household linens and nighties that used to be collected for women by their families and presented to them on marriage. What's in a modern trousseau? It's more likely to focus on lingerie than beautiful hand-embroidered linen, but don't dismiss the linens entirely . . . they're way more romantic than your average Ikea duvet cover.

Uu

Underwear (no, not lingerie)

Why did all those Hollywood sirens
look so amazing?

Because they really got what underwear could do for you.

This is not about being sexy, but making everything wrinkle-, bump-, and bulge-free. We're talking foundation garments. "BEFORE you buy a dress, or whatever you want to wear, focus on your best attributes, and buy a foundation garment that enhances them," says Asia Smaga, founder of corsetry label Ender Legard.

CORSETS: Picture Brigitte Bardot slinking around in her corset and veil in shots from *And God Created Woman* and you know what magic a corset can do. "It supports and lets you wear what you want without worrying about dress slippage, bust support, waistlines, or posture," says Smaga. "Wear one when you're trying out different dresses or when you have your first fitting. It can reduce the need for alterations or additional fittings."

> **CONS:** Not something you can slink in and out of easily on bathroom visits, especially once you've had a few drinks. In the heat, it's just one more layer to make you sweat.

"Your foundation needs to be smooth with no embellishments, because they can show through clothes. Ditch all the lace and decoration."
Asia Smaga

TOP TIP

"If you're having a dress custom made, ask about having a bra or corset built in." **Clare Mukherjee**

SHAPEWEAR: This is soft but supportive, smooths you out, puts fat somewhere else, and, in some cases, give definition to areas like the butt and bust. It's what you need for a sleek silhouette under anything remotely form-fitting. It's not just for those with a few spare pounds; it makes anyone's clothes look better.

CONS: Can make you feel like an Egyptian mummy and isn't easy to take off in a hurry or on your own.

HOW TO BUY Go to a good department store or find a specialist boutique and ask them to measure you properly. Try different brands before you buy—some have more stretch than others.

Unexpected It will happen. Guaranteed.

"I promise you something will go wrong. EXPECT IT. Be okay with it and don't let it ruin your day.

The people who have the best time at their weddings are the ones that wanted to and allowed themselves to," says planner Annie Lee.

Unique

It's only recently that highlighting your "uniqueness" has been bandied about as part of a wedding day. But weddings mark your commitment to each other, not a need to prove how interesting, fashionable, wealthy, or quirky you are. "Some people who have a beautiful life lose it when it comes to designing a wedding. They seem to be slaves of the industry magazines and throw their common sense out the door. Usually there's a certain degree of relief when they realize that all they need is a wedding that reflects their taste," says event designer Lewis Miller.

Being unique is doing what you want and not what others expect. Your wedding will be unique enough if you stay true to yourselves and draw from your own likes and dislikes, your shared personal history, food tastes, childhood memories, and family traditions.

Ushers

Their role is to show guests to their seats and act as general signposts for guests who aren't sure where to go or what to do. Is this one just for the men? Traditionally, yes, but you can invite anyone to do it—man, woman, or child—as long as they're capable of taking the lead. In fact, it's a great way to include people in your ceremony who might not otherwise have had a part to play. If the ushers aren't going to coordinate their attire with the wedding party, mark them with a simple boutonniere or corsage.

Vv

Veil

They're superpretty (like your very own tulle halo), traditional, and create a symbolic moment at the altar. . . . It doesn't matter if you're getting married for the nth time or are any age from 19 to 90: You can wear a veil if you want to.

CHOOSING YOUR VEIL

Nicole Sewall, managing director of bridal retailer BHLDN, says:

1. Go for balance. Elaborate and decorated gowns with lots of texture and detail look best with simple veils, while simple gowns can be a blank slate for a detailed veil, sprinkled with crystals or edged in lace.

2. A long tulle veil without edging is the most flattering and least intrusive style for most gowns.

3. A short veil or halo complements gowns with interesting back details and won't hinder the view from behind.

4. The color of your veil should complement your gown; it should blend in and create a soft, airy halo around you.

5. If you're planning to wear a veil with your hair down, choose one that's longer than your hair (the exceptions here are birdcage veils and blushers).

GET IT ON AND KEEP IT ON How do you attach a veil? "Fasten it at the crown of your head, three or four inches lower than the top center. This position pairs well with most hair styles. If you're wearing a high updo, place the veil just underneath it," says Sewall.

TOP 5 TIPS FOR CHOOSING YOUR VEIL

DID YOU KNOW . . .
"Updos allow for more flexibility with veil pairings, because getting a veil just right often depends more on the placement than the style." says Sewall.

Vendors

You don't need to love each other, but you do need to get along and be able to work as a team.

TOP

5

WAYS TO
GET THE
MOST
FROM
VENDORS

WAYS TO GET THE MOST FROM VENDORS

1. Be kind and polite. It will likely make them go the extra mile for you. Arrogance, bad temper, and a sense of entitlement will get you what you pay for but not one scrap more. Or they might quit.

2. Listen to them. You're paying for their advice, expertise, and years of experience. If they say you need to do something, or that something you want won't work, pay attention.

3. Be totally honest about your budget. Don't waste your time and theirs planning things you can't afford. If you need to cut the budget or if you run out of money, tell them. They've seen it all before and often have money-saving tricks up their sleeves.

4. Remember you don't own their time. You're not paying for a 24/7 on-call personal assistant. They don't have to explain where they are or why they didn't pick up your call.

5. Tell them what you don't want as much as what you do. It helps them come up with ideas, plans, and proposals that will suit you.

AVOID SHOUTY E-MAILS "If someone isn't meeting your expectations, schedule a call and explain what you're concerned about," suggests planner Sandy Malone. "A lot is lost in e-mail and your best intention of letting her know your worries could read like a giant bitch slap. I'm all for written documentation when you feel like the problem isn't being addressed, but when you kick things off that way, don't expect a warm and fuzzy response." Some things can't be undone, and vendors do ditch rude clients.

"Establish a relationship with all your vendors so that they feel invested and want to work harder for you." **Diana Schmidtke**

Venues Unless you have very particular requirements or live in a one-horse town with a single wedding venue, you could probably do with a way of simplifying the process of choosing your venue. Asking yourself these questions will help. . . .

Start to narrow down your choices:

1 How big is the guest list? Get a rough idea of numbers, then start looking. The key to a good atmosphere is nothing too big—or too small. Venues can usually tell you their optimum number of guests.

2 When's your wedding? Scratch venues that don't suit the time of year. What's perfect for an outdoor summer wedding might not have such lovely space inside. Likewise, some venues don't score high on the outside but have amazing interiors, great for winter weddings.

3 What style venue do you like? Historic, modern, city, country, beach, rodeo . . . ? Do you want somewhere that won't need much décor or would you prefer a blank slate?

4 How much help are you looking for? Do you want a full-service venue that can handle catering, cake and linens, tables, chairs, etc., or is it just the space you want?

5 Are you free to use your own vendors? Does the venue have a list of vendors you must use? If you know you want to bring in your own caterers, will the venue allow it? Some people find a list of preferred vendors really helpful; for others it's just too restrictive.

TOP TIP

Think it will never happen? Before you sign a contract, ask your venue if any building work or refurbishment is on the cards.

MORE QUESTIONS TO ASK . . . POTENTIAL VENUES

6. How many weddings will take place on the same day? And how much time between them?

7. If it's a hotel, will they cordon off space, or will you be open to public access? For any type of venue, will your guests be locked in one room or allowed to wander freely?

8. Are they licensed for alcohol? Can they provide barstaff?

9. What's extra? This could be things like cake-cutting fees, cleaning up afterward, food tasting, corkage, or fees if you overrun. Service charges? Liability insurance?

10. How long before the event can vendors get access? When can deliveries be made?

11. Are there any restrictions regarding décor/music/ fireworks? Will there be any décor in place at the time of your wedding?

12. If there's accommodation on site, what discount will they give to your guests?

Videography If you don't have the budget to hire a good videographer, stick to photographs, or get friends to film parts of the day for you. A decent videographer needs to have cinematographic skills, and too many of them don't—they're just people lugging around a couple of cameras, pointing them in your direction, and charging you lots of money for the privilege.

HOW TO CHOOSE A VIDEOGRAPHER

DO know what style you want. "Before you speak to anyone, decide if you prefer digital or film, a mix or is silent Super 8 more your style? It'll help you narrow down your search," says wedding filmmaker Joel Serrato.

DO talk through your day. "Explain the dynamic of your wedding—whether it'll be in a ballroom or outside in natural light. Ask them how they'll be prepared in different lighting situations. It's key to making sure your memories are captured properly."

TECH TALK Can't choose between normal film, digital, Super 8? Is one better than the others? "There aren't pros or cons either way," says Serrato. "It just depends what you prefer." This is a rough guide:

- **Film:** Perfect if you like soft footage with grain and realistic tones and colors that will stand the test of time.
- **Digital:** If you're looking for a sharp cinematic approach, digital might be a better fit.
- **Super 8:** The best of both worlds; organic, soft, and natural with high-definition quality. It's silent, edited to music, but can have sound recorded from another source and synched.

TOP TIP
Give your videographers advance warning if you want them in any sort of dress code.

Vintage Why is choosing vintage for your wedding so damn cool and enchanting?

❝Wearing something from the past helps keep us INDIVIDUAL in a world of cookie-cutter and ultrafast fashion.❞

AUTHOR AND FOUNDER OF DECADES VINTAGE CLOTHING STORE
CAMERON SILVER

vintage cont

IMPERFECTIONS, FLAWS, AND FIXES

Vintage clothes can be stained, worn, torn, missing buttons, or have stuck zippers. But don't let that dissuade you. A badass seamstress can accomplish a lot.

"The attraction's also an appreciation of history and the mystery of often not knowing the provenance of your vintage find," says Silver.

DOES VINTAGE REALLY ONLY SUIT A CERTAIN STYLE OR SHAPE? "There's something for everyone when it comes to vintage wedding gowns. The 20s/30s are perfect if you're looking for something beautiful in lace, the 40s for something with a wasp waist and full skirts, the 60s for retro, and the 70s for something more boho," explains Clare Borthwick, Christie's vintage couture specialist.

AGE AND BEAUTY Not all vintage is a work of art. How can you tell what to ditch? "Always go for the best quality and natural materials such as cottons, silks, and wools," says vintage expert Carmen Haid. "Stay away from polyester or any other synthetic fibers—you'll sweat, and they won't come odor-free."

WHERE TO BUY "You can find vintage anywhere from private collectors to vintage dealers, flea markets, and auctions. High-end vintage stores and sites curate their pieces and cherry-pick the best, so their prices reflect it," says Haid. Absolute bargains are the ones you'll find at thrift stores, on eBay, and at flea markets.

IF YOU . . .

- . . . feel rushed, slow down.
- . . . don't feel close, say something.
- . . . have intercourse— even for a second—use contraception. There is no "The first time is free."

Marty Klein, PhD

Virgin
If you're a virgin, says sex therapist Dr. Marty Klein . . .

- Do not have intercourse the first time you're sexual together.
- Make the first night (or day) about getting to know each other's body: look, touch, and ask questions. "Sex" can wait until tomorrow—and it will be better if you do these other things first.
- If it hurts, stop.

- Whatever sex you do have, do it with the lights on. And look at each other.
- Wash your hands before you start, smile during it, and say "thank you" afterward.
- Remember, real sex isn't like porn.

Vows

Vows are a way of sealing your partnership and the commitment you're making to each other. Your promises could be anything from religious to silly and sentimental.

FOR BETTER OR WORSE: WRITING YOUR OWN VOWS

- **Write them ahead.** Don't deliver them off the cuff. "Do not wing your vows. They SUCK every time and the entire (captive) listening audience can tell you're pulling it out of your butt," says wedding planner Sandy Malone.
- **If you feel stuck,** use the tried and tested traditional vows. And if you're writing for both of you, don't procrastinate. "My husband wrote our vows the night before, so I didn't know what I was saying until he handed them to me in front of the officiant," says coauthor Karima.
- **They don't have to stay secret.** It's okay to let your partner know what you plan to say.
- **Practice saying them (just a little).** Repeat them too much and you could end up overdelivering like a pantomime villain. Once or twice will do.

TIPS FROM A WRITER

1. **Be honest.**
2. **Be brief.**
3. **Use simple phrases**—anything too verbose will just leave you stumbling over your words.
4. **Don't try to be overly sentimental.** The moment itself provides more than enough emotion to go around.

TIMING

"If you have sex, do NOT attempt to climax at the same time. Hardly anyone does, and it's way more trouble than it's worth."
Marty Klein, PhD

WHAT CHOICES FOR VOWS DO YOU HAVE?

- Use traditional or religious vows (for a religious ceremony, will the officiant let you add or change anything?).
- Find something on the internet.
- Write your own.

DID YOU KNOW . . .

In some religions no vows are made during the wedding ceremony. For example, in Orthodox Christianity, marriage is considered a union, not a contract.

Ww

Walking down the aisle

Enjoy it; walk slowly (try not to gallop), smile, look around, see all the people who have come to celebrate with you. Think you might have an attack of nerves? Walking down the aisle isn't too far short of a model hitting the runway. And even supermodel Gisele Bündchen has admitted to butterflies before shows. Nerves are normal . . . even for the professionals.

Weather

Plans A, B, and C. And maybe D. That's how wedding planners do it when it comes to weather plans, to cover anything from too hot to too cold, or too wet or windy. Options might include finding somewhere else to have the whole wedding or take photos; temporary shelter for eating, dancing, and partying; and/or extras like parasols, AC units, rain covers, wellies, and umbrellas. See the Rain entry on page 245.

Wedding party

Who is officially part of it? Any of these people:

- **Bridesmaids:** see page 54
- **Maid of honor:** see page 201
- **Best man:** see page 41
- **Flower girl:** see page 148
- **Page boys:** see page 227
- **Ring bearer:** see page 259
- **Parents and grandparents:** see page 228
- **The officiant:** see page 221
- **Pets:** see page 20

TRIVIA

Who walked Gavin Rossdale down the aisle when he married Gwen Stefani?

ANSWER

His sheepdog, Winston.

WATCHING OVER YOU

"I have a theory, and so far it's held true . . . if one of the couple has a deceased parent, it never rains. I really think someone is looking out for them on that day."

Wedding planner Annie Lee

wedding planners

"Having a wedding planner's the equivalent of having a project manager. "

WEDDING PLANNER ANGIE NEVAREZ

306

NEED MORE CONVINCING?

We asked wedding planners themselves to sell you the benefits:

● "Enlisting someone who'll care about every detail as much, if not MORE, than you do."

Angie Nevarez

● "We eat, breathe, and live weddings, so we know what's typical, high, low, absurd, doable, etc. Especially when it comes to budget, we're going to tell you what's the best way to use it not because we get anything from it but because we want to maximize it."

Annie Lee

WHAT DO THEY DO? Take care of the boring details (scheduling, chasing people, contracts). Some will design the whole event, too, leaving you to enjoy the fun parts like shopping, turning up on the day, and eating, drinking, and dancing.

WHO DOES WHAT? Not all wedding planners are the same. Here's a rough rundown of who specializes in what, but there's a lot of crossover. Regardless of what they call themselves, the best way to gauge who's best for you is to look at what they've done before.

● **Day-of planners:** Turn up on the day and run the show. Some will help you plot out what needs to be done at the start, then take over the logistics again just beforehand.

● **Wedding planners:** Wedding specialists who'll do all the work and logistics from beginning to end. Skills may be organizational rather than artistic (but there are plenty of talented planners with design flair).

● **Event planners:** Manage lots of types of events. Experience is broader than a pure wedding planner but they might not have as much insider knowledge.

● **Event designers:** Will have a VISION. They will execute the design of your wedding from the tiniest décor detail to showstopping extras.

● **In-house planners:** Work only with that venue and the size and type of event that venue handles. They'll know the location inside out; what works, what doesn't.

QUESTIONS TO ASK . . . WEDDING PLANNERS

● **How much?** "Don't waste your time or theirs. If a planner will be more than ten percent of your budget, there is someone else for you," says Annie Lee.

● **Is this your full-time job and how many weddings have you done?** "You don't need certification to be a wedding planner," explains Lee, "so there are tons of hobbyists or recently married brides who miss wedding planning. Source a serious professional if you want the real wedding planner experience."

● **How available are you for meetings and calls?** "Some limit the number of meetings included in a package (which seems crazy pants to me). Know what hours they can be reached, what days are off days."

● **Will you be there from beginning to end?** "Even to make sure the vendors clean up," says event designer Tara Guérard.

QUESTIONS TO ASK . . . YOURSELF

● **"Can I trust this person with all my heart?** Will I be able to let go and let this person run my event? Everything else is fluff." This is the only question you need to ask about any potential planner, says event designer David Beahm.

● **Do they understand my vision?** "Ask them to talk you through their vision, and how they see your wedding day unfolding," says Angie Nevarez.

● **Do I like them?** "What's their personality like? Are they fun? Professional? Do you get a good vibe?" asks Tara Guérard.

● **Have they asked me the right questions?** "You should walk away feeling they brought to your attention a few things you hadn't realized yet, and asked comprehensive questions," says Annie Lee.

NEED MORE CONVINCING? (CONT)

● "We pay a lot of attention to an inordinate amount of detail to make sure that the couple can get hitched without any hitches. The production of the wedding event takes a great deal of preplanning as well as in-the-moment quick thinking."

● "Diplomacy. The goal is to stage a wedding, not a war. We're part general, part diplomat, and can bridge the gap between parents' wishes and brides and grooms' wishes while keeping the guests' experience in mind. (Think United Nations, with fewer languages and lovelier results!)" **Lisa Vorce**

Wedding planners:
Here's how to get the
most out of them

1 Be honest about your budget and be responsible for it. If you start running out of money or overspending, say so.

2 Acknowledge that simple does not always equal cheap. "Brides equate the word *simple* with *inexpensive,* and that's not true most of the time," says wedding planner Sandy Malone. "For example, a 'simple' bouquet of Phalaenopsis orchids is very expensive."

INDECISION AND PORN

Make decisions and stick to them. Yes, there will always be something cuter about to turn up on a blog, but let it go already. Your wedding planner can't move ahead if you're changing your mind every five minutes. See Wedding Porn, opposite . . . are you addicted?

3 Listen to what they're telling you. Some planners have four or five hundred weddings under their belt. If they say you need to do something—or do it in a particular order—it's for a good reason.

4 Do the homework they give you. "You have to work as a team," says Malone.

5 See to the big picture before you obsess about details. "Who cares if the linens touch the floor if you don't have a floor in the tent to start with? The details will come," says event designer Lewis Miller.

308

Wedding porn

Wedding porn addict = no decisions being made. "There's no end to the amount of pictures, blogs, and magazines chock full of ideas . . . too many ideas," says wedding planner Annie Lee. "Keep it relevant—I know that typewriter is cute . . . too bad it has nothing to do with you, your fiancé, either of your families, the venue . . . At some point brides need to be cut off from new wedding ideas and love the ones they've chosen."

Wedding websites

Imagine the good old days when brides and grooms and their families got asked the same questions a gazillion times over. Now your guests can access every bit of info about your wedding from ceremony details to registry, menus, accommodation, and travel on a wedding website. "They also stop you from getting bombarded with questions ranging from engagement story to airport suggestions," says Cindy Skanderup of Bliss and Bone.

FOLLOWING THE HERD
"Don't look at other people's weddings or follow trends blindly. Stay away from wedding-related stuff for a week and visit other websites."
Sarai Flores and Martha Huerta

They're totally GREEN (zero waste, no discarded stationery or carbon footprint), CHEAP to put together, and EASY for you and your guests.

More advanced ones will collect your guests' RSVPs, run live mobile updates, and share photos and social media. Search online for providers—sites run from free templates to more complex customizable designs that run to a few hundred dollars.

weight loss

MYTHS ABOUT LOSING WEIGHT

"Give yourself a year; weight loss takes a lot more time than you'd think." **Erin Flaherty**

What's the key to losing weight? Burning more calories than you put in your body. It's as simple as that.

MYTHS ABOUT LOSING WEIGHT

Chris and Heidi Powell, health and weight-loss gurus, shed some light on the hows and whys of losing weight.

MYTH 1: To lose weight, you just need to exercise a lot. Not true. While more exercise will always lead to greater fitness, when it comes to weight loss, you cannot outwork a bad diet.

MYTH 2: To lose weight, cut your carbs completely. While this may work in the short term, it is not sustainable in the long run and can lead to a metabolic slowdown . . . and a subsequent weight rebound.

MYTH 3: Thin is healthy. Not necessarily. Granted, lower body weight can put you in a category for lower health risks, but there are many thin people out there who are NOT healthy!

MYTH 4: Some people can eat anything they want and still lose weight. Nope. It all comes down to calories in vs calories out. If someone is losing weight, they are simply burning more calories than they are taking in.

MYTH 5: I can't lose weight because I have a "sluggish metabolism." The majority of your metabolism comes from your muscle mass. Most overweight or obese individuals actually have a relatively high metabolism because their body creates larger lower-body muscles to accommodate their weight. They are sitting on a V-8 engine and don't even know it!

TIPS TO LOSE THE WEIGHT The Powells share the secrets of tackling a weight-loss regime and making it stick.

- **Start small.** Focus on making one small change in diet and/or exercise, and stick to it until you feel confident in making an additional change.
- **Create an environment for success.** Clean out your home, hiding places, workplace, and car of any and all foods that will sabotage your progress. Restock with real, whole, healthy foods that will get you closer to your goals.
- **Share your goals.** Talk openly with your family and friends about your commitment to your new lifestyle.
- **Drink a lot of water.** We typically shoot for at least a gallon a day.

FOOD CHOICES MADE EASY: "If your body could speak, it would tell you it loathes sugar (it feeds anxiety and depression, ages your skin, and is bad for your digestion) and hates chemicals, colorants, and preservatives," says best-selling author Marisa Peer. Follow her easy four-step checklist to healthy eating.

- **Can you eat this food RAW?** It doesn't necessarily mean you'd like to, but if you can eat it raw, it was put on the planet for you to eat.
- **Does it ROT?** Any food that rots will be broken down in your body and used. Any food that doesn't is useless as a form of nutrition—chips, sweets, and junk food don't rot!
- **Can you RECOGNIZE the ingredients?** We can all recognize what's in a packet of almonds, a tin of tuna, or a packet of frozen peas, but you can't recognize the ingredients in a packet of Pringles or a can of Coca-Cola.
- **Does it ROAM or grow on the planet?** This means meat, chicken, fish, eggs, all nuts and seeds, olives, every fruit and vegetable. This is what your diet should be based on, and if you eat like this 80 percent of the time, you can have other foods some of the time.

BIRDS OF A FEATHER

"Surround yourself with people who are also fitness/health minded. This may be a walking group, yoga class, tennis club, or crossfit gym," say Chris and Heidi Powell.

DO THE MATH

How many calories should you eat a day?
1. Work out the minimum calories your body needs a day to maintain your current weight (basal metabolic rate) using an online calculator. Don't lie about your activity levels!
2. Eat no more than 500 calories a day fewer than your basic needs.
3. If you already exercise, keep at it or increase it. If you don't, start now to keep your body's metabolic rate up.

Weight loss:
Stop sugar cravings

Use these simple tips, says Marisa Peer:

DID YOU KNOW . . .

"Your body will crave sugar if it lacks essential nutrients and vitamins. Many vitamins can't be absorbed without fat, so don't take supplements while eating a low-fat diet. Oily fish, olives, avocados, and raw nuts and seeds have the essential oils you need in your diet. A little every day is perfect. Fat doesn't make you fat, but sugar does," says Peer.

FURTHER READING

For lots more info on getting into shape:
Detox page 112
Fitness page 147
Personal trainer page 232
Yoga page 321

1 If you crave something sweet, break a 500mg capsule of L-glutamine onto your tongue and it will end the craving immediately.

2 Sugar cravings are often a sign of being very low in zinc, magnesium, and chromium. Take a combined chromium, magnesium, and calcium supplement on a full stomach. Foods rich in magnesium include apples, avocados, Brazil nuts, celery, chocolate, parsley, and fish. Foods rich in zinc include seafood and sunflower seeds.

3 Take one B-complex vitamin every day. They're effective because they provide a boost to the adrenal system. When the adrenal system isn't functioning well, cravings for sugar increase.

4 Low serotonin levels can trigger food cravings and bingeing. Increase serotonin by taking either 5HTP or L-tryptophan. Foods that boost serotonin include eggs, coriander, bananas, avocados, poultry, pears, and celery.

5 If you must have something sweet, sprinkle a natural calorie-free sweetener like Zsweet (erythritol) onto berries.

What not to do . . .

"I have a huge list of what not to do . . . but these are the absolute top three," says Lisa Vorce.

Don't

- overschedule
- forget what the day is really about
- get lost in minutiae

White The color of purity and virginity? Nope. A centuries-old tradition? Nope. Religion? Nope. White became popular after Queen Victoria wore a white wedding dress for a surprising reason. "She chose white mostly because it allowed her to showcase the work of the handmade Honiton lace industry, which was being threatened by machine-made lace," explains textile historian Leimomi Oakes. "Before Victoria, royal brides across Europe almost exclusively wore silver and nonroyal brides the most expensive fabric they could afford in any color. It also made a point of difference between her, a reigning monarch, and other princesses (married in silver) who were merely royal consorts. Her dress had the unintended affect of bestowing a royal seal of approval on white wedding dresses. Rather than passing away as a fad, they became de rigueur for those who could afford them."

DID YOU KNOW . . .
"Mentions of white as a specific symbol of virginity are not common until post–WWII."
Leimomi Oakes

wine

"There are so many great-value wines, even under $10, there's absolutely no excuse for bad wine at weddings," says international wine expert and Master of Wine Jennifer Simonetti-Bryan. So how do you find the right wine? Throw money at it? Let your caterer or venue do it for you? It's all about "easy drinking," and most wine lists at venues are chosen with this in mind. Here are her expert tips.

FINDING THE CROWD-PLEASER

This is the holy grail of weddings . . .
finding the most enjoyable wine in your budget.

Q Does spending more money mean better and nicer wine?

A A $25 wine should taste higher quality than a $5, but does that mean you'll like the $25 better? "Not necessarily," says Simonetti-Bryan.

1. Look for grape varieties known for quality. These high-quality grapes are grown around the world and keep their flavor consistency: Chardonnay, Sauvignon Blanc, Pinot Noir, Syrah, Merlot, and Cabernet Sauvignon.

2. Look for higher-quality regions or appellations. The wine industry goes to great pains to identify and label names that are known for quality, rather than large generic areas. For example, Napa Valley is normally a higher quality wine than just California. Ask the venue or store for help if you need it.

IF YOUR VENUE HAS A SET WINE LIST . . . Using the table on page 316 and the following tips as a guide, ask what the most popular wines are and what pairs best with the menu you've chosen, advises Simonetti-Bryan. "And see what other people say about the wines on the list, at *Wine Spectator, Wine Enthusiast,* or *Wine and Spirits,* look online at www.cellartracker.com or download apps that connect to other people's tasting notes."

TRY BEFORE YOU BUY Never okay your wedding wine without tasting it first. "Not all venues will pop a cork to let you taste test every wine," says Simonetti-Bryan. "If they won't, get the list, send it around to friends, and ask each to bring a bottle from the list to a get-together. You'll find your favorites, and it's an excuse to have fun!"

A PLAN FOR ALL SEASONS
Spring: light, crisp, and fresh
- New Zealand Sauvignon Blanc
- Beaujolais

Summer: fruity and ripe
- Côtes du Rhône Blanc/Viognier
- Shiraz

Fall: plump and spicy
- California Chardonnay
- Chianti Classico

Winter: big and rich
- Napa Valley Cabernet Sauvignon
- Argentina Malbec

THE BIG CHILL These are correct wine serving temperatures, says Simonetti-Bryan.
- **Champagne or sparkling wine should be well chilled** 45°F (7°C).
- **Light-bodied white wine and rosé is chilled** 50°F (10°C).
- **Full-bodied white wine and light-bodied reds are lightly chilled** 59°F (15°C).
- **Red wine is served at room temperature** 65°F (18°C).

ASK AWAY
"Don't assume that what's on the venue's list is your only option. If you have a favorite you're dying to have at your wedding, ask if they can order it for you. Or ask for their corkage fee—which they'll charge for every bottle that you open if you order your own wine." **Jennifer Simonetti-Bryan**

ON A BUDGET?
These categories make consistently great value wines under $15, says Simonetti-Bryan:
- **Sparkling:** Prosecco
- **White:** New Zealand Sauvignon Blanc
- **Red:** Malbec

Wine

Experiment with the new-school wine pairing below, says wine expert Jennifer Simonetti-Bryan.

	OLD-SCHOOL PAIRING	NEW-SCHOOL PAIRING	GO WILD	TRY TO AVOID
White fish and shellfish: sole, shrimp	**Dry, light crisp whites:** Pinot grigio, Chablis, Sancerre	**Light crisp whites with sweetness:** German Riesling	**Bubbly:** Champagne, Prosecco, Cava	**Reds** will cover up the flavor of the fish.
Hearty fish: salmon, tuna	**Dry, medium/full-bodied whites:** Sauvignon Blanc, Chardonnay, Viognier	**Dry rosés & light reds:** Provence rosé, Beaujolais, Pinot Noir	**Bubbly:** Champagne, Prosecco, Cava, **or vodka**	**Full-bodied reds or reds with large oak influence** will overpower the dish.
Poultry and white meat: chicken breast, pork	**Whites:** dry/crisp white if poached or fried. Chardonnay with cheese or cheese sauce	**Rosés/Reds:** Dry rosé **Light reds:** Pinot Noir or Beaujolais	**Bubbly:** Champagne, Prosecco, Cava	**Intensely floral whites or heavy reds** will overpower the dish.
Poultry, dark meat: duck	**Medium to full whites or light- to medium-bodied reds:** Pinot Noir	**Spicy whites:** Gewürztraminer **Spicy reds:** Grenache, Syrah/Shiraz	**Fruit-based cocktails:** Cape Cod, Gingerberry	**Heavy reds (Cabernet Sauvignon)** will overpower the dish.
Beef	**Medium to full reds:** Syrah/Shiraz, Merlot, Cabernet Sauvignon	**Medium to full whites:** Chardonnay	**Sweet wines,** Moscato d'Asti for Szechuan	**Dry, crisp light whites.** The dish will overpower the wine.
Pasta with tomato sauce	**Moderate Italian reds:** Chianti Classico, Barbera d'Asti	**Medium to full California reds:** Pinot Noir, Syrah, Zinfandel	**Bubbly:** Champagne, Prosecco, Cava, **or beer!**	**Light whites (Pinot grigio) or very tannic red wines**

Winter

Winter weddings are beautiful—as long as you keep everyone warm all the way through. There are no what-ifs about the weather because you know to plan for the worst. Oh, and the comfort food, lots of it, twinkling lights, the preholidays feel-good mood that starts in November, and, postholidays, everyone will be thrilled to have something to get them through the crappiest months of the year.

CONS: You can rely on the weather . . . to be bad. So, yes, a pro and a con. Plan away for snow, rain, wind, ice . . . Transport can be canceled, guests stranded, and weddings called off. Take out insurance.

MONEY-SAVING TIP

Time it away from the holidays, when prices rocket for venues, travel, accommodation, and all your vendors.

Witnesses

In most states you'll need at least one, normally two, people who are over the age of 18 to witness your wedding and sign the marriage license. You don't have to know them and, as in film lore, you can pull them off the street at the last minute if they're willing. In some states, if you don't have a witness, the state will drum one up for civil ceremonies for a fee. Verify what you'll need with the county clerk's office.

Wreaths

Wreaths are hands-down the prettiest hair accessory no matter what style of wedding you're having. Wear one alone or with a veil. Queen Victoria wore a giant wreath of orange blossoms and pinned her veil low on the back of her head.

- Keep them simple or you'll look like you've picked up one of the flower arrangements by mistake.
- "Many blooms will be in a sad state by the time the aisle march begins, so use beautiful vintage silk millinery flowers for the bride, or simple white baby's breath for the little girls," advises event designer Lewis Miller.

HEADS UP

"White baby's breath makes the prettiest, most ethereal head wreaths. There are other flowers that will hold up but need to be individually wired— for example, baby roses." **Lewis Miller**

Xx

X-factor

The X-factor is all about confidence. It's the magic ingredient that can help anyone glide through life as though she's been sprinkled with stardust. If you want to walk up the aisle full of composure and self-confidence, but don't have it naturally, you just need to learn a simple trick.

GET A GRIP ON YOUR THOUGHTS: "It's all about changing your mental script," says best-selling author and therapist Marisa Peer. "Your mind does whatever you tell it to, so all your worries about not measuring up will make you look that way. There is no reason to have anything but positive thoughts and words running through your head.

Repeat things to yourself like:
- My wedding will go perfectly.
- I will look exactly as I want to.
- This day is about my lovely husband and me.

Do this constantly in your head and in the mirror leading up to your wedding day, says Peer. "Also, find a song with significant words. It will change your state if you sing the same positive line over and over. And finally, remember, the people at your wedding love and care about you."

Yy

Yoga

Feeling a bit flabby and not loving yourself, either? There's a solution that can tackle both. Yoga. "Other workouts may make you more sculpted, but they don't make you like yourself any better," says Eric Paskel, founder of Los Angeles–based Yoga Shelter. "Yoga services all your body's needs: emotional and physical. Without any weights or cardio you'll burn a whole lot of calories and create a range of motion and flexibility that's like no other workout."

That's reason enough to make it part of your routine, but it also reduces stress, increases confidence, and helps you live in the present. Don't believe us? "Do it three days a week for a month and you'll see a change in your body and emotions," promises Paskel.

Yurts (teepees and camping)

Matthew McConaughey and Camila Alves set up a minicampground with air-conditioned tents for their wedding guests. From tiny two-person teepees to yurts for 100 people for a party, they're the coolest, cutest way of providing shelter and somewhere to change or to sleep for adults and children alike. If you want to up the ante, line them with Persian rugs, install heating/AC, and create your own chill-out zone.

INSIDER ADVICE

New York event designer David Beahm asks all his couples to get a yoga habit: "I suggest every bride and groom start doing yoga at least six months before the wedding."

Zz

Zodiac What sign are you? Even if you know next to nothing about astrology, odds are that you know the signs of the zodiac and your own sun sign, and probably those of your family and close friends. What about your partner—what sign is he/she?

"Most of us marry the sign of our mother or our father because there is a familiarity there," says renowned astrologer Susan Miller.

DID YOU KNOW?
"About 80 percent of brides marry within six weeks of their birthday. It's because the sun conjunct is so powerful and favorable," says Miller.

FURTHER READING
For more information, go to Miller's website, www.astrologyzone.com.

RESOURCES

If you'd more like information or contact details for any of the experts who've given their advice throughout the book, simply run through the individual sections below. The last line with page numbers tells you exactly which entries they can be found under.

ATTIRE

Accredited Gemologists Association
www.accreditedgemologists.org
Diamonds (page 115)

American Society of Appraisers
www.appraisers.org
Diamonds (page 115)

Rebecca Apsan
Owner, La Petite Coquette boutique; author, *Lessons in Lingerie: Finding Your Perfect Shade of Seduction* (Workman Publishing)
www.thelittleflirt.com
Lingerie (page 197)

Clare Borthwick
Christie's vintage couture, accessories, and luxury handbags specialist
www.christies.com
Accessories (page 9),
Vintage (page 301)

Kelly Christy
Kelly Christy Hats
www.kellychristyhats.net
Hats (page 175)

Victor Chu
Legwork Studio
www.legworkclasses.com
Footwear (page 152)

Carmen Haid
Vintage expert and curator
carmen.haid@mac.com
Vintage (page 301)

Bec Astley Clarke, MBE
Founder, Astley Clarke luxury jewelers
www.astleyclarke.com
Engagement ring (page 131),
Jewelry (page 188)

Shea Jensen
Bridal director, Nordstrom
www.nordstrom.com
Dresses* (or anything else you want to wear) (page 118)

Martin Katz
Celebrity jeweler, Martin Katz jewels
www.martinkatz.com
Engagement ring (page 131),
Jewelry (page 188)

Desirée Lederer
Fashion stylist
www.desireelederer.com
Accessories (page 9)

Annie Lee
Founder, Daughter of Design; author, *Learn to Speak Wedding* flashcards
www.daughterofdesign.com
Peeing . . . with a wedding dress on (page 231)

Antoinette Matlins
Gem and jewelry expert and lecturer; author, *Jewelry & Gems—The Buying Guide: How to Buy Diamonds, Pearls, Colored Gemstones, Gold & Jewelry with Confidence* (Gemstone Press); *Engagement & Wedding Rings: The Definitive Buying Guide for People in Love* (Gemstone Press); *Gem Identification Made Easy: A Hands-On Guide to More Confident Buying & Selling* (Gemstone Press)
Diamonds (page 115), Engagement ring (page 131)

Stephanie McQueen
SparkleSM Bridal Sashes
www.sparklesm.com
Belts and sashes (page 40)

Lewis Miller
Event designer, Lewis Miller Design
www.lewismillerdesign.com
Wreaths (page 317)

Clare Mukherjee
Stylist and fashion expert
www.claremukherjee.com
Dresses* (or anything else you want to wear) (page 118), Stains (page 273), Underwear (no, not lingerie) (page 293)

Angie Nevarez
Event planner; owner, Baton NYC
www.batonnyc.com
Tripping and slipping (page 291)

Leimomi Oakes
Fashion and textile historian
www.thedreamstress.com
White (page 313)

Pantone
www.pantone.com
Colors (page 90)

Hattie Rickards
Fine jeweler
www.hattierickards.com
Jewelry (page 188)

Sophie Rowell
Fashion stylist
www.carolhayesmanagement.co.uk
Dresses* (or anything else you want to wear) (page 118)

Nicole Sewall
Managing director, BHLDN
www.bhldn.com
Veil (page 297)

Cameron Silver
Co-owner, vintage retailer Decades Inc; author, *Decades: A Century of Fashion* (Bloomsbury)
www.decadesinc.com
Vintage (page 301)

Asia Smaga
Founder, Ender Legard corsetry
www.enderlegard.com
Underwear (no, not lingerie) (page 293)

Tara Swennen
Celebrity stylist
www.taraswennen.com
Dresses* (or anything else you want to
wear) (page 118), Dress code (page 122)

The Royal Mint
Collector coins and gifts
www.royalmint.com
Something old, new, borrowed, blue
(page 272)

TopStick
www.vapon.com
Dresses* (or anything else you want to
wear) (page 118)

Rani Totman
President and designer, St. Pucchi
www.stpucchi.com
Dresses* (and anything else you want to
wear) (page 118)

Charlie Tuzzi
Managing director, Cameo Cleaners
www.cameocleaners.com
Dresses* (and anything else you want to
wear) (page 118), Stains (page 273)

Kelly Wearstler
Interior and fashion designer; author,
*Modern Glamour: The Art of Unexpected
Style* (Regan Books); *Hue* (Ammo Books);
Rhapsody (Rizzoli); *Domicilium Decoratus*
(Harper Design)
www.kellywearstler.com
Style (page 279), Colors (page 90)

CEREMONY

Arielle Angel
Cofounder, Ketuv: Fine Art Ketubahs
www.ketuvketubah.com
Ketubah (page 191)

Rev. Christopher Bryan
Church of the Holy Cross, Sherston, UK
Ring bearer (page 259)

Andrea Cohen
Owner, Chuppah Studio
www.chuppahstudio.com
Chuppah (page 86)

Ann Kline
Music supervisor
Choir (page 86), Music (page 214)

Sandy Malone
Wedding planner; Star of TLC's *Wedding
Island;* columnist, Huffington Post,
Brides.com, and Monsters & Critics
www.sandymalone.com
www.sandymaloneweddings.com
www.weddingsinvieques.com
Ceremony (page 80),
Vows (page 303)

Lindsey Silken
Editorial director, Interfaith Family
www.interfaithfamily.com
Interfaith (page 184)

Joanna Stephens
Founder, Canti d'Amore choir
www.wedding-choir.com
Choir (page 86)

Kristen Theisen
Director, pet care issues,
The Humane Society
www.humanesociety.org
Animals (page 20)

Universal Life Church Monastery
www.themonastery.org
Officiant (page 221)

DÉCOR

David Beahm
Event designer, David Beahm Design
www.davidbeahm.com
Décor/decorations (page 105)

Jeffrey Glassberg, Ph.D.
President, North American
Butterfly Association
www.naba.org
Butterfly release (page 59)

Holly Flora
Floral studio
www.hollyflora.com
Centerpieces (page 79)

Lindsay Landman
Event planner, Lindsay Landman Events
www.lindsaylandmanevents.com
Advice (page 14), Colors (page 90),
Décor/decorations (page 105)

Annie Lee
Founder, Daughter of Design; author,
Learn to Speak Wedding flashcards
www.daughterofdesign.com
Décor/decorations (page 105)

Jung Lee
Event designer, Fête; home and
entertaining retailer Jung Lee
www.feteny.com
www.jungleeny.com
Décor/decorations (page 105)

Ira Levy
Lighting designer, Levy Lighting
www.levylighting.com
Lighting (page 194)

Dr. Kevin McGowan
Cornell Lab of Ornithology
www.birds.cornell.edu
www.allaboutbirds.org
Rice (page 258)

Lewis Miller
Event designer, Lewis Miller Design
www.lewismillerdesign.com
Candles/candlelight (page 70),
Centerpieces (page 79), Décor/
decorations (page 105)

Pantone
www.pantone.com
Colors (page 90)

Lesley Price
Event planner, founder, In Any Event
www.inanyeventny.com
Décor/decorations (page 105)

Kelly Wearstler
Interior and fashion designer; author,
*Modern Glamour: The Art of Unexpected
Style* (Regan Books); *Hue* (Ammo Books);
Rhapsody (Rizzoli); *Domicilium Decoratus*
(Harper Design)
www.kellywearstler.com
Colors (page 90), Décor/decorations
(page 105)

DESTINATION WEDDINGS & HONEYMOONS

Amanpulo, Phillippines
Aman Canal Grande, Venice
Aman Resorts
www.amanresorts.com
Honeymoon (page 176)

David Beahm
Event designer, David Beahm Designs
www.davidbeahm.com
Destination weddings (page 108)

CDC Travelers' Health
www.nc.cdc.gov/travel
Destination weddings (page 108)

Disney's Fairy Tale Weddings
& Honeymoons
www.disneyweddings.com
Disney (page 116)

Erin Flaherty
Health and beauty director, *Marie Claire*
www.marieclaire.com
Destination weddings (page 108)

Belmond Hotel Cipriani, Venice
www.belmond.com
Honeymoon (page 176)

Laura Hutcheson
Flight services manager, Virgin Atlantic
www.virgin-atlantic.com
Flights (page 148), Mile-high club
(page 211)

Jack's Camp, Makgadikgadi Salt Pans,
Botswana
Uncharted Africa Safari Co.
www.unchartedafrica.com
Honeymoon (page 176)

North Island, Seychelles
www.north-island.com
Honeymoon (page 176)

Oberoi Amarvilas, Agra
www.oberoihotels.com
Honeymoon (page 176)

One and Only Reethi Rah, Maldives
www.oneandonlyresorts.com
Honeymoon (page 176)

Michelle Rago
Wedding planner
www.michelleragoltd.com
Destination weddings (page 108)

Diana Schmidtke
Male grooming expert; author, *Shortcuts
to a Successful Career as a Hairstylist
or Make-up Artist for the Fashion
and Entertainment Industry* (Lucy Girl
Productions)
www.dianaschmidtke.com
Destination weddings (page 108)

SeatGuru
Airline seat maps
www.seatguru.com
Flights (page 148)

Soneva Fushi, Maldives
www.soneva.com
Honeymoon (page 176)

Jody Value
Event manager, Kauai Marriott resort
www.marriotthotels.com
Destination weddings (page 108)

FLOWERS

Flyboy Naturals
Eco-friendly petals
www.flyboynaturals.com
Confetti (page 92)

Lewis Miller
Event designer, Lewis Miller Design
www.lewismillerdesign.com
Bouquet (page 50), Corsages
(page 95), Flowers (page 149)

Holly Flora
Floral studio
www.hollyflora.com
Boutonnieres (page 52), Centerpieces
(page 79), Flowers (page 149)

Liza Lubell
Owner, Peartree Flowers
www.peartreeflowers.com
Advice (page 14), Corsages (page 95),
Flowers (page 149)

FOOD & DRINK

Tony Abou-Ganim
Award-winning mixologist; author,
*The Modern Mixologist: Contemporary
Classic Cocktails* (Agate Surrey);
*Vodka Distilled: The Modern Mixologist on
Vodka and Vodka Cocktails* (Agate Surrey)
www.themodernmixologist.com
Alcohol (page 16), Cocktails (page 87)

HEALTH & BEAUTY

Mandy Aftel
Natural perfumer; founder, Aftelier Perfumes; author, *Fragrant: The Secret Life of Scent* (Riverhead), *Essence and Alchemy: A Book of Perfume* (Gibbs Smith)
www.aftelier.com
Scent (page 263)

Dr. Miles Berry MS, FRCS (Plast) Plastic and aesthetic surgeon; lecturer; coauthor, *The Good Boob Bible: Your Complete Guide to Breast Augmentation Surgery* (John Blake)
www.aurora-clinics.co.uk
Boobs (page 47), Cosmetic treatments (page 96)

Amanda Birch
Aesthetician/beauty therapist
www.beautybyamandabirch.com
Facials (page 139)

Allergan
Manufacturer of Botox™ / Vistabel™
www.allergan.com
Botox™ (page 48)

Blushington
Makeup and beauty salon
www.blushington.com
Makeup and makeup artists (page 203)

CACI
Non-surgical facial toning treatment
www.caci-international.co.uk
Facials (page 139)

Angela Chalmers
Pharmacy spokesperson, Boots UK
www.boots.com
Allergies (page 19)

Clear and Brilliant
Laser treatment
www.clearandbrilliant.com
Skin (page 270)

Marcy Cona
Global creative director of color and style, Clairol
www.clairol.com
Hair (page 168)

Dr. Thomas Connelly
Cosmetic dentist; assistant professor, Columbia Dental School; founder, 32 bad breath treatment
www.drconnelly.com
www.32oc.com
Bad breath (page 35)

Tracey Cunningham
Celebrity colorist; Redken creative consultant for Color; founder, Mèche Salon
www.mechesalonla.com
Hair (page 168)

Landy Dean
Makeup artist and eyebrow specialist
www.landydean.com
Eyebrows (page 136)

Anee de Mamiel
Acupuncturist; founder, de Mamiel health and beauty products
www.demamiel.com
Acupuncture (page 12)

Dr. Dot
Celebrity massage therapist; founder, Dr. Dot International Massage & Chiropractic Team
www.drdot.com
Massage (page 209)

Erin Flaherty
Health and beauty director, *Marie Claire*
www.marieclaire.com
Acne (page 11), Advice (page 14), Beauty (page 38), Cellulite (page 78), Skin (page 270), Weight loss (page 310)

Robert Gerstner
Cofounder, Aedes de Venustas boutique
www.aedes.com
Scent (page 263)

Shellie Goldstein
Cosmetic facial acupuncture expert; author, *Your Best Face Now: Look Younger in 20 Days With the Do-It-Yourself Acupressure Facelift* (Avery Trade)
www.hamptonsacupuncture.com
Acupuncture (page 12)

Bastien Gonzalez
Award-winning podiatrist
www.bastiengonzalez.com
Manicure (page 205)

Dr. Robert Gotkin
Plastic surgeon
www.cosmetiquemd.com
Liposuction (page 198)

Amanda Griggs
Nutritional therapist
amandagriggs@lineone.net
Cellulite (page 78), Detox (page 112), Skin (page 270)

Dr. Richard Hansler
Director, Lighting Innovations Institute, John Carroll University; cofounder,
www.lowbluelights.com
Insomnia (page 182)

Alyssa Harad
Author, *Coming to My Senses: A Story of Perfume, Pleasure, and an Unlikely Bride* (Penguin)
www.alyssaharad.com
Scent (page 263)

Jenna Hipp
Green celebrity manicurist; collaborator HIPPxRGB nail polish
www.jennahipp.com
Manicure (page 205)

Hydradermie
Lifting facial treatment, Guinot Institut Paris
www.guinotusa.com
Facials (page 139)

HydraFacial
Skin resurfacing procedure
www.hydrafacial.com
Facials (page 139)

Ipsen Biopharm
Manufacturers of Dysport™
www.ipsen.com
Botox™ (page 48)

Dr. Debra Jaliman
New York dermatologist; author, *Skin Rules: Trade Secrets from a Top New York Dermatologist* (St. Martin's Griffin)
www.drjaliman.com
Acne (page 11), Beauty sleep (page 39), Botox™ (page 48), Liposuction (page 198), Skin (page 270)

Nichola Joss
Beauty and skincare specialist; brand spokesman for St. Tropez
www.nicholajoss.com
Tanning (page 281)

Francis Kurkdjian
Bespoke perfumer; founder, Maison Francis Kurkdjian
www.franciskurkdjian.com
Scent (page 263)

Roderick Lane
Naturopath; coauthor, *Adam and Eve Diet: Your Functional Biotype Guide* (www.amazon.com)
www.rodericklane.co.uk
Acne (page 11), Allergies (page 19)

Dr. Han Lee
Cofounder, Comprehensive Dermatology Center of Pasadena; assistant professor of dermatology, USC
www.compdermcenter.com
Antiperspirant (page 26)

Dr. Jonathan Levine
Aesthetic dentist; associate professor, NYU College of Dentistry; founder, Glo Science
www.jonathanblevine.com
www.gloscience.com
Teeth (page 283)

Margo Marrone
Cofounder, The Organic Pharmacy
www.theorganicpharmacy.com
Acne (page 11), Detox (page 112)

Mizzie Logan
Makeup artist
www.mizziemakeup.com
Tattoos (page 282)

Eric Paskel
Founder, Yoga Shelter
www.yogashelter.com
Yoga (page 321)

Marisa Peer
Therapist; author, *You Can Be Thin: The Ultimate Programme to End Dieting . . . Forever* (Sphere), *Ultimate Confidence: The Secrets to Feeling Great About Yourself Every Day* (Sphere)
www.marisapeer.com
Weight loss (page 310), X-factor (page 319)

Chris and Heidi Powell
Fitness and weight-loss experts; stars of ABC's *Extreme Weight Loss*
www.heidipowell.net
chrispowell.com
Fitness (page 147), Personal trainer (page 232), Weight loss (page 310)

Marie Robinson
Celebrity colorist; founder, Marie Robinson Salon
www.marierobinsonsalon.com
Hair (page 168)

Ken Saler
Founder, Advanced Laser Tattoo Removal
www.removeyourtattoodc.com
Tattoos (page 282)

Eden Sassoon
Founder, Eden by Eden Sassoon, Pilates Plus
www.edenbyedensassoon.com
www.pp90210.com
Detox (page 112), Eyelashes (page 136), Manicure (page 205)

Diana Schmidtke
Male grooming expert; author, *Shortcuts to a Successful Career as a Hairstylist or Make-up Artist for the Fashion and Entertainment Industry* (Lucy Girl Productions)
www.dianaschmidtke.com
Male grooming (page 203)

Dr Scholl's BlisterDefense Anti-Friction Stick
Dr Scholl's For Her Rub Relief Strips
www.drscholls.com
Blisters (page 46)

Dr. Mitchell Schwartz
Board-certified dermatologist
www.dorsetstreetdermatology.com
Botox™ (page 48), Liposuction (page 198)

Dr. Daniel Sister
Cosmetic and antiaging expert; coauthor, *Your Hormone Doctor* (Penguin)
www.drdanielsister.com
Botox™ (page 48)

Jason Vale
Health and juicing expert; author,
5lbs in 5 Days: The Juice Detox Diet
(HarperCollins), *7lbs in 7 Days: The Juice
Master Diet* (Harper Thorsons), *The
Funky Fresh Juice Book* (Crown House),
*Juice Master Keeping it Simple: Over 100
Delicious Juices and Smoothies* (Harper
Thorsons)
www.juicemaster.com
Detox (page 112)

Amanda Wright
Makeup artist
www.amandawright.co.uk
Advice (page 14), Eyelashes (page 136)

MUSIC

Ann Kline
Music supervisor for film and TV
Choir (page 86), Love (page 199), Music
(page 214)

Scratch Weddings
Wedding DJ agency, part of the Scratch
group, run by Scratch DJ Academy
www.scratchweddings.com
DJ (page 116)

Spotify
Digital music service
www.spotify.com
Music (page 214)

ORGANIZATION & PLANNING

David Beahm
Event designer, David Beahm Design
www.davidbeahm.com
Host (page 179), Emergency kit
(page 127), Place cards (page 238),
Seating plan (page 264), Wedding
planners (page 306)

Dan Berger
CEO Social Tables
www.socialtables.com
Seating plan (page 264)

Kendra Cole
Manager, Skybar at Mondrian,
Los Angeles
www.morganshotelgroup.com
Bachelorette party (page 34)

Bernadette Coveney-Smith
Same-sex wedding expert; founder,
14 Stories and the Gay Wedding Institute;
author, *The Lesbian Couple's Guide to
Wedding Planning: Everything You Need
to Know About Planning Your Dream
Wedding* (Sellers Publishing), *Gay
Wedding Confidential: Adventures and
Advice from America's #1 Gay Wedding
Planner* (iUniverse.com)
www.14stories.com
www.gayweddinginstitute.com
Gay weddings (page 157)

Aaron Delesie
Photographer
www.delesieblog.com
Planning (page 238)

Brian Dorsey
Photographer
www.briandorseystudios.com
Toasts and speeches (page 288)

Sarai Flores and Martha Huerta
Event planners, Signature Event
Consulting & Design
www.signaturemexico.com
Cutting costs (page 102), Emergency kit
(page 127), Wedding porn (page 309)

Angela Gregory
Wedding coordinator,
The Riverside Church, NYC
www.theriversidechurchny.org
Gay weddings (page 157)

Tara Guérard
Event designer; owner, Tara Guérard
Soirée; coauthor, *Weddings by Tara
Guérard* (Gibbs Smith), *Southern
Weddings: New Looks from the Old South*
(Gibbs Smith)
www.taraguerardsoiree.com
www.taraguerard.com
Emergency kit (page 127), Emotion and
excitement (page 130), Escort cards
(page 132), Seating plan (page 264),
Wedding planners (page 306),

Kate Harrison
Founder, The Green Bride Guide; author,
*The Green Bride Guide: How to Create an
Earth-Friendly Wedding on Any Budget*
(Sourcebooks Casablanca)
www.greenbrideguide.com
Green weddings (page 161)

Larsen Jay
Founder and CEO,
Random Acts of Flowers
www.randomactsofflowers.org
Recycling (page 250)

Lindsay Landman
Event designer, Lindsay Landman Events
www.lindsaylandmanevents.com
Advice (page 14), Emergency kit
(page 127), Host (page 179)

Lisa Moricoli-Latham
Humorist and TV writer
www.lisalatham.com
www.askmissconduct.com
www.naughtybrideguide.com
Emergency kit (page 127)

Paula LeDuc Fine Catering
www.paulaleduc.com
Cheap and chic (page 82)

Annie Lee
Founder, Daughter of Design; author, *Learn to Speak Wedding* flashcards
www.daughterofdesign.com
Emergency kit (page 127), Escort cards (page 132), Groom (page 163), Seating plan (page 264), Tipping (page 287), Trends (page 291), Weather (page 305), Wedding planners (page 306), Wedding porn (page 309)

Jung Lee
Event designer, Fête; owner, home and entertaining retailer Jung Lee
www.feteny.com
www.jungleeny.com
Cutting costs (page 102), Traditions (page 290)

Malorie Lucich
Communications manager, Pinterest
www.pinterest.com
Mood board (page 211)

Sandy Malone
Wedding planner; star of TLC's *Wedding Island;* columnist, Huffington Post, Brides.com, and Monsters & Critics
www.sandymalone.com
www.sandymaloneweddings.com
www.weddingsinvieques.com
Checklist (page 83), Outdoor weddings (page 225), Wedding planners (page 306)

Mystic Medusa
Astrologer; founder,
www.mysticmedusa.com
Astrology (page 30)

Lewis Miller
Event designer, Lewis Miller Design
www.lewismillerdesign.com
Wedding planners (page 306)

Susan Miller
Astrologer; founder,
www.astrologyzone.com
Astrology (page 30), Zodiac (page 323)

Dr. Joseph Murphy
Author, *The Power of Your Subconscious Mind*
Organization (page 224)

Angie Nevarez
Event planner; owner, Baton NYC
www.batonnyc.com
Bridesmaids (page 54), Emergency kit (page 127), Escort cards (page 132), Toasts and speeches (page 288), Wedding planners (page 306)

Andrew Partridge
Sperry Tents
www.sperrytents.com
Tents (page 284)

Lesley Price
Event planner; founder, In Any Event
www.inanyeventny.com
Emergency kit (page 127)

Cassandra Santor
Wedding planner; founder, Cassandra & Company Weddings
www.cassandrasantor.com
Cutting costs (page 102), Emergency kit (page 127), Seating plan (page 264)

Cindy Skanderup
Cofounder, Bliss and Bone
www.blissandbone.com
Wedding websites (page 309)

Lisa Sposato
Associate director, City Harvest
www.cityharvest.org
www.feedingamerica.org
Recycling (page 250)

Diana Schmidtke
Male grooming expert; author, *Shortcuts to a Successful Career as a Hairstylist or Make-up Artist for the Fashion and Entertainment Industry* (Lucy Girl Productions)
www.dianaschmidtke.com
Vendors (page 298)

Melina Schwabinger
Event designer; cofounder, DM Events
www.dmeventsny.com
Emergency kit (page 127), Etiquette (page 133), Seating plan (page 264)

Julie Skarratt
Julie Skarratt Photography
www.julieskarratt.com
Emergency kit (page 127)

Renée Strauss
Bridal stylist; star of *Brides of Beverly Hills*
www.reneestrauss.com
Bridesmaids (page 54)

Jody Value
Event manager, Kauai Marriott Resort
www.marriotthotels.com
Accommodation (page 10)

Lisa Vorce
Event design and production, Lisa Vorce Co.
www.lisavorce.com
Emergency kit (page 127), Wedding planners (page 306)

Kelly Wearstler
Interior and fashion designer; author, *Modern Glamour: The Art of Unexpected Style* (Regan Books), *Hue* (Ammo Books), *Rhapsody* (Rizzoli), *Domicilium Decoratus* (Harper Design)
www.kellywearstler.com
Etiquette (page 133), Mood board (page 211)

PHOTOGRAPHY

Mariah Ashley
Co-owner, Snap Photography
www.snapri.com
Rain (page 245)

Corey Ann Balazowich
Photographer
www.coreyann.com
Cameras (page 69)

Liz Banfield
Photographer
www.lizbanfield.com
Photography (page 234)

Mel Barlow
Photographer
www.melbarlowandco.com
Photography (page 234)

Aaron Delesie
Photographer
www.delesieblog.com
Photography (page 234)

Brian Dorsey
Photographer
www.briandorseystudios.com
Photography (page 234)

Miguel Fairbanks
Photographer
www.miguelfairbanks.com
Photography (page 234)

Thayer Allyson Gowdy
Photographer
www.thayergowdy.com
Photography (page 234)

Corbin Gurkin
Photographer
www.corbingurkin.com
Photography (page 234)

Justin Lee
Photographer
www.justinleephotography.com
Photography (page 234)

Ian Martin
Photographer
www.ianmartinphotography.com
Advice (page 14)

Michael Simon
Photographer
www.michaelsimonweddings.com
www.msimonphoto.com
Photography (page 234)

Joel Serrato
Filmmaker
www.joelserratofilms.com
Videography (page 300)

RELATIONSHIPS

Dr. Laura Berman
Sex and relationship expert, therapist, and columnist; author, *Real Sex for Real Women* (DK Publishing), *It's Not Him, It's You!: How to Take Charge of Your Life and Create the Love and Intimacy You Deserve* (DK Adult), *Loving Sex: The Book of Joy and Passion* (DK Adult)
www.laurabermanphd.com
Marriage (page 207), Sex (page 268)

Thomas Bradbury, Ph.D.
Professor, clinical psychology UCLA; director, Relationship Institute, UCLA
www.uclarelationshipinstitute.org
Calling it off/cold feet (page 68), Compromise (page 91)

Helen Fisher, Ph.D.
Author, *Why We Love: The Nature and Chemistry of Romantic Love* (Holt Paperbacks)
www.helenfisher.com
Attraction (page 31)

Jason Good
Comedian and writer; author, *This is Ridiculous This is Amazing: Parenthood in 71 Lists* (Chronicle Books)
www.jasongood.net
Forever, fuck! (page 153)

Dr. Jane Greer
Relationship expert, marriage and family therapist, blogger, and radio host; creator, Shrink Wrap with Dr. Jane Greer; author, *What About Me? Stop Selfishness from Ruining Your Relationship* (Sourcebooks Casablanca)
www.drjanegreer.com
Attraction (page 31), Calling it off/cold feet (page 68), Expectations (page 134), Marriage (page 207)

Dr. Marty Klein
Sex therapist, marriage counselor, and psychotherapist; author, *Sexual Intelligence: What We Really Want From Sex—and How to Get It* (HarperOne), *Ask Me . . . Anything: Dr Klein Answers the Sex Questions You'd Love to Ask* (SexEd Press)
www.martyklein.com
Virgin (page 302)

Amy Nichols
Event and wedding planner
www.amynichols.com
Calling it off/cold feet (page 68)

Rabbi Dr. Jonathan Romain MBE
Rabbi, Maidenhead synagogue, UK; writer, broadcaster, and author
www.maidenheadsynagogue.org
Counseling (page 98), Marriage (page 207)

Daniel Stern
Author, *Swingland: Between the Sheets of the Secretive, Sometimes Messy, but Always Adventurous Swinging Lifestyle* (Touchstone)
Sex (page 268)

Yvonne Thomas, Ph.D.
Psychologist and therapist
www.yvonnethomasphd.com
Arguments, squabbles, and fights (page 28), Jealousy (page 187), Stepchildren (page 278)

SANITY & STRESS MANAGEMENT

David Beahm
Event designer, David Beahm Design
www.davidbeahm.com
Just one thing (page 189)

Dr. Herbert Benson
Professor of medicine, Harvard Medical School; Director Emeritus, Benson-Henry Institute for Mind Body Medicine; author, *Relaxation Revolution: The Science and Genetics of Mind Body Healing* (Scribner), *The Relaxation Response* (William Morrow Paperbacks), *The Breakout Principle: How to Activate the Natural Trigger That Maximizes Creativity, Athletic Performance, Productivity, and Personal Well-Being* (Scribner)
www.bensonhenryinstitute.org
Meditation (page 210)

Ronald Culberson
Speaker and humorist; author, *Do It Well. Make It Fun: The Key to Sucess in Life, Death, and Almost Everything in Between* (Greenleaf Group Book Press), *Is Your Glass Laugh Full? Some Thoughts on Seeing the Humor in Life* (Gilbert Belle Press)
www.ronculberson.com
Fun (page 154)

Aubrey Day
Journalist, writer, and editor
www.aubreyday.com
Films (page 143), Humor, sense of (page 179)

Mark Dinning
Former editor in chief, *Empire* magazine, editor, *Time Out Dubai*
Humor, sense of (page 179)

Erin Flaherty
Health and beauty director, *Marie Claire*
www.marieclaire.com
Big day (page 43)

Amanda Griggs
Nutritional therapist
amandagriggs@lineone.net
Stress (page 278)

Annie Lee
Founder, Daughter of Design; author, *Learn to Speak Wedding* flashcards
www.daughterofdesign.com
Unexpected (page 294)

Sandy Malone
Wedding planner; star of TLC's *Wedding Island;* columnist
www.sandymalone.com
www.sandymaloneweddings.com
www.weddingsinvieques.com
Bad behavior (page 34)

Lewis Miller
Event designer, Lewis Miller Design
www.lewismillerdesign.com
Fun (page 154), Unique (page 295)

Nev Pierce
Journalist and screenwriter; editor at large, *Empire* magazine
www.nevpierce.com
Humor, sense of (page 179)

Cassandra Santor
Cassandra & Company Weddings
www.cassandrasantor.com
Time out (page 286)

Lisa Vorce
Event design and production, Lisa Vorce Co.
www.lisavorce.com
What not to do . . . (page 313)

STATIONERY

Alexa Hirshfeld
Cofounder, Paperless Post
www.paperlesspost.com
Stationery (page 274)

Ceci Johnson
Founder, Ceci New York
www.cecinewyork.com
Invitations (page 185), Stationery (page 274)

Eunice and Sabrina Moyle
Cofounders, Hello! Lucky
www.hellolucky.com
Stationery (page 274)

Anne Robbin
Calligrapher
www.annerobbin.com
Calligraphy (page 67)

Ming Thompson
Creative director, Pounding Mill Press
www.poundingmillpress.com
Invitations (page 185), Stationery (page 274)

A very special thank-you to all of the experts who answered question after question from us and generously gave of your time and knowledge.

WE PROMISE NOT TO BOTHER YOU AGAIN FOR A BIT.

Tony Abou-Ganim, Mandy Aftel, Thayer Allyson Gowdy, Arielle Angel, Rebecca Apsan, Mariah Ashley, Bec Astley Clarke, Corey Ann Balazowich, Liz Banfield, Mel Barlow, David Beahm, Ron Ben-Israel, Dr. Herbert Benson, Dan Berger, Dr. Laura Berman, Dr. Miles Berry, Susan Bertelsen, Amanda Birch, Blushington, Clare Borthwick, Thomas Bradbury, Rev Christopher Bryan, Angela Chalmers, Kelly Christy, Victor Chu, Andrea Cohen, Kendra Cole, Marcy Cona (Clairol), Dr. Thomas Connelly, Bernadette Coveney-Smith, Ron Culberson, Tracey Cunningham, Aubrey Day, Landy Dean, Aaron Delesie, Annee de Mamiel, Mark Dinning, Brian Dorsey, Dr. Dot, Faith Durand, Miguel Fairbanks, Erin Flaherty, Sarai Flores, Fluffpop, Flyboy Naturals, Robert Gerstner, Jeffrey Glassberg, Shellie Goldstein, Bastien Gonzalez, Jason Good, Dr. Robert Gotkin, Dr. Jane Greer, Angela Gregory, Amanda Griggs, Tara Guérard, Corbin Gurkin, Carmen Haid, Dr. Richard Hansler, Alyssa Harad, Kate Harrison, Jenna Hipp, Alexa Hirshfeld, Holly Flora, Martha Huerta, Dr. Debra Jaliman, Larson Jay, Shea Jensen, Ceci Johnson, Nichola Joss, Martin Katz, Dr. Marty Klein, Ann Kline, Francis Kurkdjian, Lindsay Landman, Mizzie Logan, Liza Lubell, Roderick Lane, Desirée Lederer, Annie Lee, Dr. Han Lee, Jung Lee, Justin Lee, Dr. Jonathan Levine, Ira Levy, Mary Maher, Sandy Malone, Sara Margulis, Margo Marrone, Ian Martin, Antoinette Matlins, Dr. Kevin McGowan, Erin McKenna, Stephanie McQueen, Mystic Medusa, Lewis Miller, Susan Miller, Eunice and Sabrina Moyle, Lisa Moricoli-Latham, Clare Mukherjee, Candace Nelson, Angie Nevarez, Amy Nichols, Leimomi Oakes, Andrew Partridge, Eric Paskel, Paula LeDuc Catering, Marisa Peer, Nev Pierce, Malorie Lucich at Pinterest, Renato Poliafito, Chris and Heidi Powell, Lesley Price, Hattie Rickards, Martin Riese, Roaming Hunger, Anne Robbin, Marie Robinson, Rabbi Dr. Jonathan Romain, Sophie Rowell, Ken Saler, Cassandra Santor, Eden Sassoon, Diana Schmidtke, Melina Schwabinger, Dr. Mitchell Schwartz, Joel Serrato, Nicole Sewall, Cindy Skanderup, Cameron Silver, Michael Simon, Asia Smaga, Lisa Sposato, Daniel Stern, Tara Swennen, Scratch weddings, Julie Skarrat, Jennifer Simonetti-Bryan, Matt Simpson, Dr. Daniel Sister, Greggy Soriano, Joanna Stephens, Renée Strauss, Kristen Theisen, Yvonne Thomas, Ming Thompson, Rani Totman, Charlie Tuzzi, Urban Palate, Juliana Uruburu, Jason Vale, Jody Value, Virgin Atlantic, Lisa Vorce, Kelly Wearstler, Amanda Wright

The same huge thanks goes to all the brides and grooms and couples
who freely shared their stories, advice, insight and wisdom.

For Isabelle xoxo

For Ethan, Aidan and Aubrey I ♡ U